SYMBOLS, SIGNS
& VISUAL CODES

A PRACTICAL GUIDE TO UNDERSTANDING AND DECODING THE UNIVERSAL ICONS, SIGNS AND SYMBOLS THAT ARE USED IN LITERATURE, ART, RELIGION, ASTROLOGY, COMMUNICATION, ADVERTISING, MYTHOLOGY AND SCIENCE

ILLUSTRATED WITH OVER 350 STUNNING FINE ART PAINTINGS, ARTWORKS AND GRAPHIC IMAGES OF THE SIGNS THEMSELVES AND HOW THEY ARE USED

MARK O'CONNOR AND RAJE AIREY

southwater

This edition is published by Southwater, an imprint of Anness Publishing Ltd, Hermes House, 88–89 Blackfriars Road, London SE1 8HA
tel. 020 7401 2077; fax 020 7633 9499

www.southwaterbooks.com; www.annesspublishing.com

If you like the images in this book and would like to investigate using them for publishing, promotions or advertising, please visit our website www.practicalpictures.com for more information.

UK agent: The Manning Partnership Ltd
  tel. 01225 478444; fax 01225 478440; sales@manning-partnership.co.uk
UK distributor: Grantham Book Services Ltd
  tel. 01476 541080; fax 01476 541061; orders@gbs.tbs-ltd.co.uk
North American agent/distributor: National Book Network
  tel. 301 459 3366; fax 301 429 5746; www.nbnbooks.com
Australian agent/distributor: Pan Macmillan Australia
  tel. 1300 135 113; fax 1300 135 103; customer.service@macmillan.com.au
New Zealand agent/distributor: David Bateman Ltd
  tel. (09) 415 7664; fax (09) 415 8892

Publisher: Joanna Lorenz
Editorial Director: Helen Sudell
Editors: Joanne Rippin and Elizabeth Woodland
Designer: Adelle Morris
Editorial Reader: Lindsay Zamponi
Production Controller: Don Campaniello

ETHICAL TRADING POLICY

At Anness Publishing we believe that business should be conducted in an ethical and ecologically sustainable way, with respect for the environment and a proper regard to the replacement of the natural resources we employ.

As a publisher, we use a lot of wood pulp to make high-quality paper for printing, and that wood commonly comes from spruce trees. We are therefore currently growing more than 500,000 trees in two Scottish forest plantations near Aberdeen – Berrymoss (130 hectares/320 acres) and West Touxhill (125 hectares/305 acres). The forests we manage contain twice the number of trees employed each year in paper-making for our books.

Because of this ongoing ecological investment programme, you, as our customer, can have the pleasure and reassurance of knowing that a tree is being cultivated on your behalf to naturally replace the materials used to make the book you are holding.

Our forestry programme is run in accordance with the UK Woodland Assurance Scheme (UKWAS) and will be certified by the internationally recognized Forest Stewardship Council (FSC). The FSC is a non-government organization dedicated to promoting responsible management of the world's forests. Certification ensures forests are managed in an environmentally sustainable and socially responsible way. For further information about this scheme, go to www.annesspublishing.com/trees

ACKNOWLEDGEMENTS

THE ART ARCHIVE: front cover main image; p7t Palazzo Arco, Mantua, Italy/Dagli Orti; p10bl Cathedral Museum, Ferrara/Dagli Orti; p13t Dagli Orti; p14t (Douce OR.a3 fol 30), Bodleian Library, Oxford; p15b Stadelisches Kunstinstitut, Frankfurt; p18tr Russian Historical Museum, Moscow/Dagli Orti; p20tm Archaeological Museum, Aleppo, Syria/Dagli Orti; p21b Old Kingdom Egyptian, Saqqarah, Egypt (B.49) Musée du Louvre, Paris/Dagli Orti; p22b Médiathèque François Mitterand, Poitiers/ Dagli Orti; p23bl Warburg Institute, London/Eileen Tweedy; p29t Scrovegni Chapel, Padua/Dagli Orti; p34br Newgrange, Ireland/Dagli Orti; p40 Musée des Beaux Arts Tours /Dagli Orti; p41t Ragab Papyrus Institute, Cairo/Dagli Orti; p43t Galleria Sabauda Turin/Dagli Orti; p44 Queretaro Museum, Mexico/ Dagli Orti; p46tl Galleria Sabauda, Turin/ Dagli Orti; p48br Victoria and Albert Museum, London/Eileen Tweedy; p49tm British Library; p51t Dagli Orti; p51b British Library; p52t Musée d'Orsay, Paris/Dagli Orti; p52b British Library; p53t Musée des Arts Africaines et Océaniens/Dagli Orti; p53b Prehistoric Museum, Moesgard Højbjerg, Denmark/ Dagli Orti; p55t Dagli Orti; p55b British Museum/Eileen Tweedy; p56br Victoria and Albert Museum, London/Graham Brandon; p57 Museo Civico, Padua/Dagli Orti; p59t (Pers b1 Folio 15a) Farrukhabad, Bodleian Library, Oxford; p60t Museo del Prado, Madrid/Dagli Orti; p60b Galleria d'Arte Moderna, Rome/ Dagli Orti; p62t Canto XIII, Dante's Divine Comedy, by Gustave Dore; p63tl Musée Condé Chantilly/Dagli Orti; p63tr Ashmole 1511 folio 68r, Bodleian Library, Oxford; p64tr Museum Recklinghausen/ Harper Collins Publishers; p65b Mexican National Libary/Mireille Vautier; p74b Lucien Biton Collection Paris/Dagli Orti; p77t Dagli Orti; p79t Musée Thomas Dobrée, Nantes/Dagli Orti; p79b Palazzo Pitti Florence/Dagli Orti; p80t Tate Gallery, London/Eileen Tweedy; p83tr Médiathèque François Mitterand, Poitiers/ Dagli Orti; p84tr National Gallery, London/Eileen Tweedy; p86t National Gallery, London/Joseph Martin; p96t Buonconsiglio Castle, Trento/Dagli Orti; p102t Burnley Art Gallery/Dagli Orti; p103t British Library; p104t Culver Pictures; p105tl Galleria Borghese, Rome/ Dagli Orti; p110b Museo del Prado, Madrid/Dagli Orti; p111t Dagli Orti; p113t Archaeological Museum, Merida Spain/ Dagli Orti; p116t (Arch Bb9 plate 98), Bodleian Library, Oxford.

THE BRIDGEMAN ART LIBRARY: p7b Private Collection/Archives Charmet; p16t Private Collection; p24b The Illustrated London News Picture Library, London; p25tl Private Collection/Paul Freeman; p25tr Institut National des Jeunes Sourds, Paris/ Archives Charmet; p26b Museo de America, Madrid; p28tr Private Collection/Richard Philp, London; p31t Walker Art Gallery, National Museums, Liverpool; p33tr Palazzo Ducale, Urbino, Italy; p35t British Museum, London, UK; p36b Private Collection/The Fine Art Society, London, UK; p37t Private Collection/Christopher Wood Gallery, London, UK; p38t Private Collection; p39tr Leighton House Museum and Art Gallery, London; p50t Private Collection/Lawrence Steigrad Fine Arts, New York; p54 Private Collection; p56bl Bibliotheque de L'Arsenal, Paris, Archives Charmet; p58t Musee d'Art Thomas Henry, Cherbourg, France, Giraudon; p58b Nationalmuseum, Stockholm; p59 Bibliotheque des Arts Décoratifs, Paris, France, Archives Charmet; p61t Bibliotheque des Arts Décoratifs, Paris, Archives Charmet; p62b Royal Asiatic Society, London; p63b The Marsden Archive, UK; p70t Bibliothèque de L'Arsenal, Paris/Archives Charmet; p71t Private Collection/Stapleton Collection; p71b Private Collection/Stapleton Collection; p72bl Private Collection/Stapleton Collection; p73 Musée des Beaux-Arts, Rouen, France, Lauros/Giraudon; p76b Ms Add 24189 fol.15 Library, London; p83tl Ashmolean Museum, University of Oxford; p85b Private Collection/Stapleton Collection; p89t Lady Lever Art Gallery, National Museums, Liverpool; p93t Trustees of the Watts Gallery, Compton, Surrey, UK; p98b Private Collection/Ann & Bury Peerless Picture Library; p100t Johnny van Haeften Gallery, London; 101t Galleria degli Uffizi, Florence, Alinari; p106t Archaeological Museum of Heraklion, Crete, Greece; p106b Giraudon; p108t Musée Girodet, Montargis, France/Peter Willi; p110tr; p114b 28681 f.9 Psalter Map, British Library, London; p115 Hotel Dieu, Beaune, France/Paul Maeyaert; p118b Ms 386 fol.25r Bibliotheque Municipale, Cambrai, France, Giraudon; p120b Palazzo Pitti, Florence; 121t Louvre, Paris; p123t Nationalmuseum, Stockholm; p123b Louvre, Paris; p125b Private Collection/Index; p126b Private Collection/Bonhams, London; p127tr Musée de la Chartreuse, France/Giraudon.

CORBIS: p8t David Muench; p9tl Nik Wheeler; p9tr Dean Conger; p9b Jose Luis Pelaez, Inc.; p10bm Bob Krist; p10br Carl & Ann Purcell; p11t Michael S. Yamashita; p12t Roger Antrobus; p15t Jim Zuckerman; p17t, p18t Anthony Bannister; Gallo Images; p20tr Carmen Redondo; p23br early print shop workers at their trade, c.1800s, Bettmann; p26t Jeffrey L. Rotman; p27t Bettmann; p27b William Whitehurst; p32t Farrell Grehan; p33tl Penny Tweedie; p44 Greenhalf Photography; p45 Tranquility Base, the Moon: Apollo 11 commander Neil Armstrong takes first step on lunar surface, Bettmann; p47 Matthias Kulka; p66t Tiziana and Gianni Baldizzone; p67t Sheldan Collins; p67m Werner Forman; p69tl Jonathan Blair; p69tr Brian A. Vikander; p69b Michael S. Lewis; p72br; p75t Alison Wright; p75b Bob Krist; p81b Michael Freeman; p88t Rose Hartman; p89bl Adam Woolfitt; p90b Lindsay Hebberd; p91t Mark Cooper; p91b Norbert Schaefer; p92t Lindsay Hebberd; p93b George Huey; p94tl Lindsay Hebberd; p94tr, p98t Fabrizio Bensch; p99b Catherine Karnow; p103 Jim Zuckerman; p105 Lindsay Hebberd; p108b Werner H. Müller; p111b Michael & Patricia Fogden; p112 Archivo Icono-grafico; p113b Reuters; p116b Werner Forman; p119tr Galen Rowell; p122b Hubert Stadler; p127tl Clayton J. Price.

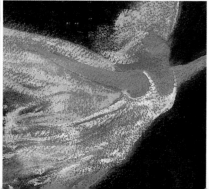

CONTENTS

INTRODUCTION

From the words on this page to the starry constellations in the night sky, from the image of a god to a sense of the divine, from the winking of an eye to a colourful ritual mask, from the figures in our dreams to the traffic lights at a street junction, signs and symbols are integral to the world in which we live.

The word "symbol" is Greek in origin and means "to throw together". Its use came from the tradition of breaking a clay tablet to mark the conclusion of a contract or agreement: each party to the agreement would be given one of the broken pieces, so that when they reconvened the pieces could be fitted together like a jigsaw. Whether consciously or unconsciously, the symbol

LEFT A door or gateway represents an entrance to another place, world or state of being. In many cultures, it is seen as a place of transition, providing an opportunity for good or evil forces to enter or leave, which is why doorways are often guarded.

carries the sense of joining things together to create a whole greater than the sum of its parts, as shades of meaning accrue to produce a complex idea. Signs are understood as something that stands for, or points to, something else in a more literal way. A sign conveys information about a specific object or idea, while a symbol tends to trigger a series of perceptions, beliefs and emotional responses.

Both signs and symbols have become part of human social and cultural identity, changing and evolving as we do. They convey information and meaning, operating on many different levels – the universal and particular, intellectual and emotional, spatial and temporal, spiritual and material. They are a way of making sense of experience. If we could not classify the world using symbolic codes and structures we would be overwhelmed by sensory data.

As well as being an essential part of human society, signs and symbols appear in nature, and may refer to pre-conscious information, as in the case of smoke signifying a fire nearby, or tracks signposting the presence of a particular animal. This book is primarily concerned with signs that have a conscious or unconscious meaning for humans, but as we are rooted in nature, we will see that there may be deeper connections between natural phenomena and the symbols that are meaningful to us.

The ability to give meaning to signs and symbols led to the possibility of communication and reflection, and

LEFT The symbol of divine will in several religions, angels are heavenly creatures in Jewish, Christian and Islamic traditions, thought to have evolved from Semitic and Egyptian winged deities. They are seen as messengers, warriors, guardians or protectors.

has enabled human beings to pass down their histories, mythologies and worldviews by means of storytelling, art and the written word. Signs and symbols have played a crucial part in furthering our scientific understanding of the world and have helped us to develop increasingly complex technologies, advancing from the invention of primitive tools to computers and spacecraft. Religious and spiritual traditions have used symbolism to help on the journey towards an understanding and experience of the divine and towards "right living". In psychology, approaches have been developed that use symbolism to work towards the alignment of mind, body and nature.

ABOUT THIS BOOK

This book looks at the power and use of symbols in many areas of life, and includes chapters on culture and communication, abstract symbols, myth and the cosmos, the human life cycle, plants and animals, and the earth.

The following pages examine the use of symbols in many different aspects of human experience – from the mundane to the sacred, from the temporal to the eternal. Some of those symbols that have the most complex meanings – such as the cross, the serpent, the rainbow and the wheel – have been singled out and are discussed more fully. Although it is impossible to include here every different nuance, the aim is to give an overview of the range of meanings individual symbols can carry.

It is hoped that the information in this book will provide a greater understanding of how communication through signs and symbols enriches our everyday lives.

ABOVE In Christianity, the chalice is a ritual cup used at Eucharist; in Medieval Europe, this cup was associated with the Holy Grail. In Japan, exchanging cups is a symbol of faithfulness and forms part of the marriage ceremony.

BELOW LEFT The standing stone circle of Stonehenge, in England, must have had great significance for those who built it, and people have speculated over it ever since.

BELOW RIGHT Candles are a symbol of spiritual illumination. The short-lived flame is a metaphor for the solitary, aspiring human soul.

EVERYDAY LIVING

THE SIGNS AND SYMBOLS THAT PERMEATE OUR CULTURE ARE OFTEN DEPENDENT ON OUR HISTORICAL AND SOCIAL CIRCUMSTANCES, BUT THERE ARE OTHERS THAT TRANSCEND CULTURE, AND ARE FAR MORE UNIVERSAL. THIS CHAPTER FOLLOWS THE COMMON THREADS THAT ARE FORMED BY THE SIGNS WE FIND IN OUR EVERYDAY LIVES.

UNIVERSAL THEMES

ABOVE The life-force and energy of nature permeates the "story" of life, in its rising and falling, birth and death.

ABOVE The swastika is an ancient nature symbol with multiple meanings, an example of how a symbol's meaning can shift and adapt. When it is facing anticlockwise it implies being against the currents of nature.

Over time, different cultures have evolved unique symbolic languages in an attempt to express their most powerful ideas, and emotional and spiritual responses to life. Symbolism displays cultural characteristics relating to the historical trends and geographical regions from which it emerges, and evolves in accordance with each culture's underlying core values and individual belief systems.

In spite of cultural differences, however, common themes also seem to underlie the world's rich diversity of symbolic expression. They may be thought of as a "living stream of dreaming" running like an invisible current through the everyday world.

ENERGETIC LIFE FORCE

Since the earliest times, people have described states and fields of energy that permeate and animate the universe. In many cultures, the universe, the Earth, and our bodies are thought to channel subtle energy, or "life force". In India this is called *prana*, in China and Japan it is *chi* or *ki*, in Polynesia it is *mana*, in the Western tradition it is etheric. In alchemy, the life force equates with the philosopher's stone, the *quinta essentia* ("fifth essence") or the "world soul".

Modern science understands that the material world, although it appears dense and solid, is fundamentally made up of energy, with atoms, protons, neutrons, electrons and particles vibrating together at different frequencies. The universe can be conceived of as held together by invisible energetic "glue". The psychologist Carl Gustav Jung saw this force in what he called the "collective unconscious", a giant reservoir of archetypal energy patterns that we tap into and express symbolically – whether in dreams, art, sacred tradition or science. This may help to explain our enduring fascination with symbols, why they appear in every conceivable form and why they have no single, correct definition.

MICROCOSM AND MACROCOSM

Attempts to explain the origins of life and the subsequent relationship between living creatures and the cosmos are two of humankind's most fundamental concerns. They lie at the root of philosophy, religion and science, and a great variety of belief systems and hypotheses have been formulated to provide explanations. A dominant theme is the idea that microcosm and macrocosm exist in parallel, so that the lives of individuals are intimately bound with the cosmos, "as above, so below". This concept existed in the ancient cultures of western Asia and has informed astrology, alchemy, divinatory systems, myth and sacred tradition throughout the world. In particular it dominated the mystical-symbolic thinking of medieval Europe, leading to ideas such as "cosmic man" – a human who embodied all the elements of the universe.

POLARITY AND WHOLENESS

Within a multitude of belief systems, another theme can be picked out: the symbolism of opposition. At almost every level, existence seems to be composed of binary pairs or opposites, such as sky/earth, man/woman, day/night. In terms of the earth's magnetic energy field, this opposition is expressed as the polarity between positive and negative, attraction and repulsion or ebb and flow. Humans define abstract concepts in a similar fashion, seeing the world in terms of good or bad, success or failure, rich or poor, beautiful or ugly. Some traditions have created from this a moral universe in which one side of the polarity is favoured over the other, with far-reaching political and social implications. For instance, much of civilization has been built on patriarchal values with women's position seen as inferior.

Some traditions, however, while recognizing the pattern of opposites in nature, have seen the value of embracing the whole as an organic unity. This is the meaning of the Chinese yin/yang symbol or the alchemical figure of the androgyne, in which male and female were conjoined in a single body. A similar idea exists in different branches of psychology. In psychoanalytic theory, neurosis occurs when parts of the personality that are considered "bad" or unacceptable are "split off" and rejected. As a model for mental health, all aspects of the psyche need awareness, as they symbolize aspects of our fundamental wholeness.

Symbolism can be used to control and influence human lives, or to help us align ourselves with our deepest nature. Indigenous and aboriginal peoples recognize the importance of a sustainable relationship with

nature, reflected in their symbolic world, which is also a living reality. They participate in the whole "web of life", honouring the Earth, sky, sun, moon, ancestors, nature spirits, fairies, animals and plants.

CHANGING SYMBOLISM

Although some symbols retain consistent meaning through cultures and ages, others rise and fall in significance, and their meaning evolves over time. An excellent example of this is how the symbolism of the goat has changed and developed through the centuries. In early Europe the male goat was a positive symbol of procreative power, the libido, fertility and the life force. The goat was particularly sacred to the Greek gods Dionysus and Pan. Pan, half man and half animal, with the horns of a goat, was the god of all things, in particular the procreative force.

In the Old Testament book of Leviticus, however, the goat became a "scapegoat" for the sins of humanity, and was sent into the wilderness, bearing this evil burden. From this point the animal increasingly came to symbolize sexual excess, with its rank smell associated with evil, until by the Middle Ages its characteristics had been attributed to the Devil. The personification of Pan, meanwhile, underwent a corresponding transformation into the goat-headed Satan. The goat has, however, maintained its positive associations in the Mediterranean, where it is viewed as a guardian, with the power to absorb malevolent influences.

DWELLINGS AS SYMBOLS

ABOVE A cave was a form of shelter, which has developed primordial symbolic significance, and can be associated with the womb.

ABOVE The house is a symbol of the self, and the way we depict it can symbolize aspects of our personality or attitudes.

BELOW Squareness in architecture may symbolize the human desire to impose ourselves on nature.

The physical structures within which we work and live possess both functional and symbolic qualities, and are usually an interweaving of both. Our homes and other buildings are indicators of rank and privilege, archetypal patterns, connection to spirits and ancestors, and our relationship with both community and nature. Homes very often have cosmological significance, mirroring a relationship to the centre while at the same time having a more personal significance for the families or individuals who live in them. The rich symbolism of the home becomes especially important when we examine the part it plays in both psychology and dream interpretation.

THE FIRST HOMES

Caves, trees and earth were important means of shelter for early humans and have provided both the inspiration and the materials for later dwellings. The dwellings of many primitive peoples are suggestive of natural arbours, with walls made from tree trunks and branches, and leaves as roofs. The trunk of the tree provides the structure while the canopy and leaves provide shelter from the elements. When the forest in which they lived was destroyed, the members of an African pygmy tribe became hugely disoriented upon leaving their vertical and horizonless world of the trees to live on the plain, demonstrating how "at home" and psychologically rooted we become in the environment, shelters and structures with which we are familiar.

The hallways and rooms in modern buildings are reminiscent of the networks of chambers in caves. The cave or cavern-like dwelling is like a womb within Mother Earth, and thus is symbolic of birth, rebirth, nurture and creativity. The home as symbolic of "mother" is a universal concept.

As early as 15,000 BC the nomadic hunters of Europe discovered the usefulness of turf and earth for building and insulation. From primitive mud huts, complex designs for earth lodges have developed throughout the world. Building with earth led to the use of clay bricks. The children's story of the three little pigs and the big bad wolf demonstrates how bricks represent security for our domestic (or pig) nature from the force of nature (or the wolf). The third pig stays safe as the wolf huffs and puffs but just can't blow down his brick house. However, while bricks can symbolize permanence and security, they are can also be used as symbols of the repression of nature through human strength and rigidity.

SYMBOLIC PLACEMENT AND ALIGNMENT

How a building or community is sited on the land is considered very important in many cultures. Houses were often built on local sacred sites, and the foundation stone of a house was similar to the omphalos, or "navel stone", of a temple – the central holy object that allowed communication with the gods. An old building tradition in Ireland involved the lighting of the "needfire" by rubbing together two of the first construction timbers in the shape of Brigit's cross. The needfire was the hearth around which the rest of the house would be focused.

Hunters and gatherers traditionally aligned their houses and communities by visualizing their territory as representing a cosmic creator or original ancestor in anthropomorphic form. The mud houses and towns of the Dogon people, who live on the Niger river at Timbuktu, are arranged according to cosmological and anthropomorphic principles. Their villages are built in pairs, signifying the relationship between Heaven and Earth. The Dogon believe that when they die they go to a paradise that is identical to their homes in life.

In China, where the art of feng shui is practised, the "bagua" is a template for buildings, with eight "guas" surrounding the centre. Each of its zones corresponds to

an area of life: prosperity, fame and reputation, relationship, family, health, creativity and children, knowledge and skills, work, and helpers. The dwelling needs to be designed in a proper relationship to the four directions, in such a way that chi flows freely through the different zones for the wellbeing of the inhabitants.

In India, *vasta purusa* is the spirit of the house, described as a tightly coiled male body. To ensure good fortune, the house must be aligned with his body in such a way that his head, heart and limbs are not disturbed.

The Mongol yurt is a microcosmic representation of the macrocosm, with the sacred hearth on the square earth, the circular roof as the sky, and the smoke-hole in the roof as the eye of Heaven through which comes the light of the sun. The yurt is divided into living quadrants, each relating to the roles of the family or community.

The book *A Pattern Language*, by Christopher Alexander, Sara Ishikawa and Murray Silverstein (1977), describes patterns common to many buildings and towns throughout the world. The authors spent years attempting to formulate a language of patterns that when lived in, are conducive to the well-being of individuals, families and community. They feel that many of these patterns are archetypal in nature, connecting humanity with the essential nature of things. An example is

the alcove, or smaller space within a room, which enables a family to be together while at the same time being involved in different activities; this is an archetypal pattern as relevant to the yurt-dweller as to those who live in a castle.

THE SYMBOLIC VALUE OF THE HOME

Psychologists often view the house as symbolic of a person's inner being, so that when a client draws a house, or describes a dream about a part of it, they are describing their psychic structure. The outside of the house can be seen as representing their outer personality, with the windows and doors showing their relationship to others and the world.

Attics and basements are places where the light of consciousness does not shine. They can symbolize spiritual elevation and the unconscious. In his autobiography, C.G. Jung described going to the basement of a building where he discovered a primitive part of himself. The foundations of a house can symbolize our relationship to the collective unconscious, our ancient beginnings and the non-human realms.

The kitchen, where things are cooked, is a place of alchemical transformation where nurturing takes place, so it may have associations with good or poor parenting. In the hearth or fireplace, glowing embers or

flickering flames are the source of life and dreaming, and may also refer to the spark of imagination or genius. Almost every culture has valued the hearth as the heart of the home, though in modern times it seems to have been replaced by the television set, which also glows and flickers with symbolic stories.

The significance of bedrooms depends upon their occupants. A child's room may represent a place of play or fantasy, while adult bedrooms may point towards sexuality and a person's relationship to sex.

As with all psychological interpretations there is never really any fixed meaning to any of these symbols. What is most important in determining the significance of aspects of the home is the individual's associations with those areas. For example, two people may visualize the front doors of their houses closed. If the first person has always lived in houses where the front door stood open and people were always welcome, whereas the second has lived in houses where the back door was the place of relationship, and the front door was always closed, these similar images need to be interepreted differently. Similar differences in interpreting the same symbols will occur in dream analysis, where the meaning of each home-based image will depend on the person who has dreamed it.

ABOVE Mongolian yurts are circular dwellings constructed from wood and felt, serving both as nomadic homes and symbols of the cosmos.

ABOVE LEFT The Dogon village is an earth-bound representation of what the Dogon people believe paradise to look like.

ABOVE Tree-houses symbolize a relationship between humans and nature, and offer spaces in which children can free their imagination.

BELOW In modern times the television has replaced the hearth as a source of focus and symbolism for the family.

THE GATEWAY

JANUS, GOD OF THE GATE

One of the most ancient gods of Rome, Janus was the warden of all gateways and master of initiation into the mysteries. Often carved on gateposts and doorways, his two faces meant that he could simultaneously see all who were coming and going, looking into both the past and the future. His attributes were the doorkeeper's keys and staff. He presided over beginnings, so that the first day of each month was sacred to him, as was the first month of the year. In the Gregorian calendar, January is named after him.

RIGHT The entrance to this cave in Bali is a monster's mouth with guardian statues protecting the threshold.

There are many symbols of transition, but the gateway or door is an archetypal motif that represents an entrance to another world (a room, a city, a palace, a temple, a social institution) or another state of being that may be either heavenly or hellish, a paradise or a prison. To pass through a gateway is to cross a threshold, to move from the known to the unknown. Gateways may be open but are often closed and guarded, so that the traveller needs a key or password, or must undergo a test, in order to pass through. Hence gateways are also a symbol of initiation: typically there may be a series of gates or worlds to be negotiated, each one leading to greater wisdom, before the ultimate state of bliss is reached.

HEAVEN AND HELL

There are many examples in religion of Heaven and Hell being entered through a gateway or door. In Judaism, for instance, it is believed that there is one gate to the Garden of Eden (a symbol of paradise), but 40,000 to Hell, showing how much more difficult it is to find and enter Heaven. For Christians, Jesus is the entrance to salvation: "I am the door: by me if any man enter in, he shall be saved." (John 10:9). In Muslim tradition, different levels of paradise are reached through a series of gates, with 100 steps leading up to each level before the ultimate seventh heaven is attained. One teaching states that the key to these gates has three prongs: proclamation of Allah's oneness, obedience to Allah and abstinence from evildoing.

BIRTH AND DEATH

Doorways are often associated with death and also with rebirth. In ancient Egypt, the sun god Ra travelled through the underworld each night, passing through 12 gates representing the 12 hours of darkness before being reborn each morning. Ancient Egyptian coffins were sometimes painted with a small false door, symbolically allowing the *ha* (soul) to fly through. In ancient Rome the dead were often depicted in art as standing in front of half-open doors. The Hebrew word for "door" – *daleth* – also means "womb", the gateway of life.

GUARDIANS

Both good and evil influences can pass through a gateway, so guardians or protective deities may be assigned to oversee them. The gates of Chinese cities were set at the four compass points, watched over by fierce lions who attracted good but repelled evil influences, while the entrances to Babylonian and Assyrian palaces were guarded by gigantic winged lion-man sculptures called *lamassu*. In Asian temples, warrior figures called *dvarapala* performed the same function. Cerberus, the three-headed dog of Greek myth, guards the gates of Hades (the underworld of Greek legend), and his secondary function is to make sure that once admitted no one ever leaves.

In ancient Rome every section of a doorway was guarded by numina (minor deities); the god Forculus oversaw the door's panels, for instance, while the goddess Cardea looked after its hinges. The two-faced god Janus (see box) was the chief deity of

BELOW In myth and story, a small or hidden doorway can represent a secret entrance to a magical otherworld.

the gate. In China, it is the custom to paste images of the two Door Gods on the house door on New Year's eve, then lock it until midnight so that no evil spirits can enter, while in Japan *kadomatsu* – decorations made from the boughs of evergreen trees – are placed at the entrance to attract the gods and bring good luck. A similar tradition, linked to pagan customs, is practised in the West, where holly wreaths or bunches of mistletoe are put on front doors during the Christmas and New Year holiday: holly is associated with protection and good fortune, and mistletoe with magic and medicine – it was a symbol of immortality for the Celtic druids.

A cave mouth in Chalcatzingo, Mexico, has a monster's face carved around it, symbolizing the protection of the entrance as well as the transition from one world to another. In the Hindu tradition, a gateway also sometimes takes the form of a monster's mouth through which one must pass when travelling from life to death.

GATEWAYS OF VICTORY

Sometimes gateways are used as symbols of victory and power, both temporal and spiritual. For instance, the Ishtar Gate in ancient Babylonia (in modern Iraq) was built to glorify both the mother-goddess Ishtar and the great city of Babylon. It straddled the Processional Way, and provided an entrance to the city, which had walls so thick that two chariots could drive side by side along the top. In Beijing, the gates

RIGHT The Tori Gate is the largest Shinto *tori* in Japan. A tori is an open gateway symbolizing the transition from mundane to holy.

of the Forbidden City represented the Chinese emperor's might, while the triumphal arches of ancient Rome embodied national and political power. More recently, Napoleon (1769–1821), who emulated Roman imperialism when he became emperor of France, began the construction of the Arc de Triomphe in Paris, in anticipation of a victory that never happened. Subsequently the arch became a war memorial dedicated to the soldiers killed in World War I (1914–18).

HIDDEN DOORWAYS

Gateways do not always have to be large and ornate to be significant. Sometimes small or hidden doorways provide access to other, often magical worlds. The entrance to Wonderland in Lewis Carroll's Alice stories (1832 –98) is first down a rabbit hole and then through a tiny door, which Alice cannot get through until she shrinks. In *The Lion, the Witch and the Wardrobe* by C. S. Lewis (1899–1963) the gateway to the magic land is through a wardrobe. Many enchanted gardens of European folklore are reached through tiny gates that are often obscured; for instance, in the tale of Sleeping Beauty the

entrance to the palace where the princess sleeps is overgrown by briars, which the hero-prince must cut through to reach her.

OPEN OR CLOSED DOORS

In Japan open archways known as *tori* mark the entrance to Shinto shrines. They represent a divine state of perpetual openness, and symbolize the point at which a visitor passes from the everyday world to the sacred. In Chinese tradition, an open door is thought of as active, or yang, and a closed door as passive, or yin. The opening and closing of a door represents the cosmic dance between yin and yang, where first one and then the other holds sway. In Taoism, the opening and closing of the Gates of Heaven are related to human respiration, so that holding the breath equates with shutting the doors, and breathing with opening them.

KEYS

In Japan, the key is a symbol of happiness because it opens up the door to the rice pantry, symbolic of the source of life. In the Christian tradition St Peter is often depicted with the keys to Heaven. The Church adopted keys as symbols of authority: the papal coat of arms shows two keys, one silver, one gold, previously emblems of the Roman god Janus.

SEXUAL SYMBOLISM

The vulva can also be likened to a gateway, as it is both the passageway into life at birth, and the entrance to the vagina during coitus. In Eastern traditions such as Taoism and Tantra, sexual union is itself a gateway of transcendence, through which it is possible to achieve an altered state of consciousness and experience the "bliss body". The mythical Yellow Emperor, Huang-tsi, one of the Eight Taoist Immortals, ascended to Heaven on the back of a dragon partly because of his skill in the art of loving, while early Chinese "bedchamber books" refer to the penis as the jade stalk and the vagina as the jade gateway, jade being the stone of Heaven and a symbol of perfection and immortality.

TRAVELLING AND JOURNEYS

ABOVE A winding road symbolizes the twists and turns of the pathway through life.

ABOVE In myth and story, shoes can possess magical properties, enabling the traveller to cross great distances speedily and safely.

BELOW The chariot is a solar symbol and as such is used as the vehicle of gods, kings and warriors in many traditions.

Journeys symbolize quests for personal advancement, either material or spiritual, or both. To travel is to tread the (potentially hazardous) path through life in which the ultimate destination is not death but spiritual enlightenment, mythically embodied as a promised land (such as the Isles of the Immortals in Chinese tales or religious sites of pilgrimage) or a precious object with special powers (such as the Holy Grail or the Golden Fleece). Sometimes journeys are subterranean, symbolizing entry into the underworld, and sometimes through the air, suggesting spiritual aspiration.

THE TRAVELLER

Boots or shoes are a symbol of the traveller. The might of the Roman army was built on walking power, symbolized by the soldier's boot. Many stories of Western folklore involve "seven-league boots" that magically enable the traveller to cover great distances at great speed without becoming tired, while Hermes the Greek god of travel wore winged sandals. In many cultures charms and talismans are carried on a journey for luck and protection, and the traveller is wished "good speed" (or "God speed").

THE HORSE

The animal that is the most archetypal symbol of travel is probably the horse. In Celtic culture, white horses were sacred and drew the chariots of priests and kings. They were associated with the goddess Epona, one of the few Celtic deities to be worshipped by the Romans. In the 16th century, Europeans introduced the horse to North America (though it may have existed there previously and died out), and its arrival had a profound effect on many native tribes. For them, horses became associated with thunder because of the sound of their running hooves, and the horse became a symbol of wealth and power.

Horses feature in many myths of otherworldly transport, often pulling the chariots of the gods, and are endowed with mythical characteristics. Slepnir, the mount of the Norse god Odin, has eight legs, while in Greek myth Pegasus has wings and pulls the chariot that brings Zeus his thunder and lightning. Mohammed is said to have ascended to Heaven riding on the hybrid creature Borak (whose name means "lightning"), a winged horse with a human head and a peacock's tail.

THE CHARIOT

Chariots, or "triumphal cars", are the carriers of rulers and gods – in Renaissance art they are shown carrying deities such as Venus, Jupiter and Mars. Chariots symbolize the power to lead and vanquish and are often associated with warfare: the Celtic battle leader, Boudicca, is usually depicted in her chariot, while the Achaemenids, the rulers of ancient Persia, are described as going into battle accompanied by the chariot of the supreme god, Ahura Mazda, drawn by eight white horses. The chariots of Indian deities, sometimes lotus-shaped, are drawn by different animals, such as horses for Agni and Surya, and geese for Brahma. The English word "juggernaut" is derived from the massive chariot of the Hindu god Jagganath.

TRAVEL BY WATER

Sailing ships, boats and canoes are all used to symbolize the journey through life. In ancient Egypt, sails symbolized wind and breath, representing the fickle "winds of fate" that can blow a traveller off course. In Egypt, and later in Rome, a new ship was sacrificed each year to ensure fair winds and calm seas: inscribed with holy words, laden with perfumes and baskets of flowers, it was launched into the sea for the winds to take it.

Voyages across water are frequently associated with death and transformation, and symbolic ships of the dead are common to many civilizations. In Indonesia, the dead are exposed in canoes, and in ritual practice the shaman uses a boat to "travel through the air" in search of his patient's soul. In ancient Egypt, the sun god Ra travelled through the underworld

ABOVE Boats can symbolize death, and in ancient Egypt were believed to carry the souls of the dead.

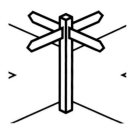

THE CROSSROADS

Traditionally a crossroads marks an important point of decision, and sacred monuments or shrines have been erected at such sites: for instance, votive stones left by travellers in the Peruvian Andes have built up into pyramids. The crossroads is a place of transition, a symbol of risk, opportunity, change, choice and transformation. Being the point where divergent pathways intersect, it is an important place of encounter, traditionally associated with otherworldly powers (both good and evil). In many places, crossroads are associated with ghosts, witches and troublesome spirits: in Europe, statues to Hecate, the Greek "dark" goddess, were erected at crossroad sites, while in Africa, the Bambara from Mali make offerings of tools, cotton and cloth to the Soba spirits who are thought to meddle in human affairs. Crossroads are also widely linked with divination: in Japan, people would go there at dusk, when the words of passers-by would reveal what fate might bring. This was linked to a belief that travellers might be deities bringing good fortune, and evolved into the custom of selling rice-crackers containing paper fortunes at crossroads.

and across the sky in the "boat of a million years", while in China and Japan, paper boats are used as conveyances for spirits. Hindus use miniature flame-carrying boats symbolically to carry solar energy or prayers.

There are also many accounts of heroic journeys in ships such as the Argos, in which Jason searched for the Golden Fleece, or the Pridwen, taken by King Arthur and his men on their journey to the underworld. The sea represents the perils of the unknown, and apart from the danger of shipwreck the journey may bring encounters with mythical beasts such as sea monsters or demons.

For island peoples, boats are particularly important. For instance, Maori war canoes are said to bestow mana (prestige) on all those who own or sail in them, an idea similar to one held by the Vikings. Sea vessels are also symbolic containers and emblems of security: in Judaeo-Christian belief it is Noah's ark that preserves humanity against disaster by saving a breeding pair of every living creature.

MODERN TRANSPORT

Cars, buses, trains and aircraft have symbolic associations that are usually seen in psychological terms. Driving a car can be seen as a metaphor for an individual travelling through life in conscious control of their direction; issues of safety and danger, of conformity or rebellion (obeying or ignoring the rules of the road), of having a sense of direction or of being lost can all be highlighted. Unlike the car, the bus is a public vehicle and can suggest a person's relationship to society, so that difficulties in boarding or wanting to get off can be significant.

Trains operate according to fixed rules. Being late, missing or only just catching a train, travelling without a ticket or in a lower or higher-class carriage can all be interpreted in terms of a person's relationship to the world. Many psychologists believe that the departure platform is a symbol of the unconscious, the starting point of literal and metaphorical journeys, and luggage a symbol of what is being "carried" by the psyche, so that heavy bags can signify psychological burdens, while light bags may indicate inner freedom.

The desire for flight is archetypal. Aircraft (and spacecraft) can symbolize spiritual aspiration, transcending human limitations by defying gravity, rising up to the purifying reaches of the sky and beyond. Aircraft can also be symbols of independence, freedom and speed. Running out of fuel, crashing or falling can suggest being brought "down to earth", a punishment perhaps for over-ambition, just as Icarus in Greek myth fell to his death after flying too close to the sun, which melted the wax of his wings.

ABOVE The horse is an archetypal motif. It symbolizes life-giving but dangerous forces, as well as power and strength.

BELOW A red car symbolizes male sexual potency and drive. It also suggests the thrill of speed and power.

THE GARDEN

Almost universally, the garden is a symbol of earthly and heavenly paradise – the word "paradise" comes from *pairidaeza*, the old Persian word for a garden. Within the garden, the design and plants contribute to its symbolism. The first gardens were probably made in China around 4,000 years ago. From there they spread to the Mediterranean and Near East, and since then almost every culture that survives above a subsistence level has created gardens.

HEAVEN ON EARTH

Gardens are sacred symbols in many spiritual traditions. The Judaeo-Christian Garden of Eden is the ultimate Heaven on earth, created by God for man (Adam) and woman (Eve) to live in. Eden symbolizes the primordial state of divine innocence, when humans existed in harmony with God, nature and one another before they fell from grace after eating the forbidden fruit of the Tree of Life. The theme of Eden and the Fall is a favourite motif in

Western art and literature; representations include *The Garden of Earthly Delights* by the Dutch painter Hieronymus Bosch (c.1450–1516), and the epic poem *Paradise Lost* by John Milton (1608–74). In Islam, too, heavenly bliss is interpreted in the Qur'an as a garden, a home for the elect beyond the grave, and Allah is sometimes referred to as "the Gardener". In ancient Greece, the Elysian Fields, the place where the virtuous go after death, was also represented as a garden.

In China, the traditional lake-and-island garden was invented to attract the Eight Immortals – a group of Taoist saints alleged to live on the Mystic Isles – to Earth. The Emperor Wu Di's gardens of the 2nd century BC contained palaces and pavilions built on man-made mountains and connected by bridges to the islands that stood in the middle of a huge artificial lake.

PLEASURE GARDENS

In ancient Egypt, gardens were places of recreation. Pictures of gardens with pools and banks of flowers decorated tombs, suggesting the joys of the afterlife, as well as palace walls and floors. The Romans carried garden design to sophisticated heights, incorporating buildings, statues, stairways, colonnaded walkways, springs, grottoes, wells and fountains, and the garden became one of the symbols of civilization. This theme was developed during the European Renaissance, with the formal symmetrical designs of many gardens, such as the spectacular Italian gardens at Villa

Lante (Bagnaia) or Villa d'Este (Tivoli) symbolizing human power to tame nature.

In Mexico, the royal pleasure gardens of the Aztec emperor Montezuma combined the functions of a private garden with those of the botanical garden and zoo, preserving not only plants but also birds and animals, with some 600 keepers to tend them. Humans with unusual physical characteristics (such as dwarfs or albinos) were also housed there.

Gardens are widely associated with sensual pleasure, love and seduction. For instance, the classic Arabian erotic text on lovemaking is entitled *The Perfumed Garden*, while many of the great lovers of myth and legend (such as Rama and Sita in India) are frequently portrayed in a garden setting.

PARADISE GARDENS

In many cultures, the garden exists as a type of dream world, designed as an escape from the "real" world and intended to lift the senses from the mundane to the sublime. This is epitomized by the archetypal Persian garden, planted with fruit trees and sweetly scented plants and intersected by streams. In the hot desert land, both water (a symbol of life) and shade are important garden features.

The garden is enclosed and is usually entered by a magnificent gateway, a symbol of transition from one world to another. It is often designed around a large central pool, sometimes lined with blue tiles to create an impression of depth, with four

channels flowing from it; in large gardens, the grid pattern may be repeated, with fountains marking the intersections between the watercourses. As well as being cooling and refreshing, fountains symbolize the flow of life, while the intersections represent the connection between the everyday and the eternal. The geometric design is softened with vine fruits and flowers, particularly bunches of grapes and roses – in Persian, the words for flower and rose are the same.

In the Persian garden, moon-gazing was an important activity. Roses were planted to attract nightingales; the nocturnal habits of these birds linked them to the moon, while their song associated them with love and longing. Gazebos in the corners of the garden provided shelter for those viewing the night sky. The word "gazebo" is derived from a Persian word meaning "a platform for viewing the moon"; traditionally the structure would have a central hole in the roof through which the sky could be seen.

The gardens of Persia provided an oasis of inspiration for poetry, music and art. In his collection of poems and stories called the *Gulistan* ("The Rose Garden") the 13th-century poet Sa'di likened his thoughts to rose petals collected from the garden of his meditations. Persian garden

designs influenced some of the most famous gardens in the world, including the gardens of the Alhambra Palace in Spain, and the Mogul Taj Mahal in India.

THE ZEN GARDEN

In the East there is a saying that a sacred space is complete only when there is nothing more that can be taken away from it. The first Zen gardens in Japan were created by Buddhist monks as places of contemplation, designed to bring the mind to a point of stillness through simple but profound design. In a Zen garden nothing is left to chance and every element is significant. The aim is to create a harmony between the two cosmic forces of yin and yang, water and land. Traditionally, water is symbolized by gravel or sand, raked to form ripple patterns, while large stones

represent land. When plants are used, shrubs such as azaleas, cut-leaf maples, conifers and bamboos represent land, while moss represents water. Space is an integral part of the Zen garden, allowing the spirit of nature to move between yin and yang.

Unlike gardens in the West, which are designed to celebrate the changing seasons, Zen gardens are designed with permanence in mind, so they are more or less the same today as when they were first designed hundreds of years ago, and even the gravel is raked in the same patterns. This permanence symbolizes the transcendent spirit unbound by time or space.

BELOW In medieval times, the walled garden was a symbol of refuge. Here the Virgin Mary is shown surrounded by roses, symbols of her purity.

ABOVE The Court of the Lions at the Alhambra Palace in Granada is rich in symbolism, suggesting spiritual attainment and leadership.

THE HOME

The traditional centre of domestic life is the hearth, an archetypal symbol, but many other common household objects enjoy a rich symbolic tradition: they include the broom and mirror, cooking pots, baskets and items of furniture. In the West some of these items – notably the hearth – are no longer in general use, but they retain their symbolic power.

THE HEARTH

As a source of light, heat and food, the hearth represents home and community, warmth, safety and family life. It has figured in the myths and religions of many civilizations. In Aztec tradition it was sacred to the androgynous Two-Lord Ometecuhtli, who was believed to live at the heart of the universe, while in both China and Japan the hearth gods attract abundance and good fortune to the household, with the Japanese god of the hearth residing in the hook on which the cooking pot is suspended over the fire.

THE BROOM

A humble piece of household equipment, the broom is also a symbol of sacred power and new beginnings. In some North African agricultural societies, the broom used to sweep the threshing floor is a cult object. In ancient Rome, houses were swept after funerals to clean away any bad spirits and symbolize a fresh start, and the Chinese observe a similar custom at the end of the year, sweeping the house to remove any bad luck in preparation for the next year.

THE CAULDRON

The freestanding cooking pot, or cauldron, is another powerful, cross-cultural and archetypal symbol. In Indo-European traditions, it is an instrument of mystical and magical power and transformation. In Celtic myth there are three types of cauldron: the Dagda's cauldron of plenty – an eternal source of food and knowledge; a cauldron of sacrificial death, in which the king of the old year was drowned while his palace was burned; and a cauldron of rebirth in which the dead could be revived.

In China, a three-legged cauldron had the power to bestow the ability of divination, the control of the seasonal cycle, and to grant immortality. The hero Yu the Great, founder of the Chinese Empire, cast nine sacred bronze cauldrons that were said to boil without fire and were filled by celestial powers. It was said that if the people of the Earth turned from virtue to vice, the cauldrons would disappear.

CONTAINING VESSELS

Aside from the cauldron, there are many other archetypal containers, including urns, vases, jars and bowls, as well as caskets, boxes, baskets and coffers, all of which have symbolic significance. In many cultures, rigid vessels are associated with death. The ancient Egyptians, when they mummified the dead, placed the heart and other internal organs in canopic jars – magical vessels that would protect the contents from evil influences. In Europe the dead are usually enclosed in a coffin before burial or cremation, and their ashes may be placed in an urn. In some South American countries, a broken vessel placed on a grave indicates the transition between life and death.

Urns and vases are also life symbols: the Mesopotamian goddess Ishtar is often depicted carrying an urn containing the waters of life. In the Kabbalah, the vase symbolizes spiritual treasure – a symbolism echoed in the Grail legends of medieval European literature, in which the Grail is the chalice or goblet said to contain the blood of Christ and with it the secret of immortality. In the Jewish Temple, golden bowls – a metaphor for vessels containing life – were used for ritual offerings.

Containers are also associated with the feminine principle. In the Americas, stories about baskets and basket-making are often related to women: for instance, in a Pawnee myth, Basket Woman is the mother of the moon and stars. The basket is a symbol of the womb and the attribute of many goddesses, including Diana of Ephesus, whose priestesses wore their hair dressed in a basket shape. Among the Shona of Zimbabwe, pottery bowls are sometimes shaped like a woman's body parts, and there is a saying that a husband must treat his wife with respect to prevent her from "turning the bowl upside down", or denying him access to her sexuality. Similarly, in the Japanese tea ceremony, the tea bowl represents the moon and yin, or the feminine essence.

MIRRORS

The Latin word for mirror is "speculum", and speculation – now an intellectual activity – originally meant using a mirror to scan the sky and stars. Mirrors – especially darkened mirrors – have also been used in divination, by gazing into them until visions were revealed: the Aztecs made polished black obsidian mirrors for this purpose, dedicated to the god Tezcatlipoca, or Smoking Mirror. In some Native American traditions, a blackened medicine bowl would be filled with water to create the same effect.

Sometimes mirrors are seen as reflecting the truth: in Greek myth, Medusa, whose gaze could turn others to stone, was turned to stone herself when presented with her reflection in Perseus' shield. The Chinese hang octagonal mirrors inscribed with the *Pa Gua* above the entry to a house, in the belief that by revealing the nature of evil influences the mirror will drive them away.

RIGHT The carpets of Arabia are associated with the home, and the colours and patterns used in their weaving are rich in symbolism. Every carpet has a mistake to illustrate the Islamic belief that only Allah can create perfection.

Mirrors are symbols of spiritual wisdom, knowledge and enlightenment: in Tibetan Buddhism, the Wisdom of the Great Mirror teaches that the world of shapes reflected in it is illusory, while for Taoists the mirror of the heart reflects Heaven and earth. Through its association with heavenly intelligence, the mirror is often a solar symbol: Japanese myth tells how the sun goddess Amaterasu was enticed from her cave by a sacred mirror to reflect her light upon the world. The mirror is also a female, lunar, symbol, and has associations with luck and superstition. In China, a mirror is a sign of harmony and happy marriage, with a broken mirror suggesting separation. In Western folklore, a broken mirror is said to bring seven years of bad luck to the person who broke it.

FURNITURE

In ancient Rome, emperors sat upon stools, while thrones were reserved for the gods. Today in parts of Africa stools are symbols of kingly office, while the golden stool of the Ashanti in Ghana is believed to enshrine the nation's soul. Because they elevate the sitter, chairs are associated with status and authority. In the Christian tradition, the Latin name for a bishop's chair was a "cathedrum" (from the Greek for chair, "kathedra"); churches presided over by bishops were therefore called cathedrals.

A table is a focal point, a meeting place where people

gather together to eat or talk. For Jewish people, the family dining table assumes the role of an altar when it is sanctified by ritual and prayer during the Sabbath meal. The Round Table of the Arthurian legends represented a select community, an idea echoed in business today when board meetings are held around a table.

Both carpets and curtains have sacred and secular associations. In the Middle East, carpets are associated with the home and with the mosque, and are used to beautify and delineate domestic and holy spaces. Together with screens and veils, curtains provide concealment and define space. In the Temple in Jerusalem, a curtain was drawn over the Holy of Holies, the innermost sanctum that only the Jewish high priest could enter, while in certain Muslim societies, curtains are central to the practice of purdah, which involves concealing women from public view. To perpetuate their holy authority, the emperors of China always kept a veil between themselves and their visitors so that they could see their guests without being seen.

ABOVE The mirror has many complex meanings, associated with both the sun and moon.

ABOVE Curtains symbolize separation between different realms, either opening them up or concealing them.

STATUS AND WEALTH

ABOVE Beaded jewellery is a mark of status among many African peoples.

ANOINTING WITH OIL

In many cultures oil is thought to bear special powers. Olive oil in particular is a symbol of both spiritual power and prosperity. In the Judaeo-Christian tradition, kings and priests were ritually anointed with oil as a sign of divine blessing and God-given authority, power and glory. The Greek word "christos" and the Hebrew "messiah" mean "the anointed". They are used for Jesus as symbols of his royal, prophetic and priestly authority.

Symbols can be used to communicate power and authority – both temporal and spiritual. Every culture has developed symbols of power and rank that accord with its social values, beliefs and customs. Many are associated with royalty and office or with wealth and possessions. Traditionally, valuable commodities have been used to signify wealth and rank. What the specific items are may depend on cultural values – the wealth of nomadic peoples, for instance, may be measured in terms of camels or sheep.

PRECIOUS COMMODITY

Some of humankind's most precious commodities – such as gold, silver and gemstones – are valued both for their beauty and their rarity. A symbol of purity and incorruptibility, gold is associated with divinity, royalty, the sun and the highest aspirations of the spirit. The golden apples of the Nordic heaven, Asgard, like those of the Hesperides in Greek mythology, prevent the gods from growing old, while images of the Buddha are often gilded as a sign of enlightenment and perfection. As a traditional symbol of wealth, gold features in the regalia of monarchy and high office, and it is also used to symbolize human achievement – as in a gold medal or, figuratively, in the notion of a "golden age".

Like gold, silver is also related to immortality; the ancient Egyptians, for instance, believed their gods had golden flesh and silver bones. Silver is associated

ABOVE A lavish portrait of Russian Empress, Catherine the Great, is full of the symbols of kingship, including crown, sceptre and orb.

with the moon, the element of water, female energies and purity; it is also symbolic of wealth, used in currency and given in tribute.

In ancient Mesoamerica jade was valued more highly than gold or silver; it was a symbol of purity and life and the preserve of royalty. Animals and plants have also yielded precious substances – pearls and ivory, musk and ambergris, spices, resins and oils. Liquid chocolate was used by the Maya as currency, while pepper was such a valuable spice that, in the 5th century, Attila the Hun is reputed to have demanded 1350kg (3000lb) of peppercorns as ransom for the city of Rome.

MONEY

As production of goods and services became more diverse and specialized, trade by simple barter ceased to be practical. Universally recognized tokens, which gradually developed into money, solved the problem: as long as everyone accepted the symbolic value of the tokens they could be exchanged for anything. Items such as shells and beads were used by some societies, but metal, when it was available, was more versatile and was most commonly used. Originally coins represented the intrinsic worth of the metal from which they were made, but the value of modern coinage, and of banknotes, is purely symbolic.

Designs impressed on the faces of coins usually signified the authority of the ruling body (typically the ruler's head). They also bore iconographic signs of the culture – such as horses, boars and trees on many Gaulish coins – a tradition that continues to this day. Chinese cash had a square hole in the centre symbolizing Earth surrounded by the circle of Heaven, with a superscription of the emperor, son of Heaven and Earth.

REGALIA OF OFFICE

One way of distinguishing rank is through ceremonial dress and accessories. The head is often seen as the "seat of the soul" and the noblest part of the body, and elaborate headdresses are almost universally used to indicate high status – the leader being the "head" of the group. They range from the elaborate feathered headdress of a Native American chief to the richly jewelled crown of a monarch. Many leaders carry a golden globe, or orb (a piece of regalia first used by Roman emperors to show their dominion over the world), and a sceptre similar to a staff. In Japan, one of the items of imperial regalia is a bronze mirror, associated with the goddess Amaterasu and passed down to the imperial family, who claim descent from her.

The principal item of clothing forming part of the regalia is typically a robe or cape. The

Chinese emperor's robe had a round collar with a square hem, identifying its wearer as the intermediary between Heaven and Earth. The robe of a shaman bears a wealth of symbolism: in ancient Uralo-Altaic cultures, for example, it was decorated with a three-branched emblem known as the mark of the bustard, which symbolized the communication between the worlds of death and rebirth. Today in the West, white ermine, symbolic of moral purity and justice, is still used to decorate the robes of state, judicial, ecclesiastical and academic dignitaries.

The trappings of power help to maintain the mystique of those who occupy a "seat of office" that sets them apart from the lowly rank and file. This "chair" takes many different guises: the chairperson is the head of an organization, while in academia, the holder of a chair in a particular subject is at the very top of that discipline. A throne is a special chair that symbolizes the authority of a god or sovereign. It is often positioned on a raised platform to signify the ruler's elevated status, and is usually richly embellished. In the Bible, King Solomon's throne is described as being of ivory, overlaid with gold, standing at the top of six steps, flanked by a pair of golden lions. The intricately decorated beadwork thrones of

the Bamum kingdom in Cameroon incorporate the figures of men and women to illustrate the monarch's wealth in people, while the beads themselves, the preserve of royalty, symbolize his material wealth.

SEALS

An ancient symbol of identity and authority is the seal, a small object carved with a unique design, which could be pressed into a soft clay tablet or into melted wax. It was used like a signature to guarantee the authenticity of a document such as a royal decree, and it could also ensure the security of a document in transit: when stamped into sealing wax securing folded or rolled paper, the seal could not be broken undetected. To this day seals are still used on legal documents, such as wills. Seals were sometimes worn in the form of rings, and inscribed with the names of deities or passages from holy texts, leading to their use as talismans.

ABOVE A sceptre or staff is a symbol of authority and rulership.

TOP A throne is the seat of power and authority in both the temporal and spiritual realm.

BELOW Traditionally, seals were symbols of authority and identity.

ALPHABETS AND WRITING

ABOVE The runic alphabet was used for a written, not spoken, language that was associated with magic, religion and prophecy.

ABOVE The Roman letter A stands for first grade or top class. It also symbolizes beginnings.

BELOW More than merely a writing system for the communication of information, Chinese script has been elevated into a poetic art form.

In almost every culture, alphabets and letters are laden with symbolic meaning. In ancient times, they were particularly associated with magic, divination and sacred knowledge. Knowing how to read and write was a mark of privilege and a source of power – something that still holds true today, when almost half the world's adult population cannot, or can only just, write. Written language also made possible the dissemination of knowledge and information, first through written documents and centuries later through printed books.

WRITING

Communication through writing relies on an agreed repertoire of formal signs or symbols that can be used in different combinations to reproduce the ideas the writer wants to express. It seems likely that the earliest writing systems – the cuneiform pictographs of ancient Mesopotamia, Egyptian hieroglyphs and Chinese ideograms – developed from the signs and paintings of pre-history.

When alphabets were developed (some time around 1000 BC) the number of different characters needed was drastically reduced: the Roman alphabet, which we still use today, contains 26 letters, while 1,000 basic signs are needed for writing Chinese.

ABOVE The pictorial cuneiform script could be used to infinite purpose. This inscription, dating back to the 13th century BC, is a contract for the sale of children.

EARLY INSCRIPTIONS

The population of Mesopotamia consisted largely of shepherds and farmers, and one of the first uses of writing seems to have been for agricultural accounts: the earliest known Sumerian clay tablets list sacks of grain and herds of cattle. Cuneiform script was based on pictograms, so that, for instance, the outline of the head of a cow stood for the animal, but ideas as well as objects could be represented: a bird and an egg side by side meant "fertility".

The characters used by the ancient Egyptians are known as hieroglyphs, from two Greek words meaning "holy engravings". Hieroglyphs were created from stylized drawings – of human heads, birds, animals, plants and flowers, as well as some man-made objects – and were written in different directions, depending

ABOVE The first letter-based alphabet, reading from right to left, was probably the Phoenician one, from which Hebrew, Aramaic and Arabic scripts developed.

on the text and where it was used. Like the Egyptians, the Chinese attributed a legendary origin to writing: according to one story the Emperor Huang-Tsi discovered it after studying the heavenly bodies and objects in nature, particularly bird and animal footprints. While hieroglyphs and cuneiform script were eventually supplanted by Arabic script, the system of writing invented by the Chinese remains essentially unchanged: the pictograms for words such as sun, tree, mountain, field and door have changed very little in 3,000 years.

ALPHABETS

The Phoenician alphabet is generally considered to have been the first, comprising 22 consonant characters and written from right to left. From

ILLITERACY AND THE SPOKEN WORD

In modern Western culture, illiteracy tends to be linked – erroneously – with ignorance. However, many great spiritual leaders, including Mohammed, the Zen master Hui Neng and the Indian sage Ramakrishna, were illiterate, indicating their direct and intuitive perception of divine reality, which does not rely on the written word. In some ways, writing can be seen as a debased form of speech, a symbol of loss of presence and the missing spoken word. The Buddha, Jesus and Socrates left no written works, while many of the world's great myths and cultures have their roots in oral rather than written traditions. Linguists have identified around 3,000 spoken languages in use in the world today, of which only about 100 are normally written down.

ABOVE In the ancient world, scribes formed an elite, high-status, social class, sometimes holding more state power and knowledge than the sovereign himself.

Phoenician, scripts such as Aramaic, Hebrew and Arabic developed, all of which are read from right to left, as well as some lesser-known writing systems, some of which have survived. These include Tifnagh, the script used by the Tuareg people of northern Africa, which is distinctive because of its highly geometric form. It is also very unusual as its use is confined to women, Tuareg society being matriarchal: a good example of the connection between literacy and social power. Other alphabets include Greek, Roman (which forms the basis of the English alphabet), Sanskrit and Cyrillic.

Individual letters of an alphabet may possess symbolic value. Scholars have noted that in many ancient alphabets most letters depicted an animal, a human gesture or a physical object, while some alphabets, for example Hebrew and runic, are a sequence of specific words rather than letters. The Hebrew alphabet begins, aleph (ox), beth (house), gimel (camel), and not A, B, G.

EUROPEAN TRADITIONS

Runes are the oldest scripted signs of the ancient Germans. The word *runa* means "secret" in Middle High German, and was borrowed by Finnish as *runo*, meaning "song". Allegedly created by the Norse god Odin, the 24 letters of the runic alphabet incorporate fertility symbols from prehistoric rock carvings and represent letters, words and symbolic concepts. For instance, the rune Ansuz (the equivalent of A) was concerned with messages and signals and was associated with the mouth as a source of divine speech, as well as the mouths of rivers, and the Norse trickster god Loki. The runic alphabet was linked to religious beliefs and magical practices, and was never used to represent a spoken language. Norse expeditions carried the runes to other places – Anglo-Saxon England, Iceland, Russia and possibly even North America.

Distantly related to the runes, the letters of the Celtic Irish or Ogham "tree" alphabet consist of 25 symbols, each made up of a series of horizontal or diagonal notches or lines. Originally cut into wood or stone, each glyph is named after a tree. One variation of the Ogham alphabet is named after its first three letters: beith (birch), luis (rowan) and nion (ash). The Ogham symbols were believed to come under the aegis of Ogma, the god of speech. Like runes, the Ogham alphabet was primarily a method of inscription and augury used by druids, seers and poets, rather than a system of ordinary writing.

ABOVE The letter Z comes at the end of the Roman alphabet and symbolizes endings.

BELOW A portrait of a scribe named Mery, head of the royal archives at Saqqarah, mid-4th dynasty (c.2575–2450 BC), on the door of his tomb. The fact that Mery had his own richly decorated tomb shows his high status in ancient Egyptian society. The relief shows Mery at work, making an inscription on a writing tablet, his stylus tucked behind his ear.

THE LETTER X

Many different symbolic associations are ascribed to the letter X. In countries where the Roman alphabet was used, illiterate people used it instead of their signature on legal documents such as birth certificates. After they had made their mark, it was customary to kiss it as a sign of their sincerity, which is why we use X to represent a kiss. In Roman numerals, X is the number 10, while in mathematics it denotes multiplication, or in algebra, a variable in a function. The latter, indicating an unknown quantity, has led to expressions such as "Mr X", where X expresses the idea of anonymity. The use of X to guarantee anonymity also occurs when voting. In contrast to a tick, indicating "correct", X is used to mark an error. On road and other signs it is a warning that something is forbidden or has been cancelled, and the use of crossed lines to pinpoint a position on a map has led to the expression "X marks the spot".

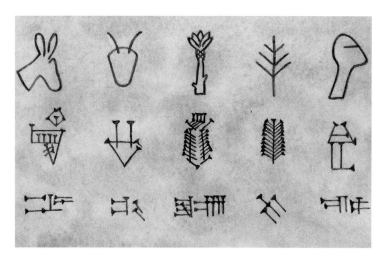

RIGHT These ancient Mesopotamian pictographs show the development of writing. The top row shows a simple drawing (donkey, ox, date palm, barley, head), while the next two rows show how the picture developed into cuneiform script.

BOOKS

The book is an important symbol in many traditions, variously linked with religion, wisdom, scholarship and divination. Judaism, Christianity and Islam are all "religions of the book", based on the holy texts or scriptures (meaning "writing") that have God-given status. Codes of conduct have evolved concerning the handling of holy texts: Moslems observe rituals of cleanliness before studying the Qur'an, and it is never put on the floor; in synagogues, books or scrolls that are too worn out to read, or pieces of paper bearing holy words, are not discarded but kept in a special box that is ceremonially buried when it is full.

In China, books were associated with Taoist sages and were symbols of great learning. In the ancient world, the Sibylline Books were believed to contain prophecies of Rome's destiny and were consulted by the Roman senate in times of emergency, while in medieval Europe books were thought to have divinatory powers, so that if a book was opened at random and a grain of wheat dropped on to a page, the text on which the grain landed would point to a future course of events or answer a question. Words from books have even been eaten as auspicious talismans, a way of ingesting the wisdom and power of the written word.

WRITING MATERIALS

Many different materials have been used for writing on, including papyrus (ancient Egypt), tablets of baked clay (Mesopotamia), marble (Greece), deerskin (Mexico), bamboo (Polynesia), silk (China) and wood (Scandinavia). Each material has called for the use of suitable writing implements, of which the most widely used are the pen and the brush.

In Islamic traditions, the pen (qalam) is highly symbolic. An agent of divine revelation, it was made of light and created by Allah to write upon the "book" or tablet. In Classical mythology, the stylus pen and tablet are attributes of Calliope, the Muse of Epic Poetry, and in Christian iconography the four Evangelists are sometimes associated with a quill pen.

In China, the writing brush, together with its accompanying ink and inkstone, are important symbols. With paper, they make up the "Four Treasures of the Study", symbols of the scholarly class that ruled China from the 2nd century BC, and they were used in calligraphy, in which writing was transformed into an art form practised by the elite. Calligraphy was also accorded high status in other Eastern countries, such as Japan, and in Islam, where inscriptions of texts from the Qur'an were used instead of religious imagery.

RELIGIOUS TRADITIONS

Almost universally, writing has been linked with sacred tradition. In ancient Egypt it was thought that writing was the gift of the god Thoth to humanity, while in India, Sarasvati, the goddess of speech, is also called the alphabet goddess; her consort Brahma, the creator god, is sometimes shown wearing a garland of 50 letters. According to the Biblical account, the Ten Commandments were presented to Moses inscribed on tablets of stone (which Moses symbolically broke when the precepts were not followed), together with the Torah, the primary document of Judaism.

For Kabbalists, the letters of the Hebrew alphabet are linked with numbers and thought to possess powers of creation, while in Islamic mystical traditions there is also a highly refined science of letters based upon their symbolic qualities. In Sufism, the letters of the Arabic alphabet can be classified according to the four elements (fire, air, earth and water), each of which, as a material representation of the divine word, bears a specific meaning. Some traditions have viewed vowels and consonants in terms of "spirit" and "matter" respectively. In antiquity, the seven Greek vowels were thought to symbolize the seven spheres of Heaven and the seven sets of stars moving within them.

SECRET CODES

Writing has always been linked with magic and the occult (meaning "hidden") and has been used in symbols purposefully created to conceal information from all but initiates or the learned, especially in esoteric traditions whose ideas go against mainstream thought. For instance, Hebrew letters, Latin words and Kabbalistic signs have sometimes been used in five-pointed magical seals called pentacles, impressed on virgin parchment or engraved on precious metals. These symbolize occult powers and have been used in spells and magic.

The Western occult or "hermetic" tradition traces its origins to the Hermetica, writings of the 1st–3rd centuries AD that allegedly contain the teachings of Hermes Trismegistus (the Greek name for the Egyptian deity Thoth, god of wisdom and writing). They enshrine a number of concepts central to many esoteric and occult traditions – for instance, the duality of matter and spirit, and the idea that salvation can be achieved through self-knowledge rather than through faith or belief. During the Middle Ages, magical "recipe books" called "grimoires" set out a system in which self-knowledge could be attained using the power of symbols to invoke spirits that the magician then had to confront and overcome. Today psychologists might interpret these as facets of the magician's own personality. Many magical symbols (known as "sigils") were devised during the 15th and 16th centuries, such as those created by Dr John Dee, astrologer to the English court of Elizabeth I. Some of Dee's sigils bear a resemblance to letters, such as an inverted L or Y or a back-to-front Z.

ALPHA AND OMEGA

The first and last letters of the Greek alphabet symbolize that which is all-encompassing, the two poles of the universe between which is contained the totality of knowledge, being, time and space. In the Christian tradition, they are ascribed to Jesus Christ, who, in the Book of Revelation declares: "I am alpha and omega, the beginning and the ending... which is, and which was, and which is to come" (1:8). In modern parlance, the phrase "from A to Z" means "completely, thoroughly and in detail".

ABOVE Today runes are popular as a divination device, with each symbol inscribed on a stone and then "picked".

FAR LEFT This frontispiece to John Dee's *Little Book of Love* shows Venus with magic sigils on her scroll and trumpet.

LEFT The printing press revolutionized the production of books, making the written word more widely available.

BODY LANGUAGE

ABOVE This Indian gesture, known as namaste, symbolizes the reconciliation of the duality in nature. It is also used as a greeting in China.

ABOVE The CND sign was devised using the semaphore signals for the letters N and D.

RIGHT The V for victory sign, two fingers raised in a "V" shape, palms outwards, was first used by Winston Churchill, Britain's prime minister, during the First World War. It is now used as a sign for triumph over adversity all over the world.

The body is a channel of communication, whether the information it conveys is conscious or unconscious, intended or unintentional. Its language is organized both by culturally constructed meaning and symbolism and by the symbolism of the unconscious, or the realm of dreaming. The body is a great source of symbolic expression, communicating both to ourselves, in the form of "body wisdom", and to others. Expressions such as "You are a pain in the neck", "I will hold you in my heart", "I feel it in my bones" and many more, suggest that our bodies can be channels of meaningful and symbolic information.

GESTURE AND GESTICULATION

The intended language of the body appears in gesture and gesticulation. In early humans, the use of both tools and symbols became possible when moving on two limbs freed the hands so that humans were able to physically and mentally "grasp" or apprehend the world.

Gestures play a part in creating and communicating meaning. In India and China, placing the hands together in a praying position at chest height is the "namaste" gesture, which can be interpreted as "The god in me greets the god in you" and also symbolizes the reconciliation of the duality of nature. Some gestures – such as a deferential stoop or bow, smiling or shrugging – appear truly universal, yet even the

commonest signs can have different meanings in different cultures. Though nodding the head signifies assent in most parts of the world, in India it is communicated by shaking the head from side to side.

Raising the thumb stands for "OK" in the USA, but is obscene or very impolite in Brazil, Russia and Greece. In Colombia, this sign placed over the nose implies that someone is a homosexual. Gestures implying a man finds a woman pretty vary widely: they include raising the eyebrows in America and Britain, grasping the beard in the Arab world, rotating a finger in the cheek in Italy and kissing the fingertips in France.

Sticking out ones tongue at someone can be seen as cheeky, provocative or insulting in many cultures. In Tibet, however, it is used as a polite greeting. In New Zealand, the Maori use it as a ceremonial warning. When visitors arrive a Maori warrior approaches them in a warlike manner, with bulging eyes and extended tongue, meaning, "We are willing to attack if you do not

come in friendship." If the visitors react passively they are then welcomed warmly.

The v-sign, popularized by Britain's wartime leader Winston Churchill, is now used throughout the world as a sign for victory, or triumph over adversity. If the sign is reversed, with the palm facing inwards, however, it is seen as rude and offensive.

Gesticulations are bodily gestures that accompany and enhance verbal communication. They are used everywhere but are particularly prominent in Italy, where every conversation is seasoned with such a wide array of hand signals that it is possible to understand its thrust from the other side of a piazza. As an example, a hand drawn away from the chin as if growing a beard means, "You are boring."

SIGN LANGUAGE

Formal body language systems may involve gestures that depict objects and ideas iconically, or communicate by spelling out words. The Native Americans of the Plains used a complex, mainly

MUDRAS

The mudras are symbolic and meaningful hand gestures of the Buddha, portrayed in Buddhist statues since the 5th century AD. *Dhyana* mudra indicates balance and meditation. *Ksepana* mudra means the sprinkling of the nectar of immortality. *Varada* mudra signifies charity and the fulfilment of all wishes. *Uttarabodhi* mudra represents supreme enlightenment.

iconic, system of signing for communication between tribes without a common language. In 1755 the Abbé Charles Michel de l'Epée developed a system of signing for the deaf, which has been the foundation for many modern sign languages.

The semaphore signalling system, originally developed for maritime purposes, uses arm positions and flags to communicate letters of the alphabet. Semaphore is the source of the campaign for nuclear disarmament (CND) symbol, which combines the signals for the letters "N" and "D": two arms in a downwards facing "V" shape for "N", and one arm pointing straight up and the other straight down for "D".

RIGHT Charles Michel de l'Epée, the French educationalist who invented a system of signing for the deaf, teaches a group of students.

DOUBLE SIGNALS

When we communicate two or more different things at the same time, we are double-signalling. Body language may disturb the intended communication, as when we say to someone, "It's nice to meet you", but simultaneously turn away, so that our body conveys the message "I am not interested in meeting you", or "My focus is elsewhere."

NON-VERBAL COMMUNICATION

Communication theory understands communication as the exchange of discrete pieces of information through signals. We communicate linguistically through words and language, but also "non-verbally" through our tone of voice, posture, movement or positioning of our body, the direction of our gaze, and touch.

Our interpretations of other people's non-verbal signals may be very accurate, or they may fall wide of the mark due to our own preconceptions, projections or cultural variations. For example, the behaviour of the eyes can communicate relative social ranking, dominance, submission or respect. They can also signal aggression, love and sexual interest or disinterest. For black Americans, lack of eye contact shows respect, but this may be misinterpreted by white Americans, who expect a direct gaze. Maintaining eye contact in conversation is respectful or can indicate trustworthiness for Arabs, Latin Americans and southern Europeans, while for East Asians and Indians

"peripheral gaze" or no eye contact is more acceptable. In Greece, it is common for people to stare at others in public, and Greeks can feel invisible or ignored in a country such as Britain, where it is rude to stare.

PERSONAL SPACE

Customs, conventions and body language exist in order to define personal or community space. Each community has different symbolic rituals and methods of engaging with visitors and enemies at the edge of their defined territory. Every individual has different needs for personal space, and these change according to time and circumstance. For example, monarchs and political leaders commonly command a wide berth in public life, unless they are making significant gestures such as the symbolic embrace and handshakes of two leaders, or conferring an honour on one of their subjects. In a different situation, with friends or family, the same individual will reduce their personal space to allow greater intimacy.

ABOVE Eye contact is an important part of non-verbal communication.

BELOW The handshake is valuable both for guarding personal space and also for breaking through spatial barriers.

Body Art

ABOVE Painting the body with henna is an ancient art originating in Mesopotamia, and still practised in parts of India, as at this Hindu wedding, and the Middle East. It is the henna itself that symbolizes love, happiness and protection.

BELOW In this earliest known painting from South America, dated 1599, an Ecuadorian from Quito wears European dress but has the body piercings and jewellery of his own tribal tradition.

DON P. Z ZA S.

Though fashions and customs vary, people of all cultures use the body to express their identity and to mark rites of passage. They alter and adorn it in both permanent and temporary ways, from tattoos, decorative scarring and piercings, to jewellery, hairstyles, make-up and clothes. Body art is used to symbolize social and cultural allegiance and difference, to denote rank or power, to accentuate beauty, and to make a statement about gender and sexual availability. It also plays an important part in ritual and ceremony.

DRESS AND TABOO

Aside from their practical use as protection from the elements, clothes have a moral significance in many cultures. In Victorian Britain it was considered risqué for a woman to show her ankle, while one of the symbols of the "sexual revolution" of the 1960s was the mini-skirt. In cultures that do not view nakedness as something to hide, clothing signifies an embellishment of the human form.

Dress can show adherence to a specific body of belief or part of society. Teenagers in the West choose clothes that conform to a recognizable style to indicate their social allegiance. In many religious traditions, the robes of monks or nuns symbolize their non-attachment to the material world and a lack of concern with individual characteristics, focusing instead on their relationship with the divine.

BODY PAINTING

In many parts of the world women dye their skin with henna. In parts of India this practice, known as *mehndi*, has been a tradition for more than 5,000 years. The drawing of intricate patterns over the hands and forearms or feet forms part of the wedding ceremony, and it is thought that the deeper the colour on the skin, the longer the love will last between a couple. In Morocco, henna symbolically blesses the wearer and is said to protect from evil and promote fertility and good fortune. In Sudan, the wearing of henna is an expression of happiness and of a wife's love for her husband, while not wearing it is thought to represent grief or lack of love.

Make-up is used to accentuate desirable facial features but also as a disguise. Often it is a means of conforming to current fashions and ideas about what constitutes beauty, but today's Goths, for example, use white face make-up and black or purple lipstick as a way of challenging the dominant culture. In Japan, where white make-up represents a traditional ideal of beauty and is still the mask of the geisha, it was once customary for upper-class women to shave off their eyebrows and blacken their teeth as a sign that they had come of age.

BODY PIERCING

The piercing of the body as a symbolic act is common to many cultures. In South America, the Carafa Indians insert a thin cane into their lower lip to show that they are in the prime of life. Tongue piercing was practised in a ritual form by the Aztecs and Maya as well as by some Native American tribes such as the Tlingit and Kwakiutul. Among the Berber, Beja and Bedouin of the Middle East, nose rings are very common: the size of the ring denotes the wealth of the family, and when a man marries he gives his ring to his wife as a security if she is divorced or widowed. In India, it is common for women to wear nose studs on their left nostril; this is because in Ayurvedic medicine, the traditional healing system of India, it is believed to connect with the female reproductive organs via the body's subtle energy system, so the piercing is thought to ease menstrual pain and facilitate childbirth.

Body piercings are also governed by aesthetic standards. For instance, the women of the Makololo of Malawi wear plates called *pelele* in the upper lip to enhance their beauty. Body piercing is also associated with erotica: the Kama Sutra, the Indian text on the art of lovemaking, talks of *apadravya*, a vertical barbell inserted through the glans of the penis for increased arousal, while in 19th-century Europe the "bosom ring" was worn by women in high society to enlarge their nipples and keep them in a state of excitement. Today in the West, body piercing involving the lips, tongue, eyebrows, nose, navel, nipples and labia is enjoying a revival. Some people think this represents a need to connect to something more enduring than the ephemera of consumer society; it is also associated with asserting individual and group identity, rebellion against society's "norms" and sexual fetish.

SCARIFICATION

For many indigenous peoples the practice of scarification (deliberate scarring of the body) is highly symbolic. Among the Karo in Ethiopia a scarified line on a man's chest shows that he has killed an enemy from another tribe and is a mark of respect, while Karo women enhance their beauty and sensuality with deep cuts made into their chest and torso. In initiation ceremonies practised by the Barabaig of East Africa, pubescent boys' heads are shaved and their foreheads are cut with three incisions from ear to ear to mark their entry into manhood. In West Africa, young girls have scarification marks around the navel as a reminder of

their ancestral mother, while the Djuka people of Dutch Guiana in the West Indies mark faces, shoulders and arms with Kaffa designs handed down from their African ancestors.

TATTOOS

Mummified bodies found in many parts of the world, including Egypt, South America, Africa, Russia and Europe, suggest that tattooing is an ancient art linked to ritual and sacred ceremony. The body of a Bronze Age man preserved in ice in the Austrian Alps had a total of 57 tattoos, thought to be connected with healing. The Inuit and some Native Americans use them to protect against disease, and in the Sudan, Nubian girls have "welts" thought to strengthen their immune systems while pregnant.

The word tattoo is from the Samoan *ta tau*, which means "balanced" and "fitting". The *ta tau* is used as a sign of maturity, demonstrating a readiness for life. Male *ta tau* are applied in a particular order, starting at the small of the back, with the navel design (*pute*) always applied last. Female Samoans always have a diamond-shaped design (*malu*) on the backs of their knees. Any *ta tau* that remains unfinished is considered shameful as it indicates an uncompleted ceremony. In Maori culture, intricate tattoos known as *ta moko* signify achievements and social rank. Lines and spirals are worn on the face and buttocks of men, and on the chin, lips and shoulders of women. Those of high rank also have *ta moko* on

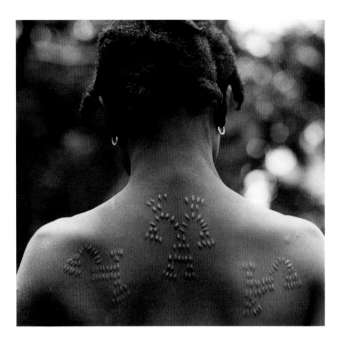

their faces, the left side relating to the father's line, and the right side to the mother's.

Tattoos may denote allegiance to tribes, clans or gangs. For instance, in America a winged skull tattoo is the emblem of the Hell's Angels motorcycle gang. A tattoo common among Hispanic gang members is the pachucho cross, placed on the hand between thumb and index finger; another consists of three dots in a pyramid shape, which means *mi vida loca* or my crazy life.

A tattoo establishes a symbolic link between its wearer and what it depicts, which acts as a totem. This means tattoos may have a protective function: Melanesian fisherman use a dolphin tattoo to avoid shark attack. Alternatively, tattoos can be symbols of aggression: in the West, designs include eagles with their talons drawn to attack, black panthers, scorpions, skulls, or images of death and demons. Tattoos can also symbolize love and allegiance, so another popular design in the West is a heart pierced by an arrow, inscribed with the beloved's name.

ABOVE The Kaffa designs on the shoulders of a young Djuka girl are made by cuts filled with ashes that are allowed to heal and then recut and refilled until the scars reach the right level.

BELOW Tattoos have become common in the youth culture of the West as an identity statement or to enhance eroticism and beauty.

PATTERNS AND GRAPHICS

SOME OF THE MOST COMPELLING SYMBOLS RELY ONLY ON PATTERN OR COLOUR, LINE OR GEOMETRIC SHAPE, AND IT IS OFTEN THESE MOST BASIC SYMBOLS THAT REPRESENT THE GRANDEST CONCEPTS, SUCH AS ETERNITY BEING REPRESENTED AS A SIMPLE DOT, OR THE SPIRAL CONVEYING THE VERY RHYTHM OF BREATHING AND LIFE ITSELF.

NUMBERS

The complex symbolism of numbers stretches back into antiquity. In many traditions, they are linked with cosmic principles that give order and structure to the universe, governing the movement of the moon and planets as well as plant, animal and human life. In ancient Greece, Pythagoras (c.569–475 BC), sometimes described as the first pure mathematician, is quoted as saying, "Numbers rule all things."

Numerology is one of the oldest sciences of symbols. Cultures all over the world have used individual numbers symbolically: here are some of the main associations for one to ten.

1 Number one represents beginnings and the primal cause. It is a symbol of creation and the human species, and is depicted in the standing stone, the upright staff and the erect phallus. In monotheistic religions one is the number of God, while in Jungian psychology it is a unifying symbol. In the Native American Earth Count, one represents Grandfather Sun and fire, the spark of life. We use the expression "number one" to refer to our own importance as an individual. In Pythagorean theory one represents the male principle.

2 Chinese numerology is based on the number two, for in Taoist belief the universe is made up of polarity, expressed in the complementary forces yin and yang. Two represents pairs and duality, separating creator and created, spirit and matter, man and woman, light and dark. Many cultures regard sets of two, such as twins, as especially lucky. In the Native American Earth Count, two represents Grandmother Earth, the body, Earth, death and introspection. For Pythagoreans it represents the female principle.

3 Number three expresses all aspects of creation, including birth, life and death; past, present and future; and mind, body and soul. To the Chinese it is a perfect number, expressing wholeness and fulfilment through the joining together of Heaven, Earth and humanity. In Pythagorean theory it represents perfect harmony, the union of unity (one) and diversity (two). In Islam the number three represents the soul, and for Native Americans it is linked with water and the emotions. Among the Dogon it symbolizes the male principle. The symbolism of three is linked with the triangle.

ABOVE A six-pointed star is a symbol of balance and harmony. It is also an emblem of Judaism.

TOP Number one is the symbol of beginnings.

TOP RIGHT As a symbol of two, twins represent doubled force, but also symbolize warring spirits.

ZERO

The use of zero developed far later than our system for representing numbers, though Babylonion scribes sometimes left a blank space where it was intended to go. In ancient Egypt, there was no hieroglyph for nought. The Maya understood the concept of zero, and represented it as a spiral, suggesting the womb symbolism of the shell and foetal life. Zero represents the blank space of infinity, the void from which life arises and to which it returns. Zero is the symbol of complete potentiality.

$1\ 2\ 3\ 4\ 5\ 6\ 7\ 8\ 9\ 0$

4 The number four is related to the cardinal directions, the seasons, the elements and the phases of the moon. In Pythagorean theory, as the first square it represents perfection, and in the Native American Earth Count it symbolizes harmony. Its symbolism is connected with both the cross and the square, suggesting order, stability and solidity. In Islam it is related to matter, and in Christianity to the four Evangelists. It is a sacred number in the Hindu Vedas, which are themselves divided into four parts. The Japanese word for four, *shi*, sounds like the word for death, so it is replaced in conversation by *yo* or *yon*.

5 According to Pythagoras, five is the number of humanity, the human body with its four limbs and head fits inside a pentagram, or five-pointed star. In the Native American Earth Count, five denotes the human as a sacred being, bridging the gap between earth and sky, past and future and the material and spirit worlds. In China, it is the number of the harmonic union of yin (two) and yang (three), while in India and China it represents the elements – fire, air, earth, water and ether.

6 In China, six is the number of celestial power and longevity. In the Native American Earth Count it is associated with the ancestors. Expressed as a hexagon or six-pointed star, it signifies harmony and balance and is linked with the universal human, and in Pythagorean theory with justice. In Buddhism, there are several

groupings of six, including the six realms of existence. Six is associated with sin in the New Testament Book of Revelation: as 666, it becomes the number of the beast of the Apocalypse.

7 Seven has widespread significance in magic and divine mystery. It is the number of the planets known in antiquity (Sun, Moon, Mercury, Venus, Mars, Jupiter and Saturn) and of the days of the week. There are seven branches to the shaman's cosmic tree, seven colours to a rainbow, and seven main chakras in the human body. In ancient Egypt, there were seven gods of light and seven of darkness, and seven was a symbol of eternal life. In Judaism the New Year begins in the seventh month of the Jewish calendar. Muslims believe there are seven heavens, seven hells and seven earths, while for Christians it is the number of heavenly virtues as well as deadly sins.

8 Almost universally, eight is the number of cosmic balance. For Native Americans it is the number of all natural laws. In Buddhism it relates to the dharmachakra, or eight-spoked wheel of life, and the eight petals of the lotus, representing the eight paths to spiritual perfection. Taoists revere the Eight Immortals and Eight Precious Things, while the Hindu god Vishnu has eight arms

corresponding to the eight guardians of space. Eight is also an important number in African belief: among the Dogon there are eight hero-creators and eight primal ancestors, and eight is associated with water and semen.

9 The number nine relates to the symbolism of the triple power of three – the three trimesters (three-month periods) of pregnancy or the three triads of the nine orders of angels. In China it is highly auspicious because it is the number of the celestial spheres. Among the Aztecs, a nine-storey temple echoed the nine heavens or stages through which the soul must pass. In the Native American Earth Count, nine signifies the moon, change and movement.

10 In Pythagorean theory, ten represents divine power. In the Biblical tradition it is the number of God's commandments, and in Native American tradition it represents the intellect.

ABOVE Through its association with pregnancy, the number nine is associated with gestation and the fulfilment of creation.

TOP In antiquity, there were seven known planets, and the days of the week were named after them.

TWELVE

In Christian symbolism, twelve is a number of universal fulfilment, being the number of Christ's disciples, as well as the Tribes of Israel. There are also twelve gates to the Heavenly City of Jerusalem, and the "Tree of Life" bore twelve fruits. In many traditions, it relates to the space-time continuum (with the zodiac and the months of the year) and represents a completed cycle.

THIRTEEN

In the West the number 13 is generally considered unlucky. This superstition may derive from the 13 people (Christ and his 12 disciples) who were present at the fateful Last Supper. The Kabbalah lists 13 spirits of evil. In other cultures the number is considered sacred. In ancient Greece it represented Zeus, the 13th deity, and it is an important number in ancient Mexican astronomy, calendars and theology. In the Native American Earth Count 13 represents the Goddess.

DOTS AND LINES

ABOVE In the Hindu tradition, the dot, or *bindu,* is a sacred symbol and is often worn in the position of the third eye.

It may be hard to conceive that markings as basic as dots and lines could have any particular symbolic significance, yet these simple graphics are some of the earliest and possibly most profound symbols. As well as being important in their own right, they also form an integral part of many other symbol systems, including the visual arts, writing, mathematics, geometry and various forms of divination, as well as informing sacred traditions all over the world.

THE DOT

Like a star in the sky, the dot or point is the first emanation to appear from the infinite void, a pinprick of light from the world of spirit. It symbolizes the centre or source from which all life begins and to which it must one day return. It is emblematic of the bud or seed, symbolizing the start of a new life, of hope and promise for the future. It is the first sign of a presence and a source of power – the centre from which all else radiates and the essence that remains when all else is removed. It is the pupil at the centre of an eye and the navel in the middle of

the body – a visual reminder of the umbilical cord that connected the unborn child to life. As the full point at the end of a statement it can represent an ending, but also presupposes a new beginning with the start of the next sentence.

In Hindu teaching the dot is known as the *bindu* (from a Sanskrit word meaning "drop") and is a symbol of the absolute. It is represented in the yantra (a type of mandala) by the point at which the two triangles representing Shiva and Shakti (god and goddess of the universe) meet. The *bindu* is often seen painted or worn on the face at the "third eye" in the centre of the forehead. In Hindu and Buddhist traditions the *bindu* is the source of meditation and a symbol of spiritual integration or enlightenment; it is the centre at which all experience is compacted into total concentration before imploding back to its origin – the void or a transcendental state of consciousness. In Islamic mysticism it is a symbol of the creator and the eternal. Numerically it is related to the symbolism of zero.

BELOW A zigzag pattern is one of the oldest known geometric shapes, thought to represent snakes or water.

COUNTING STICKS AND STONES

The Ishango Bone from the Congo, dating back to c.25,000–20,000 BC, is thought to be one of the earliest examples of a counting stick. Because of the series of horizontal notches that are carved into the bone, it is thought to be a lunar calendar, each notch representing a day in the lunar cycle. An even older bone piece found in Abri Blanchard in France, dating back to c.32,000–25,000 BC, shows a series of meandering dot patterns and is thought to represent a two-month lunar calendar. Neolithic pebbles with geometric line designs, such as those found at Susa in Iran, are thought to be counting stones or *calculi* – the word "calculate" is from the Latin *calculus*, meaning "stone".

HORIZONTAL AND VERTICAL LINES

As its name suggests, a horizontal line follows the direction of the horizon. It represents the division between earth and sky, the dividing line between human life and the realms of the gods, and

RIGHT The horizon is the line that appears to divide the earth from the sky, or, figuratively, the human and spiritual realms.

ABOVE The straight line is one of the five basic elements in Western ideography. These are six of the most common variations. From left (1) to right (6): 1. The base; 2. Unity; 3. Equals sign; 4. Complete entities; 5. Similarity in one dimension; 6. The same as.

the base or ground we stand on. As an axis of direction, the horizontal line symbolizes movement on the earth plane: from left to right (west to east) or right to left (east to west), as well as movement in time. It is concerned with the temporal realm, with matter and substance, balance and stability. Traditionally it is linked with the female or receptive element, although in China it is a yang symbol, denoting active, masculine power. In mathematics, a short horizontal line is a minus sign.

If the horizontal line is associated with matter, then the vertical line embraces spirit and provides the link between the higher and lower worlds. It is associated with the male principle and describes the movement from above to below, from Heaven to Earth, from the nadir to the zenith and vice versa. Related symbols include the spine in the human body, the trunk of the World Tree, the staff, stave, sceptre or wand, and many different phallic symbols. It is also widely used in many alphabets: in the Roman alphabet it forms the letter "I", where it represents the authority of the self. In Greek it forms the letter "iota", which the ancient Greeks considered to be representative of destiny or fate. The vertical line is related numerically to the number one.

ZIGZAG LINES

One of the earliest carvings known is more than 300,000 years old. It appears on a bone fragment from Pech de l'Aze, in France, and shows a zigzag or meander pattern. A set of similar symbolic designs more than 40,000 years old was found in Bacho Kiro, in Bulgaria. It is thought that the zigzags represent either snakes or water: in ancient Egypt, the zigzag was the hieroglyph for water, while a horizontal parallel zigzag formation is used to represent the sign of Aquarius, the water carrier in Western astrology.

PARALLEL LINES

Running side by side and never meeting, parallel lines are symbolic of opposites as well as balance and equality. In early cuneiform script, parallel lines signified "friendship" while crossed lines meant "enmity".

Vertical parallel lines can be observed in pillars or columns, which in the architecture of the ancient and classical world were associated with both temporal and spiritual authority. Double pillars also appear in esoteric symbolism. For example, in the Tarot, the High Priestess is shown sitting between two columns, one black, one white, symbolizing the polarities of male and female, positive and negative, life and death, creation and destruction. This symbolism is echoed in esoteric Jewish lore with the two columns on the façade of Solomon's Temple in Jerusalem. The left-hand column, made of black stone, corresponded to the moon, decay, the waning year and cursing and was called Jachin, meaning "it shall stand"; the right-hand column, made of white stone, was called Boaz, meaning "in strength" and corresponded to the sun, the waxing year and blessing.

ABOVE Buildings are constructed by combining horizontal and vertical lines or planes. The horizontal planes of floors and ceilings provide grounding and enclosure or protection, while the vertical planes represent stature, growth and aspiration.

DOTS AND LINES IN DIVINATION

The Chinese I Ching, one of the world's oldest divinatory texts, is based on a series of hexagrams composed of broken and unbroken horizontal lines. An unbroken line is yang and relates to the sun, daytime and the heavens, while a broken line is yin and relates to the moon, night and the earth. The patterns made by dots have also been used in divination, originally in the form of stones, nuts or seeds, which were thrown on to the earth and then interpreted. Dot patterns were later transferred to dice or dominoes, where they are used in gaming as well as prediction.

THE CROSS

ABOVE The ankh is the Egyptian version of the cross, and is one of its most ancient manifestations.

ABOVE The equilateral or Greek cross forms the ground plan of many early Greek churches, and is the motif of the Red Cross organization.

In Western culture, the cross has become almost inseparable from Christianity, yet it is actually one of the oldest and most all-encompassing symbols. Carved in stone or wood or worked in metal or bone, richly decorated or simply drawn, the cross has appeared all over the world. A stone disc with a carved cross, found in the Tata Cave, in Hungary, is estimated to be around 100,000 years old, while crosses carved on a mammoth statuette from Vogelherd, in Germany, date back more than 30,000 years. The cross is found in the ancient civilizations of China, Egypt and Central America, is a frequent motif in African art, and appears on Celtic pottery, jewels and coins. It is widely considered to be one of four basic symbols with the point, the circle and the square, to which it is also linked.

EMBRACING THE WHOLE

The cross creates a totality. Its intersection of two lines can be seen as the uniting of the male principle (the vertical) with the female (the horizontal). The two axes also stand for the dimensions of time and space, matter and spirit, body and soul, as well as the equinoxes and solstices.

THE CROSS AND HEALING

Because of its various spiritual and esoteric associations, the cross is connected with healing and miraculous powers. At one time, the cross was considered to offer protection against disorders such as epileptic fits, or to have the power to ward off supernatural phenomena such as vampires and devils. It is now associated with medicine and nursing through the Red Cross charity, which provides care for victims of war and famine.

Crossing horizontal and vertical lines are the basis of a "stick person", one of the most basic representations of the human figure, found in prehistoric rock art, and in children's drawings ever since. When aligned with the four cardinal points, the cross becomes a symbol of orientation to the terrestrial directions of north, south, east and west, which in turn informs the symbolism of the Native American Medicine Wheel. A cross within a circle also mediates between the square and the circle, emphasizing the connection between sky and earth. It has been suggested that the four arms of the cross represent the four phases of the moon, as well as the four elements, the four winds and the four seasons. Together with the square, the cross is closely linked to the symbolism of four, a number signifying wholeness and universality, although in China the number of the cross is five, the perfect number of the human being as microcosm. This is because the midpoint (where the two lines intersect) is also counted – emphasizing the centre or source to which everything is connected.

WORLD SYMBOL

In China the early symbolism of the cross was expressed in the ideogram meaning "Earth": an equilateral cross within a square. According to a traditional Chinese saying, God fashioned the Earth in the form of a cross. A similar view emerges in ancient Mexican mythic tradition, where the cross symbolizes the world in its

totality. The 1st-century Christian theologian, St Jerome, came to the same conclusion when he wrote, "What is it but the form of the world in its four directions?"

Although there are literally hundreds of different types of cross, several appear to be particularly significant.

THE GREEK OR EQUILATERIAL CROSS

The equal-armed cross is one of the simplest. When enclosed in a circle it becomes the solar cross or sun-disc, a symbol similar to that adopted by the Assyrians to represent the sun god Shamash. In this form the circle emphasizes the cyclical nature of the seasons, while the four-armed cross represents the shadows cast by the rising and setting sun at the two solstices. This may explain why the cross appears in many examples of megalithic rock art. The Neolithic structure at Loughcrew, in Ireland, was made in the shape of a cross, with the central passage aligned to the equinoctial sunrise.

Centuries later, the Celts combined the cross and circle in a distinctive pattern that originally had links with fertility – the cross symbolizing the male generative power, and the circle, the female. In time the Celtic cross was used as a Christian symbol to represent the union of Heaven and Earth.

THE SWASTIKA

The Sanskrit *svastika* means "well being", and in India the swastika is a symbol of fertility and good fortune. It appears extensively throughout Asia, in both secular

LEFT In Central Australia the Aborigines use the form of a cross to control the composition of many sacred works of art.

and religious contexts. It is an ancient and widely used form of solar cross. Some of the earliest European examples appear on Bronze Age pottery found in Anatolia, in central Turkey, dating from about 3000 BC. It also appears on bronze articles among the Ashanti in Africa and was used by the Maya and Navajo.

Essentially the swastika is a spinning cross, with the angles at the end of each arm suggesting streaming light as it turns, just as the sun's rays light up the earth. Spinning anticlockwise it is said to represent the female principle, and clockwise, the male. The anticlockwise swastika appears in Buddhism, Taoism and in Native American cultures. In the modern Western world, however, the symbol tends to be associated with anti-Semitism because of its adoption by the German Nazi party in the 20th century.

THE T-CROSS

The Tau, or T-cross, is another very ancient cross symbol. It may have developed from the axe, a widespread and ancient symbol of the sun god, and appears to be phallocentric, its shape denoting testicles and penis. It forms the

basis of the Egyptian ankh, in which the upper arm is replaced by a loop. A symbol of immortality in ancient Egypt, the ankh was adopted by the Coptic Church as its unique form of the Christian cross. The handled cross also occurs in America, where it has been found engraved on monuments in the ruins of Palenque, in Mexico, as well as on pieces of pottery.

THE LATIN CROSS

There is disagreement about the type of cross that was used for the crucifixion of Christ. It was as late as the mid-2nd century that translators of the Gospels first used "crux" in descriptions of death by crucifixion. Many images show Christ hung either from a Y-shaped structure (*furca*) or a T-shaped cross, as well as the more familiar Latin cross, where the cross-bar is set approximately two-thirds of the way up. Over time, the Latin cross became the central symbol of Christianity. Some believe this coincided with the gradual tendency in the early Church to separate the spiritual and material realms in accordance with Christ's saying, "My kingdom is not of this world." This view has dominated ideas about spirituality in much of the Christian world, where earthly life (including nature), the world and the body have been seen as forces that have to be overcome, rather than parts of an organic whole.

For Christians, the crucifix is a seminal symbol, representing Christ's death, resurrection, the victory of spirit over matter and the redemption of humanity.

CROSS OF LORRAINE

A single vertical crossed by two horizontals (the upper shorter than the lower) is known as the double cross, or cross of Lorraine. When a third, smaller, horizontal bar is added, it becomes a triple cross, associated with the papacy. The cross of Lorraine is believed to represent the crucifixion, with the upper bar added for the inscription "INRI" (the Latin abbreviation for "Jesus of Nazareth, King of the Jews"), fixed above Christ by Pontius Pilate. The cross of Lorraine was the emblem of the medieval Dukes of Anjou, later the Dukes of Lorraine, and in World War II became the symbol of the Free French, in opposition to the swastika of the Nazis.

ABOVE The cross has become the most widely used version in depictions of the crucifixion of Christ, and as such has become perhaps the most widely recognized symbol of Christianity.

ABOVE For the early Christians the three directions of the Tau cross linked it with the Holy Trinity.

SPIRALS AND CIRCLES

ABOVE Because of their circular shape, rings can symbolize eternity, hence their use as love tokens.

TOP Like the Earth, the circle is a primordial symbol of perfection.

TOP RIGHT This triple spiral at a Stone Age burial site at Newgrange, in Ireland, is believed to symbolize the Celtic triple goddess.

BELOW Megalithic monuments were often arranged in a circle pattern that aligned with the sun's movement through the sky.

Both the spiral and the circle occur in nature as well as in art, myth and sacred tradition. The earliest known use of these shapes was in the Paleolithic age, when they were carved into bone or stone or painted on cave walls. Antler bone batons found in a cave at Isturitz, in France, dating back to c.25,000–20,000 BC, bear a relief forming a complex pattern of concentric arcs and spirals. A disc from the same period, found in Brno, in the Czech Republic, has a vertical line incised from the edge to the centre and is thought to be an abstract representation of a vulva, suggesting a link with the goddess worship characteristic of this period.

THE NATURAL WORLD

The sun, moon and planets all appear circular in shape, while spiral galaxies form some of the most breathtaking patterns in space. In the plant and animal kingdoms, spirals and circles appear in many guises, such as the concentric pattern of tree-rings, the centre of a flower, the shape of a bird's nest, the spiral of a snail or conch-shell, a coiled serpent or a twining plant stem.

Weather and water patterns also form spirals and circles in tornadoes, whirlpools, ripples on a pond and ocean waves. Nature itself circles and cycles through the changing seasons and the endless rhythm of night and day.

THE SPIRAL

Beginning with a single dot, the spiral develops from the initial seed and moves forwards in a clockwise or anticlockwise direction; thus it is connected with movement, energy and growth. Since the earliest times it has been a favourite ornamental motif linked with the symbolism of the moon and with cyclic development, involution and evolution, resurrection and renewal. It has also been linked to the erotic symbolism of the vulva, female sexuality and fertility, while many cultures believe the spiral represents the soul's journey after death. The motif is widely used in Oceanic art, where it is carved into door handles or canoe prows or tattooed on the body. To the Maori the spiral represents creation, and in Polynesia it is thought to be the key to immortality.

DOUBLE SPIRALS

Spirals often appear conjoined in twos and threes. The double spiral is said to symbolize duality and balance. It is also moving simultaneously in two directions – towards involution and evolution, contraction and expansion, or birth and death. This motif is seen in the wreathing of the twin serpents around the caduceus (the rod of

Hermes), or the double helix around the Brahman's staff. In Aztec mythology, the S-shaped counter-rotating double spiral is a symbol of thunder and of the phases of the moon. Spiral oculi (double twists resembling eyes) appear on entrances to sacred sites throughout Europe and are thought to be associated with the equinoxes, when day and night are of equal length.

TRIPLE SPIRALS

The triple spiral is often referred to as the spiral of life and was used consistently in Celtic art for nearly 3,000 years. One of the most famous examples appears in the "womb" chamber of the megalithic structure at Newgrange, Ireland (c.3200 BC), where a shaft of sunlight falls upon it once a year, at the winter solstice. It represents the Triple Goddess – maiden, mother and crone – who in turn is associated with the phases of the moon (waxing, full and waning) as well as the birth-death-rebirth cycle. It has been suggested that triple spirals might also be connected with the three trimesters of human gestation.

SACRED DANCES

Initiation rites and sacred dances often follow a spiral pattern that represents death and rebirth. Spiral formation dances can be a way of acknowledging and celebrating life's pattern of change and evolution. For instance, at New Year the Zuni (Pueblo) Indians chant "spiral" songs and dance spiral dances. One of the best-known forms of sacred spiral dance is that practised by the *mevlevi*, or "whirling dervishes" in Turkey, who spin round and round like a top. Exactly like the centre of the spinning top, the trunk of the whirling dancer symbolizes the still point in the midst of dynamic movement, the eye at the centre of the storm. Circle dances also symbolize life's pattern of change and flow.

A STAIRWAY TO HEAVEN

In ancient times it was thought that the heavens were reached by climbing a spiral path that ascended to a wheeling circle of stars. Souls ascended to Heaven along this pathway in the skies, which was mirrored on Earth as a spiral path up a sacred mountain, or the spiral staircase around a structure such as a ziggurat.

THE CIRCLE

With no beginning and no end, the circle has been used to signify eternity and wholeness, the heavens, the cosmos, the absolute and perfection. In Islam, the circle is seen as the perfect shape, and poets praise the circle formed by the lips as one of its most beautiful representations. In many cultures the circle represents the continuing cycle of the seasons and the sun's endless progression through the skies. It is often used as a symbol for the sun (itself a symbol of perfection) as well as for the full moon.

THE POWER OF THE WORLD

In Native North American traditions, the circle is perhaps the most important shape, related to the Sacred Hoop or Medicine Wheel: the Lakota Sioux shaman Black Elk (1863–1950) asserted that the power of the world works in circles, and that the circle contains all things.

In social and political life the circle is the preferred shape for an assembly of equals: the campfire circle, the council circle, the Round Table of the Arthurian legend. It is the easiest geometric shape to draw accurately, with stick and string, and may also represent the idea of a home or dwelling place, which in early societies was often constructed on a circular ground plan. In Australian Aboriginal art from the Western Desert, concentric circles were often used to represent sanctuaries or camping places, while lines between them were the paths and tracks of people or mythological beings. Here, the circles suggest places where ancestral power can surface from the Earth and return again.

POWER AND PROTECTION

Being a closed circuit and all-embracing, the circle is associated with protection, providing safety for all who put themselves within its boundary. The magic circle is used in occult traditions to guard against negative psychic forces, and the protective circle can also be worn – as a ring, necklace, bracelet, girdle or crown.

SPIRITUAL HIERARCHIES

Drawings of concentric circles have been used as a teaching device to symbolize different stages of spiritual development in Zen Buddhism, as well as in esoteric Christian schools such as Rosicrucianism. In Christian symbology, hierarchies of angels are sometimes shown arranged in circles around God and Christ, while in the Divine Comedy, the Italian poet Dante (1265–1321) describes Heaven, purgatory and Hell as being divided into different circles or levels.

ABOVE In ancient tradition the path to Heaven was seen as a spiral, reflecting nature's whirling patterns, an idea used by William Blake in his 18th-century painting of Jacob's ladder.

BELOW The spiral symbolizes movement, energy and connection with nature.

TRIANGLES AND SQUARES

ABOVE The triangle is often associated with sacred mountains.

PYTHAGOREAN TRIANGLE

The Pythagorean triangle was an important symbol to the Egyptians, who regarded the vertical and horizontal sides as the male and female forces respectively, and the hypotenuse as their "offspring". This triangle symbolizes construction and development.

BELOW The pyramids of Egypt were symbols of the creative power of the sun and the primal mound.

The triangle and the square are universally important motifs. They are connected to the symbolism of three and four and everything to which these numbers relate, and can only be separated from them in terms of their relationship with other geometrical figures. The triangle appears frequently in everyday life, for example on road signs or washing instructions, while, after the circle, the square is the most common geometric shape printed on textiles. Many buildings have a square plan and, in urban design, a central square is often a focus of activity, such as a town square.

THE TRIANGLE

An equilateral triangle has three sides of equal length. In Christianity it is a symbol of the Trinity, while in Islamic art it symbolizes human consciousness and the principle of harmony. The triangle features in many alphabets. It is the ancient Maya hieroglyph for the sunray, and in the Greek alphabet it represents the letter "delta", which for the ancient Greeks symbolized the four elements and hence was linked with completion and wholeness. Today the word "delta" is used in English to describe a triangular tract of land at the mouth of a river (such as the Nile Delta), which is often very fertile. The connection of the triangle with the four elements also appears in alchemy, where it is used in various formations to symbolize them.

UPWARD AND DOWNWARD TRIANGLES

The Maya likened the shape of the upward-pointing triangle to a shoot of maize as it breaks through the surface of the soil, linking it with fertility, and also the male principle (the erect phallus). For the ancient Hittites an upward-pointing triangle was a symbol of the king and of health. Among the Pueblo people of the south-western United States it represents a sacred mountain, while a downward-pointing triangle represents clouds.

The inverted triangle is also associated with female fertility, as it resembles an image of a woman's pubic region and her internal sex organs – the triangle formed by the two ovaries and the womb. The Sumerians used a downward-pointing triangle to represent woman, and it is also a feminine symbol in China. In ancient Greece, Rome and India triangles were often used as decorative motifs in friezes. In all instances they seem to signify the same: pointing upwards, they stand for fire and the male sexual organs; pointing down they represent water and the female sexual organs. In more general terms, an upward-pointing triangle can symbolize reaching for the sky and so may be associated with aspirations, the attainment of goals, and new possibilities. It is also associated with arrowheads and the theme of spiritual quest. A downward-pointing triangle, on the other hand, is associated with receptivity, movement inwards rather than outwards, and consequently is often used as a meditation symbol.

CONJOINED TRIANGLES

The tips of triangles touching, one pointing up and one pointing down, can be used to denote sexual union, while intersecting triangles represent synthesis. Positioned with their bases meeting, two triangles can also represent the waxing and waning phases of the moon.

The six-pointed star combines two overlapping equilateral triangles and so relates to the symbolism of the triangle. It is an alchemical symbol for conjunction, relating to the union of the four elements. As the Star of David, it is the pre-eminent symbol of Judaism, while as the Seal of Solomon in Judaic mysticism it stands for the sacred number seven, represented by the

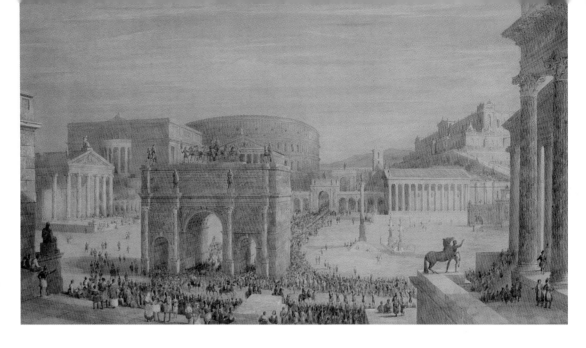

six points plus the space at the centre, the place of transformation. In India, a six-pointed star is known as the Star of Lakshmi (the goddess of prosperity and abundance) and is often drawn in powder on doorways or village thresholds to keep away hostile spirits.

THE SQUARE

The ancient Greek philosopher Plato thought that, together with the circle, the square embodied beauty and perfection, while in ancient Egypt it represented achievement. It is one of the most common abstract symbols, representing Earth, material existence and the created universe. The square's shape suggests structure, order and stability, but also limitations – echoed in the expression of feeling "boxed in" to describe being trapped and constrained. It is often seen in relation and in contrast to the circle of the heavens, or of the limited in contrast to the unlimited, of matter as opposed to spirit, of static versus dynamic.

A quadrangular form has often been used for areas set apart for sacred or other reasons, such as altars, temples, castles or military camps. City squares traditionally lie at the heart of urban life. The Forum in ancient Rome was the market square at the heart of the capital, through which the Sacred Way ran up to the Capitoline Hill and the temple of Jupiter; the ancient Greek equivalent was the Agora, the commercial centre of Athens, surrounded by temples and public buildings.

MYSTICAL SYMBOLISM

The symbolism of the square is connected with its four corners, which suggest the foundations and sum of life: the four elements, the four seasons, the four stages of life (childhood, adolescence, adulthood, old age) and the four cardinal directions.

In ancient China, space was measured by the four yang or square directions; the earth god was represented by a square mound, and the capital city and imperial palace were both square, with the emperor at the centre. In Hinduism the square is the anchor that assures the order of the universe, while in Islam the human heart is symbolized as a square, as it is thought to be open to four possible sources of influence: divine, angelic, human or devilish. In contrast, the heart of a prophet is triangular as it is immune to the devil's attacks.

RELATED SHAPES

It is the number of sides of a geometric shape that gives it its symbolic significance. Other important shapes include the pentagon (with five sides) and hexagon (six), as well as three-dimensional shapes such as the cube and pyramid. In the mystical Kabbalah, the pentagon relates to the fifth sephira on the tree of life, associated with justice, war and the planet Mars, while in Islamic mysticism, it is a symbol of the five elements (fire, water, earth, air and ether) and of the five senses. The hexagon is also associated with Islamic esoteric teachings, symbolizing the six directions of movement (up, down, forwards, backwards, left and right).

A cube is a six-sided solid figure representing the three-dimensional physical world. It also symbolizes the six directions of movement. In Islam it represents perfection: the Ka'ba in Mecca, said to be the centre of the world, is a black cube. In Freemasonry a cube of ashlar (smooth dressed stone) stands for the perfected human being.

With four triangular sides and a square base, the pyramid synthesizes the symbolism of both shapes, as well as the numbers three, four and five, connecting with the Pythagorean "tetrakis". The square base represents the earth plane, while the four upward-pointing triangles of the pyramid's sides meet to form a fifth point, suggesting the fifth element: ether. As the pyramid reaches up to the sky, its point represents the human soul striving to unite with the Cosmic One.

ABOVE Perhaps the most famous city square in history, Rome's vast Forum lay at the heart of the city's religious, commercial, ceremonial and public life.

ABOVE The cube's six sides make it a symbol of stability and truth.

THE TETRAKIS

The sum of the numbers 1+2+3+4=10. In Pythagorean theory, ten is a holy number representing divine power and the quintessence of perfection. It can be represented as a triangle of dots, four to each side and one in the centre, called the tetrakis.

Colour

ABOVE Red is the colour of sexual and romantic love, and symbolizes intense passion.

Together with shape, colour is one of the fundamental building blocks of visual symbols. It is also closely associated with mental and emotional states, and can affect them profoundly. The seven colours seen in the rainbow correspond with the mystical number seven and other groups of seven, such as the number of notes on a musical scale or the number of chakras in the body.

COLOUR SHORTHAND

Different colours are often used as a shorthand to describe emotional states, gender or social and political status. In the West colours are traditionally used to distinguish between the sexes – pink for a girl and blue for a boy – and colours are chosen to differentiate sports teams from each other.

Colloquial English expressions that describe states of feeling in colour terms include "in the pink", "green with envy", "in a black mood", "feeling blue",

"seeing red" or "off colour". During the 20th century red was linked to the Communist party, while the green movement aims to put environmental issues on the political agenda. Similarly, colour is used to denote race, so that "black" and "white" carry social and political meanings depending on their context.

RED

As the colour of blood and fire, red is widely associated with life and warmth. In Paleolithic times, red ochre was mined and ground into powder. It seems to have been endowed with life-giving powers, and its presence in Neolithic graves may have been to help the dead in the afterlife. Thousands of years later, in Anglo-Saxon times, red was believed to protect against evil and objects, trees and even animals were painted red, while warriors covered their axes and spears in red paint to endow them with magic powers – a custom also practised by some Australian Aboriginals.

Red is linked with love and fertility. In ancient Rome, brides were wrapped in a fiery reddish-orange veil (the *flammeum*), a custom still observed in parts of Greece, Albania and Armenia, while in China, the wedding gown and veil are red. Red eggs are offered to the couple when a child is born. Red has been used to suggest passion and erotica in Indian and western tradition, or to suggest high energy and speed.

Red is associated with danger (the most serious crisis is described as a "red alert"), anger

and aggression (it is linked with Mars, the Roman god of war), or wickedness or evil. In ancient Egypt red was an accursed colour. associated with the destructive god Set, and "making red" was synonymous with killing someone. Evil doings were referred to as "red affairs" and scribes used special red ink when writing words of ill omen.

YELLOW

Closely related to the symbolism of gold, yellow is associated with the sun and its life-giving generative powers. In the Aztec pantheon, Huitzilopochtli, the victorious warrior god of the midday sun, was depicted in blue and yellow, while in Mexican cosmology, the earth's "new skin" (before the rain comes and turns it green) was golden yellow.

In China, yellow was associated with the centre of the universe, and one creation myth describes how the first humans were made out of yellow clay. It was the sacred colour of the emperor. Australian Aboriginals use yellow ochre to symbolize death.

Sometimes a distinction is made between different shades of yellow: in Islam, golden yellow symbolizes wisdom, whereas pale yellow indicates treachery. In Egypt and medieval Europe, yellow was the colour of envy; it also signified disgrace, and is still associated with cowardice.

GREEN

The colour of plant life, green can stand for awakenings, new beginnings and growth: in China and Japan it relates to spring. The

ORANGE

Midway between red and yellow, orange represents a point of balance between the libido and spirit: in India, it is the colour of the second chakra, associated with sexual energy and emotional relatedness. Through its association with the fruit, orange also symbolizes fertility and abundance.

Celtic Green Man is an important vegetation and fertility god, and there are many instances of green being linked with superhuman powers. In ancient Egypt, cats with green eyes were feared, and in medieval Europe green was associated with the Devil and wearing it was considered unlucky. The "green ray" is an extremely rare manifestation of light that can be observed occasionally at sunrise and sunset, and in alchemy, the secret fire, or the living spirit, was envisaged as a translucent green stone. In Islam, green is the most important colour: Mohammed's green cloak represented paradise, renewal and spiritual refreshment.

BLUE

Whether celestial or oceanic, blue evokes wide, open spaces and is linked with infinity and primordial emptiness. The blue of the sky has been associated with the male principle, distance and the gods. In ancient Egypt, gods and kings were often depicted with blue beards and wigs, and the Hindu divinity Krishna is portrayed as blue. Still, deep water, on the other hand, also associates blue with the female principle. As a symbol of peace and purity, it is the colour of the Virgin Mary. Blue is associated with dreamlike states, contemplation, introspection and yearning. In parts of the Arab

world blue is thought to offer protection against the evil eye, and the old English custom of brides wearing "something blue" is meant to ensure fidelity.

PURPLE

Historically, in the West, purple dye was the most expensive to produce as it was made from *Murex* or *Purpura* molluscs, which were rare and also costly to process. Only the rich could afford purple garments, hence the colour's symbolic association with royalty and the priesthood. It was the preferred colour of the Byzantine and Roman emperors.

In China, purple was the colour of the North Star, the centre of Heaven and the site of the "purple palace" of the heavenly emperor. To identify the temporal emperor as the Son of Heaven, his imperial palace compound at Beijing was called the Purple Forbidden City. Buddhists regard purple as a sacred colour, and in Thailand it is worn by mourning widows.

BLACK AND WHITE

In some parts of the Arab world, black animals are regarded as unlucky: black dogs bring death in the family, and black hens are used in witchcraft. White, the colour of light, is considered lucky. However, black is also a symbol of power and authority: it became an emblem of the Caliphate in the 1st century AD.

Death and mourning are symbolized in the West by black and in the East by white. In Africa, white is the colour of the dead, but is also believed to have the power to drive death away and so is associated with healing.

In ancient Egypt, black was the colour of resurrection and eternal life, perhaps because new life was seen as emerging from the darkness. It is associated with the mother goddess and fertility, when it is sometimes linked to red, the colour of blood. In China, black represents the feminine principle (yin), with its opposite being yellow.

In the West, white symbolizes spiritual purity and innocence, and is the colour traditionally worn for baptism robes and wedding dresses.

ABOVE Berenice (c.273–21 BC), Queen of Cyrene and Egypt, wears a purple toga as a symbol of her imperial status.

TOP LEFT Blue symbolizes divinity and peace.

TOP MIDDLE In the West, white symbolizes innocence and purity,

GREY

Traditionally, grey is associated with old age and with the planet Saturn. Saturn, or Cronos, was lord of time in the Greco-Roman pantheon, and wisdom was one of his attributes. On the Kabbalastic tree of life, grey is also linked with wisdom.

MYTH AND THE COSMOS

THE CREATIVE PROCESS

Creation may be described as one huge cosmic event, or a process in stages in which things become increasingly differentiated, sometimes leading to a natural hierarchy and at others to a sacred interrelationship between all aspects of nature. Whether the mythological creation of human beings coincides with the actual event of creation, or emerges slowly over time, the original man and the original woman are always seen as central symbols of primordial humanity.

BELOW This painting of God creating the world is rich with Christian symbolism, including the globe, symbol of power and totality, held by Adam, the Greek letters alpha and omega on the front of God's book, represent God's role as the beginning and the end, and the animals and plants, symbolizing the abundance and variety of God's created world.

THE CREATOR GODS

Creation is often actively brought about through the actions, dreams or reflections of divine beings. The Upanishads, Hindu scriptures of the 9th century BC, describe the Divine Self or Supreme Being who created the universe by reflecting upon nothingness and finding only itself. This fundamental act of self-consciousness led to the first word: "This am I." In Samoan mythology, the supreme god Tangaroa created the world from nothingness by thinking of it.

Australian Aboriginal stories more than 150,000 years old attribute creation to Ancestors living in the mythical space and time known as the "Dreaming". These beings lived much like their human counterparts, travelling, hunting, loving and fighting, and shaping the landscape through their "walkabouts". In sleep the ancestors dreamed the events of the next day, dreaming up all living beings, the sun, moon and stars. Australian Aboriginals believe that every being shares a fundamental connection with the source of creation, reflecting their deep respect for nature.

The book of Genesis describes God bringing about all of creation single-handedly. He completed his work on the sixth day with the creation of humans, who were to "have dominion" over all life. Thus the Judaeo-Christian cosmology gives humanity a special place under God in the hierarchy of nature.

CREATION FROM CHAOS OR THE VOID

The Greek term "chaos" refers to an initial dark, formless universe. From it sprang Eros, a fertility deity later associated with erotic love, but initially the creative urge behind life and nature. With Eros came Gaia, earth goddess, and Tartarus, god of the underworld. Gaia's son Uranus impregnated her, giving rise to the Titans and the Cyclops and then to the seas, land and other natural features.

Since oceans encircle the world, in many creation myths the universe arises from a chaotic body of water. The creation of the Egyptian world from water is fitting in a land that depended on the periodic flooding of the Nile: from Nu, the original water, a hill of dry land emerged, followed by the first sunrise on the new horizon, then the rest of creation.

The Japanese gods Izanagi and Izanami disturbed the primordial waters with a spear, and the drips from it coalesced to form the island of Onokoro. The Arunta people of central Australia tell of

LEFT The Egyptian sky goddess, Nut, whose body is arched over the earth, is separated from Geb, the Earth god.

a world covered with salt water that was gradually drawn back by the people in the north, revealing the first land. The myth of the Altaic shamans of Central Asia tells of a time before creation in which there was no earth, only endless water, over which flew a white gander, the god Kara-han.

CREATION FROM SEPARATION

The theme of separation explains the origins of life in terms of the splitting of a primordial state of unity. Usually this involves the rending apart of a male sky god and a female earth goddess, though in some cultures the male is associated with earth and the female with sky.

In Maori and other Polynesian myths the universe originally consisted of an eternal night or gloom. Eventually Rangi, the sky father, and Papa, the earth mother, coupled, creating the land and many divine offspring. They lived in darkness until it was decided to split the parents apart. Tu Matauenga, the god of war, hacked at the sinews joining his parents, which bled with the sacred colour of red ochre. But it was only Tane Mahuta, god of the forest, who was able to separate them, drawing them apart to allow light and air in between sky and earth. In a similar Egyptian myth, the sky goddess Nut and the earth god Geb were separated by their offspring.

CREATION THROUGH DISMEMBERMENT

A common theme is of creation emerging from the death and dismemberment of a primordial being. Such myths may help people to reconcile themselves with the violent preconditions of life and the need for death in order to sustain life.

According to Norse creation mythology, Odin, Vili and Ve killed the giant Ymir, from whose body the world emerged. His flesh formed the land, the sea and rivers flowed from his blood, his bones became mountains and trees grew from his hair. Ymir's huge skull became the heavens. Similarly, when the Chinese primordial being P'an-Ku died, his breath became the winds, his voice the thunder, his blood the water and his muscles the fertile land. His happy moods caused the sun to shine and his anger produced thunder and lightning. The Babylonian epic Enuma Elish, composed in the 12th century BC, tells of the god Marduk killing and cutting in two the body of Tiamat, the goddess of the ocean. The two halves became the sky and the earth.

Indonesian mythology tells of a time before creation in which there was no time, no birth or death, and no sex. Then a great cosmic dance occurred during which a single dancer was trampled and his body torn into pieces. Time began with this murder and immediately brought about the separation of the sexes. From the buried body parts of the dancer grew plants and trees. And so the first death simultaneously produced the beginning of time, growth and procreation.

FIRST MAN AND WOMAN

The origin of humankind is symbolized worldwide in the images of the "first man" and the "first woman", representing the blueprint of humanity. But with humans comes the creation of evil or forces of torment with which they must contend.

In Sumerian mythology of the 3rd millennium BC, Enki, the fun-loving god of wisdom, with his mother/lover, the earth goddess Ninhursag, and twelve other goddesses, moulded the first humans out of clay from the bed of the river Euphrates. Having created perfect people, they had a contest to create people for whom the others could find no role, giving rise to human imperfection.

In the Biblical account, Adam (whose name means "made of clay") is created from the dust of the earth by Yahweh, the creator God, who breathes life into him. He is then given a female companion, Eve, who will be the mother of all humanity.

Although in both these myths the first humans are created from the substance of the earth, there are differences between them. Sumerian humans were created to be made slaves of the gods, Adam and Eve were created by one God and given dominion, and their task was to "subdue" nature.

FORBIDDEN FRUIT

The story of Adam and Eve living in the Garden of Eden represents them in a state of innocence in which there is no awareness of difference, sexuality, good or evil. By eating the fruit of the tree of the knowledge, the one thing God has forbidden, they gain a moral sense and are responsible for the corruption of human nature. It is often the apple that is portrayed as the forbidden fruit, but this probably dates from medieval rather than Biblical times, when artistic interpretations of The Fall were created. The pomegranate rather than the apple is often favoured by Hebrew scholars.

BELOW The idea of the first human beings, one man and one woman, is common throughout many world mythologies.

The Sun

ABOVE Sunset symbolizes old age, endings and death in many cultures.

ABOVE The Eye of Horus was a symbol of royalty and immortality, and a talisman for protection.

MIDDLE The sun is an archetypal symbol, worshipped as a deity by many peoples.

TOP The lion is a solar symbol, a sign of power and leadership.

As our only source of light and heat the sun is crucial to life on earth and is one of the most important symbols in all world cultures. It is typically associated with power, manifesting both as a supreme deity and in emperors or kings. Its active energy is usually (though not always) regarded as male, and is associated with immediate, intuitive knowledge or cosmic intellect. The sun's counterpart in the heavens is the moon (often seen as female), and solar and lunar symbolism is contrasted by nearly all cultures. The solar principle is associated with animals, birds and plants (such as the lion, eagle and sunflower), with gold, and with colours such as yellow, orange and red. The sun is an important symbol in astrology, alchemy and psychology, where it represents the undivided self.

THE EYE OF THE WORLD

In many cultures the sun is likened to an all-seeing divine eye. It was the "eye" of the Greek god Zeus (and his Roman equivalent Jupiter), the Egyptian god Horus, the Hindu Varuna, the Norse Odin and the Islamic Allah. The Samoyed of the Arctic region regard the sun and moon as the two eyes of Num (the heavens), the sun being the good and the moon the evil eye. According to a myth of the Fulani of West Africa, when Gueno (the supreme deity) had finished the work of creation he took the sun out of his eye-socket and placed it in the heavens. He then became the one-eyed king, one eye being enough to see with, the other

providing light and heat. In many traditions the sun is poetically referred to as the "eye of the day".

SOLAR DEITIES

The link between the sun and divinity is archetypal, and many cultures have worshipped solar deities, including Shamash (Babylonian), Ra (Egyptian), Mithras (Persian) and Apollo (Greek and Roman). In Eastern traditions, the sun is the emblem of the Hindu god Vishnu and of the Buddha, whom some Chinese writers refer to as "Sun-Buddha" or "Golden Man". The Jewish High Priest wore a golden disc on his chest as a symbol of the divine sun, and Christ is sometimes compared to the spiritual sun at the heart of the world and called Sol Justitiae (Sun of Justice) or Sol Invictus (Invincible Sun), with the twelve disciples compared to the sun's rays.

Although the sun is usually regarded as male, in some cultures (African, Native American, Maori, Australian Aboriginal, Japanese and Germanic) the solar deity is female, because the female principle is seen as active through its life-giving powers. Japan's sun goddess, Amaterasu, retreats to a cave in protest at the neglect of his duties by her brother the storm god, and is enticed back out by other gods making much noise. In the cosmology of the Dogon of Mali, the sun is described as a white-hot earthenware pot (a symbol of the womb) surrounded by a spiral of red copper, representing the semen that will make it fertile.

TEMPORAL POWER

Many cultures and their rulers have claimed ancestry from the sun, including the Incas, the pharaohs of ancient Egypt, the Chinese and the Japanese. The Japanese imperial family are said to be direct descendants of the sun goddess Amaterasu, and the rising sun (represented by a red disc) is not only the Japanese national emblem but also the country's name (Nihon).

The rising sun is generally regarded as a symbol of hope and new beginnings, in contrast to a rayed sun, which signifies illumination. In China the sun was a symbol of the emperor who wore a sun design (a circle containing a three-legged crow) on his robes. Sun symbolism is a common motif on regalia. It appears on the thrones of the Kubu of southern Africa, while the Ashanti of West Africa use a gold sun disc to represent the king's soul. Modelling himself on the sun god Apollo, the French king Louis XIV (1638-1715) was known as the "Sun King", and court life revolved around him like planets around the sun, at his opulent palace at Versailles.

SUNRISE AND SUNSET

The disappearance of the sun each evening and its apparent rebirth the next morning make it a potent symbol of death, resurrection and immortality. This forms the basis of many myths and sacred rituals. In ancient Egypt the sun god Ra made a terrifying journey each night through the underworld, encountering his arch-enemy, the

RIGHT Apollo, the sun god of
classical antiquity, drives his solar
chariot across the sky.

monstrous snake Apophis, before
rising again in the east; if Apophis
were ever to defeat Ra, the sun
would not rise and the earth
would be plunged into darkness.
In the Native American Cherokee
tradition the sun is female, and
when her daughter dies from a
snake bite the sun covers her face
in grief and the world becomes
dark. To console her, the people
dance and sing, whereupon she
uncovers her face and the world
becomes light. The Sun Dance of
the Plains Indians is linked to this
symbolism.

THE BLACK SUN

Some cultures refer to a black
sun. The Aztecs showed it being
carried on the back of the god of
the underworld, while the Maya
depicted it as a jaguar. As the
antithesis of the midday sun at
the height of its creative, life-
affirming powers, the black sun is
associated with death and
destruction, foreshadowing the
unleashing of disaster. Solar
eclipses are therefore almost
universally regarded as bad
omens, heralding cataclysmic
events that bring a cycle to an
end: for instance, at the moment
of Christ's crucifixion, the sun

ABOVE In many traditions, a solar
eclipse was viewed with dismay
and fear as a symbol of misfortune.

went dark. In alchemy, a black
sun stands for unworked, primal
matter yet to be refined; to the
psychologist, it is an emblem of
the elemental unconscious.

PSYCHOLOGICAL
SYMBOLISM

The sun is often associated with
the principle of authority, of
which the father is the first
embodiment. It is linked with
individuality, will, ego and
personality, at the highest level
striving for psychic integration or
enlightenment or at a lower level
indulging in egomania, excessive
pride and authoritarianism. The
sun is also linked with creative
energy, health and vitality,
influencing both physical and
psychological development. As
the embodiment of male energy, it
can be seen as a representation of
the animus and may appear in
dreams and myths as an emperor,
king, god or hero figure.

SOLAR SYMBOLS

Symbols of the sun include a disc,
a point within a circle (used in
astronomy and astrology), a
spoked wheel (a Celtic symbol)
and a chariot – in many traditions
(including Norse, ancient
Egyptian and ancient Greek) the
sun is viewed as a deity
transported across the sky in a
chariot. A rayed sun suggests
illumination; a common graphic
symbol is a circle with rays
presented as alternating straight
and wavy lines, suggesting the
sun's power to generate light and
heat. Traditionally there were
seven rays, for the six directions
of space and the seventh, cosmic,
dimension. Sometimes the sun is
depicted with a face – among the
Native American Hopi, for
instance, as well as in Western
iconography. In Celtic myth, the
sun was personified by Lug
("Light"), sometimes referred to as
Grianainech ("Sun Face").

THE SUN AS
DESTROYER

The sun's power
causes drought. In
ancient China, people
would shoot arrows
at it to hold it in
check, while in
Cambodia rain-
making rituals
involved the sacrifice
of a "solar" animal.

ABOVE A halo of sunrays
surrounds Amaterasu,
sun goddess of Japan.

THE MOON

BLUE MOON

Two full moons within the same calendar month constitute a blue moon, a phenomenon that occurs every two or three years. Therefore "once in a blue moon" means hardly ever. In the Wiccan tradition an esbat (lunar festival) is celebrated in that year, on top of the usual 12, at which rituals and invocations are thought to have doubled power.

Being about 400,000 km/250,000 miles from the Earth, the moon exerts a powerful gravitational pull on both land and water. Its influence is most noticeable in the ocean tides, but many believe that plants and animals, including humans, are also affected. Next to the sun, the moon is the most obvious heavenly body, and its periodicity was of central importance in early concepts of time. The fact that its rhythms correspond almost exactly to the female menstrual cycle, and to the seasons and the annual cycle, led to obvious associations with the feminine and with earth or nature. The moon doesn't emit its own light, but reflects the light of the sun: the quality of this light has itself been a great source of religious and artistic inspiration.

THE MOON AND THE FEMININE

The symbolism attributed to the moon is predominantly (but not exclusively) associated with the feminine. The moon is connected to the imagination, intuition, psychic powers and dreaming, and is particularly associated with women, fertility and birth. Ancient civilizations performed fertility rituals and celebrated the moon at annual festivals dedicated to the goddess, to seek her help with conception. The time of ovulation for women was thought to occur during a full moon, and it was believed that during her time of menstruation a woman's powers of perception were heightened.

Moon goddesses are found in many ancient cultures. The moon is revered as a many-breasted mother of all, creator of all life on earth. The Greek goddess Artemis (the Roman Diana) is depicted with many breasts and with animals and plants springing from her head, limbs and chest. The Chinese moon goddess gave birth to all things after a flood; similarly, moon goddesses of Western Asia and Europe were the source of all living creatures. Inca beliefs about the moon changed over time: at first a goddess with no connection to the sun, she later became the sun's wife and the goddess of marriage. Her children were the stars. Finally she was thought to be her brother the sun's incestuous bride.

INNER WISDOM

The moon is a great reflector and embodies the qualities of receptiveness that are necessary for the intuitive process and to experience feelings. This receptiveness is another aspect of moon deities.

The moon is often associated with wisdom. The Greek and Egyptian goddess Sophia, or Lady Wisdom, is a moon goddess and the personification of divine knowledge. Shing Moo, a Chinese moon goddess, is called the goddess of perfect intelligence, and the Virgin Mary, sometimes called the Moon of the Church, is said to have perfect wisdom.

THE MOON AND THE MIND

As the moon pulls on the tides it can also be understood to pull on our emotions, which are often associated with water. Although the moon is sometimes linked with the acquisition of knowledge, it is more often associated with feeling, irrationality, and the unconscious or hidden. To be "under the influence of the moon" is to lose your reason, to be taken with moods and feelings, overwhelmed by the unconscious, which in its most extreme form manifests as madness or lunacy. (Despite all the folklore relating the two, there is very little reliable scientific evidence of a connection between the moon and madness.)

In early Japanese mythology the light from Tsukuyomi, Shinto god of the moon, could induce hallucinations and delusions. Hecate, the Greek goddess of the dark moon, bestowed visions but could also strike people down with madness. The same is true for most of the moon deities, with a thin line dividing inspiration and lunacy. There are stories of frenzied demons that are strongly influenced by the moon. The

BELOW The stones of Stonehenge are believed to have served to astronomically measure the phases of the moon.

ABOVE Since medieval times the Virgin Mary was associated with the crescent moon, in her role as reflector of the light of Christ.

Slavs tell of werewolves – people who are transformed into wolves by the light of the full moon. They are a great threat to people and are invulnerable to all weapons except for those made from silver, a moon metal.

PHASES OF THE MOON

The moon reflects the rhythms of life, undergoing an endless process of death and rebirth in its 28-day cycle; it therefore often represents transition and renewal and has come to symbolize cyclical time. The moon actually has 28 phases in its daily rising and setting, during which it passes through the entire zodiac. However it is more common to refer to four phases or quarters of the moon: waxing, full, waning, and the new or dark moon.

The waxing of the moon is associated with rising energy – mirroring pregnancy – and is often thought to be a good time to embark on new projects. The moon is at its strongest when it is full: it represents the fullness of female energy and echoes the symbolism of the circle, signifying wholeness. The waning moon is the time of decreasing, for letting go of things. The new moon is associated with restfulness and the beginning of the ascent from the underworld or death.

THE CRESCENT

As an emblem, the crescent moon is pre-eminently associated with female deities. The virgin goddess Artemis (or the Roman equivalent Diana) is usually depicted either holding a crescent or wearing one on her head. The upturned crescent is an attribute of the Egyptian goddess Isis, and in Christian iconography the Virgin Mary, inheriting some of the symbolism of Isis, is also sometimes shown on an upturned crescent. It is an attribute of the High Priestess of the Tarot, who is associated with mystery, intuition and the powers of the unconscious. In Hinduism the crescent moon is the emblem of Shiva, the god of transformation.

The crescent moon is a very important symbol in the Islamic world, symbolizing openness and concentration. Generally accompanied by a star, it is a symbol of paradise and of resurrection, frequently carved or painted on minarets and tombs. In the Arabic alphabet, the letter "n", shaped like a crescent with a dot above it, is the letter of resurrection, and prayers for the dead are written to rhyme with it; the letter is pronounced "nun", which is also the Arabic word for fish, and the fish is a symbol of eternal life in the Qur'an.

LUNAR MYTHS

In Nordic myth, Mani the moon and Sol the sun were created by the gods and put in chariots to cross the sky. Mani's chariot often came close to the earth so that his light could have greater influence on those below. On one occasion he snatched two children who were fetching water, Hiuki and Bil, to be his companions, and they became the waxing and waning moon. Mani was often chased by the wolf Hati – when he caught him the atmosphere would become ghostly, and when he managed to drag him to the ground there was an eclipse.

TOP The new moon symbolizes the resting point of the cycle of life.

ABOVE A waning moon represents 'letting go' and 'decrease'.

THE STARS

ABOVE Stars are connected with spiritual illumination and divine presence.

RIGHT In the Christian tradition, it was a star that guided the Magi to the newborn baby Jesus, to whom they gave their gifts of gold, myrrh and frankincense.

ABOVE A five-pointed star was the emblem of the Assyrian goddess Ishtar (later Isis, Venus). It became a widespread symbol for spiritual and military ascendancy.

As pinpoints of light that illuminate the darkness, the stars have almost always been seen as heavenly symbols, signifiers of divine presence. They are archetypal symbols, appearing in sacred and secular traditions all over the world. According to the Yakut shamans of Siberia, stars were the windows of the universe. Their fleeting opening and closing gave or denied access to the upper world. In early societies, sky-watching was an important part of life, and astrology and astronomy were one. Celestial phenomena were of great practical significance, marking seasonal changes and providing a calendar for hunting and planting. As people noticed that certain occurrences in the heavens coincided with events on Earth, the parallels became fused into omens – a blood-red moon, for instance, was taken to indicate natural disaster or war.

STAR MYTHS

Many stories are told about the symbolism of stars. According to the Kalevala, the national epic of Finland, the stars were made from shell fragments flung out when the World Egg cracked. Among the Aztecs the Milky Way was called *mixcoatl* ("cloud-serpent"), and gave its name to Mixcoatl, the god of the Pole Star and of the hunt, who was thought to dwell in the stars. In the hieroglyphics of the Maya, stars are often depicted with rays of light shooting out from them. According to folk-belief in Guatemala and Peru, stars represent the souls of the righteous dead, while among the Inca the cosmic symbolism of stars extends to include not only humans but also animals and birds: they believed that in the heavens there was a double of every creature on Earth, responsible for their birth and increase. In the Christian tradition, the birth of Christ was heralded by the appearance of the Star of Bethlehem. Today, stars are associated with dreams and wishes and the belief that if you make a wish when you see a shooting star it will come true.

THE MORNING STAR

Because the orbit of Venus lies within that of Earth it always appears fairly near the sun in the sky, and depending on its cycle it is seen near either the rising or the setting sun. It is therefore called both the Morning and the Evening Star. In Babylonian and

SHOOTING STARS

Generally regarded as a sign of divinity, shooting stars have been interpreted as sparks of heavenly fire or seeds of the godhead. They are said to perform a similar function to angels, acting as messengers between Heaven and earth and reminding human beings of their connection with spirit.

RIGHT In Native American traditions stars are seen as the campfires of the ancestors.

Assyrian mythology, Ishtar, the goddess of love associated with Venus, descended to the underworld in search of her lover then returned to life, just as the Evening Star disappeaed from view for a period, before reappearing as the Morning Star to herald the rising sun.

Among the Plains Indians the Morning Star is a symbol of the life principle – because it heralds the dawn and the rebirth of daylight – while the Cora Indians of the south-western United States give it equal importance with the sun and moon, with which it forms a heavenly trinity in their mythology. In the Mexican tradition, however, the Morning Star was thought to unleash disease, and doors and windows were closed at daybreak to protect against its dangerous light; in Mexican folk art it is often depicted with a bow and arrow and wearing a skull-mask. In the Christian tradition, one name for the devil is Lucifer, which means Morning Star.

THE POLE STAR

The Pole Star symbolizes the fixed and eternal point at the centre, around which the cosmos revolves. In many parts of Europe and Asia it is variously referred to as a pivot, hub, navel, life-centre or gate of Heaven. In the Turkic tradition it is described as the "tent-pole" of the heavens; the Mongols refer to it as a golden pillar, and the Saami of northern Scandinavia call it the Pillar of the World. In most northern Asiatic traditions it is placed over the summit of the World Mountain,

pinpointing the residence of the almighty god in the skies; consequently in these regions altars are usually set at the northern end of a temple.

The symbolism of the Pole Star as the apex of the heavens mirrors human hierarchies. In China, for example, the heavens, with the rest of the stars fixed according to their relationship with the Pole Star, are seen in terms of the structure of society, in which the emperor and ruling classes were the pivotal point around which everyone else revolved, each in their correct place. In India, the Pole Star is invoked in Vedic marriage ceremonies, representing the bridegroom as the pivotal point of the relationship.

STAR SYMBOLS

A five-pointed star is known as a pentagram and is an ancient magical sign. It is a shape that appears in art and classical architecture, as well as in nature (in starfish and certain flowers). The lines joining its five points divide each other in the ratio known as the Golden Mean or Divine Proportion, making it a symbol of wholeness and perfection. When drawn pointing upwards the pentagram is said to

be a symbol of the cosmic human, and in Christian tradition it is a symbol of Christ as "Alpha and Omega", beginning and end.

The followers of Pythagoras used the pentagram as an identifying sign, and it also appears frequently as an emblem in the regalia of Freemasonry, a society that traces its history back to the Pythagoreans.

In medieval Europe the pentagram was used as a talisman against evil to ward off demonic powers. When inverted, however, with two points uppermost, the pentagram was associated with the devil, the points being seen as signifying his horns.

ABOVE Two versions of the eight-pointed Star of Ishtar, used throughout the Near East for many centuries before the birth of Christ. The top star is a Babylonian version, the bottom is Phoenician.

THE PENTACLE

In the Western occult tradition upright five-pointed stars were engraved on discs of precious metals such as silver or gold to create a magic seal known as a pentacle. Hebrew letters, Latin  words and Kabbalistic signs were sometimes inscribed within the star shape. The seal symbolized the power of the occult, and was believed to be able to cause earthquakes, inspire love, cause misfortune and cast spells, as well as offer protection against evil. The sign of the pentacle appears on the walls of ancient temples, carved into the stones of churches and as a pattern in stained-glass windows. When an apple is cut in half across the core, the shape of the pentacle is revealed: the European Roma call this the Star of Knowledge.

THE ZODIAC

ABOVE Aries resembles the head of a ram but also the fountain of life.

ABOVE Taurus resembles the head and the horns of an ox.

ABOVE Gemini symbolizes duality.

ABOVE Cancer suggests crab claws, and may represent a change in direction.

ABOVE Leo represents the lion's mane, or creative energy similar to the snake's.

ABOVE Virgo could be celestial wings, a woman holding a wheatsheaf or a snake.

Both a symbol in its own right and a collection of symbols, the zodiac is a belt of stars on either side of the "ecliptic", the apparent path across the sky of the sun, moon and planets. It is divided into 12 constellations or signs. "Zodiac" is derived from the Greek and means circle of living things. It is a concept that originated at a time when people thought that each heavenly body was inhabited by an astral spirit, and stems from a world-view that sees creation as a vast web of interconnected forces, reflecting or even influencing life and events on Earth. The constellations became associated with various life forms and objects, acquiring mystical significance in explaining human destiny and the complexities that make up human character. The signs are divided among the four elements, and each is given one of three "qualities": cardinal (creating or initiating), fixed (maintaining) and mutable (changing). Each sign is "ruled" by a celestial body.

ARIES, RAM
(21 MARCH–20 APRIL)

The astrological year begins at the spring equinox (in the Northern Hemisphere) when the sun enters Aries the ram. The ram is often shown running forwards but looking backwards. The sign is headstrong, enthusiastic, independent, ambitious and easily bored. Mars is the ruler of Aries; anatomically it relates to the head and face, its element is fire, its quality cardinal and its gemstone is the diamond.

TAURUS, BULL
(21 APRIL–21 MAY)

An ancient symbol of virility and fertility. Taureans are loyal, practical, calm, generous, understanding and patient. They enjoy sensuous pleasures, but can become stubborn and rigid. The ruler of Taurus is Venus; anatomically it relates to the throat and neck, its element is earth, its quality fixed and its gemstone emerald. A festival celebrating the Buddha's birth occurs on the first full moon after the sun enters Taurus.

GEMINI, TWINS
(22 MAY–21 JUNE)

As twins, Gemini signifies opposites and duality. Some traditions depict the sign as a man and woman, or as a pair of lovers. Gemini is associated with human contact, communication and the intellect. Its element is air, its quality mutable and its ruler Mercury. Anatomically it relates to the lungs, arms and shoulders, and its gemstone is agate. In India, the constellation is linked with Aditi, the Vedic mother-goddess.

CANCER, CRAB
(22 JUNE–23 JULY)

Cancerians are sensitive, moody, imaginative, romantic, protective and nurturing but can become possessive and overly emotional. Cancer is associated with the mother archetype; its ruler is the moon, its element water and its

RIGHT The zodiac circle is a symbol system representing cycles, stages of development, and aspects of the male and the female.

quality cardinal. Anatomically it relates to the chest and stomach and its gemstone is moonstone.

LEO, THE LION
(24 JULY–23 AUG)

When the sun enters Leo its power (in the Northern Hemisphere) is at its zenith and the sign is associated with warmth, generosity, creativity, courage and leadership, although it can also be egotistical, proud and autocratic. Its ruler is the sun, its element fire and its quality fixed. Anatomically Leo is related to the heart, and its gemstone is ruby.

VIRGO, VIRGIN
(24 AUG 23 SEPT)

Virgo, the virgin (in the sense of "independent woman"), comes at harvest. It has been associated with most major Western female goddesses, including Isis, Demeter and the Virgin Mary.

Virgoans are practical, discriminating, analytical and precise, but can be pedantic and critical. Ruled by Mercury, Virgo is related to the intestine, spleen and solar plexus. Its element is earth, its quality mutable and its gemstone carnelian.

LIBRA, SCALES (24 SEPT–23 OCT)

When the sun enters Libra it is at the mid-point of the astronomical year when days and nights are of equal length. Librans are artistic, refined and good peacemakers, but can be indecisive. The ruling planet of Libra is Venus, its element is air, and its quality is cardinal; its gemstone is sapphire and anatomically it is related to the spine, kidneys and liver.

SCORPIO, SCORPION (24 OCT–22 NOV)

The venomous scorpion is ruled by Mars and Pluto. It is associated in many cultures with decay and death. Scorpios are determined, forceful and inquisitive, with intense sexual energy and passion, although inclined to jealousy. Anatomically, Scorpio governs the kidneys and genitals, its gemstone is opal, its element water and its quality fixed. An eagle, phoenix or snake sometimes represents the sign.

SAGITTARIUS, ARCHER (23 NOV–21 DEC)

The ninth sign, Sagittarius, represents the perfect human, a combination of animal and spiritual power and divine potential. It is usually shown as a centaur bearing a bow and arrow; its glyph represents the latter, a symbol of humanity aiming for the stars. Sagittarius is a symbol of higher wisdom, the spiritual seeker, philosophy, learning and travel, but Sagittarians can also be unrealistic and unreliable. Its ruling planet is Jupiter, its element fire, its quality mutable and its gemstone topaz. Anatomically, Sagittarius governs the liver, thighs and pelvic region.

CAPRICORN, GOAT (22 DEC–20 JAN)

Capricorn, the goat, is ruled by Saturn, and heralds the depth of winter. Its element is earth, its quality cardinal, its gemstone garnet; anatomically it rules the knees, teeth and bones. Capricorn represents order, structure and stability, as well as ambition and hard work. Its name is linked to Capricornus, the mythological goatfish, and its glyph reflects the shape of both fish and horns.

AQUARIUS, WATER CARRIER (21 JAN–19 FEBRUARY)

The water carrier's glyph represents water and communication. Saturn and Uranus govern Aquarius, which is

ABOVE The zodiac represents a perfect cycle, and its symbolism is therefore related to the wheel and to the circle.

usually linked with humanitarian ideals, freedom, eccentricity and original thinking. Anatomically it is related to the lower legs, and blood. Its element is air, its quality fixed and its gemstone is the amethyst.

PISCES, FISH (20 FEB–20 MARCH)

The 12th sign is Pisces, symbolized by a pair of conjoined fish swimming in opposite directions, with its glyph representing this contradictory aspect. Pisceans often feel tugged in two directions and are typically dreamy, intuitive, artistic and impressionable, their psychic sensitivies making it difficult for them to live in the everyday world. Jupiter and Neptune, god of the sea, rule Pisces, its element is water and its quality mutable. Anatomically it governs the lymphatic system and feet and its gemstone is bloodstone. As the last sign of the zodiac, Pisces represents dissolution, the return to the watery abyss before the creative cycle begins afresh.

ABOVE Libra depicts a pair of scales and also a sunset.

ABOVE Scorpio is based on the Hebrew letter *mem*, and the arrow represents the sting in the scorpion's tail.

ABOVE Sagittarius signifies projection.

ABOVE Capricorn links the goat's horns with the fish's tail.

ABOVE Aquarius's glyph represents water, and conveys the idea of passive dualism.

ABOVE Pisces is two fish swimming away.

GODS AND GODDESSES

ABOVE Zeus sits in victorious judgement with the rest of the Olympians, and banishes the last of the Titans to Tarterus. As a supreme god, Zeus symbolized male power and authority for both divine and human worlds.

Every culture has created its own mythology, theology and sacred rituals in its quest to come to terms with the mysteries of the universe. Although these are rooted in and specific to the culture in which they arise, there are nevertheless many striking similarities in the various deities of the world, making them powerful archetypal symbols that explore some of the most profound ideas of humankind.

SUPREME GODS

The idea of a supreme creator god is universal, symbolizing the primeval force from which all life begins. In many traditions, the deity is self-created and appears magically: for instance, in ancient Egypt, Atum (whose name means "the all") arose as a mound or hill from the chaos of the watery abyss, while the Zulu Unkulunkulu created himself from the vast swamp of coloured reeds that existed at the beginning of the world.

The supreme god frequently symbolizes male power and authority and is linked with the archetypes of father, king and warrior leader. He is seen as omnipotent and omnipresent, exercising authority over nature, animals and human beings. Odin, the warrior god of the Norse pantheon, was known as the "all-father". The Celtic Dagda, whose name means "all-powerful god", controlled the weather and the crops and offered his people protection and benediction. Both Odin and Dagda were renowned for their wisdom, another feature of supreme gods. At times the supreme god embodies righteous fury at human misdemeanours: the thunderbolt, which the god brandished when he was enraged, was an attribute of both Zeus, the ancient Greek ruler of Heaven and Earth, and the Inca creator god Viracocha ("lord of the world"). Other examples of supreme gods include Quetzalcoatl (Aztec), Vishnu (India) and Tangaroa (Polynesia).

Not all supreme deities are male, however. The Chinese goddess Nu Gua, whose lower body was that of a snake or fish, made all living things as she transformed herself into a multitude of shapes, while in the Native American Navajo tradition, Spider Woman (or Changing Woman) brought creation into existence by weaving patterns of fate just as a spider spins its web. The Japanese creator deities, Izanagi and Izanami, were twins, a brother and sister who created the land by stirring the waters of the primeval ocean with a spear.

THE GREAT GODDESS

The concept of an all-powerful goddess is very ancient. Worshipped as the great goddess or the mother goddess, she is typically identified with nature or the earth. In South America, the fertile earth goddess was Pachamama (her cult was adapted to the Virgin Mary in the colonial period), and among the Maori was Papatuanuku (or Papa), the goddess of earth and rock and mother of the people.

The goddess is not only the creator whose limitless fertility and generous abundance generates, feeds and sustains life, but is also the destroyer, who demands tribute as part of nature's regenerative cycle of birth, growth, death and rebirth. She is often associated with the moon, reflecting her cyclical

QUETZALCOATL

One of the major deities of the Aztec pantheon, Quetzalcoatl created humans by sprinkling bones from the dead of the previous creation with his blood. He was also lord of knowledge, god of the wind and the zodiac, vegetation and the arts. He was a compassionate deity who taught peace and was a force for good. His emblems were a turquoise-encrusted snake and a cloak.

nature and her light and dark attributes. In some early societies she was represented by a cone or pillar of stone, sometimes white and sometimes black, corresponding to her bright and dark aspects. In Chaldea, in Babylonia (modern Iraq), the goddess was worshipped in the form of a sacred black stone, which some scholars believe is the same holy stone that has become central to the Islamic faith, the Ka'ba in Mecca.

Representations of the Great Goddess include Selene (Greco-Roman), Isis (ancient Egyptian) and Ishtar (Babylonian). In India the Great Goddess is known variously as Shakti – the ultimate creative force – Devi or Maha-Devi ("great Devi") and is regarded as a personification of the feminine principle and the mother of all things. In her dark aspect she takes on ferocious forms, including Durga, the warrior goddess, and Kali, the goddess of death. Durga is usually depicted riding a tiger and carrying weapons in each of her ten hands, with which she slays her enemies, while Kali is shown with a garland of skulls, brandishing a sword in one hand and a severed head in the other.

THE TRIPLE GODDESS

In many traditions the goddess is split into separate entities, typically three – maiden, mother and crone – corresponding to the waxing, full and waning phases of the moon. In the Greco-Roman pantheon, Artemis (Roman Diana), Demeter (Ceres) and Hecate represent the three aspects of the Triple Goddess. Sister to Apollo, who is associated with the sun, the virgin hunter goddess Artemis is often shown carrying a silver bow and arrow, which she uses to protect but also to kill. Demeter is the goddess of the fruits of the earth, and her attributes are the wheatsheaf, sickle and cornucopia (horn of plenty). Hecate, goddess of night, darkness and death, is sometimes portrayed with three bodies or faces to symbolize her links with the moon. She is linked with places of transition as guardian of the gates of Hades, and goddess of the crossroads. Hecate is associated with magic and witchcraft in occult traditions.

LESSER DEITIES

There are gods and goddesses connected with practically every dimension of life – both in the natural world and in human society. Nature gods include deities of the skies, oceans and vegetation. For instance, Uranus (ancient Greek) and Rangi (Maori) are sky gods, Poseidon or Neptune (Greco-Roman) and Susanowo (Japanese) rule the oceans, while Tammuz (Sumerian) and the Green Man (Celtic) are fertility gods connected with nature and the renewal of life in the spring.

Although the Earth and the moon are typically associated with female deities, in some traditions they are male gods. Among the Inuit people, Igaluk, the spirit of the moon and a powerful and skilful hunter, is male, while in ancient Egypt the Earth was personified by Geb,

THE GODDESS ISIS

Isis was one of the most important deities of the ancient world. Her name means "seat" or "throne", and sometimes she is depicted wearing a throne on her headdress. She is also shown wearing a headdress of a pair of cow horns with a sun disc between them, linking her to Hathor, goddess of love and fertility. Isis was associated with magic motherhood, and nature. For the Greeks she offered protection to sailors, while in ancient Rome roses were her attribute.

who is usually depicted with a green body, to represent the earth's vegetation, and an erect phallus, showing his desire to reach Nut, goddess of the sky.

There are also deities of agriculture and fishing, mountains and forests, volcanoes and earthquakes, rivers and fish, the weather and wild beasts. Examples of these nature gods include the Hindu goddess Parvati, the consort of Shiva, whose name means "mountain daughter"; Pele, the Hawaiian god of volcanic fire; Chac, the Maya rain god; Thor, the Norse god of thunder; Sedna, the Inuit goddess of sea creatures; and the Native North American Selu, or Corn Woman, who brings the gift of knowledge of the cultivation of corn to her people.

In Africa, earth and water are invariably goddesses: among the Yoruba of West Africa, Ile is the mother goddess of the Earth and Yemoja is the goddess of water. Yemoja's messengers are the hippopotamus and crocodile, and her daughter is Aje, goddess of the river Niger.

BELOW The Hindu mother goddess Mahadevi is depicted here in her benign aspect, as Parvati (consort of Shiva), while the weapon-bearing arms symbolize Durga, the warrior goddess.

ABOVE According to legend, Venus, goddess of love, was born from the sea. She is shown here with the abundant, long hair that symbolizes her maidenhood.

GODS AND HUMANITY

Many cultures honour deities connected with society and human values. There are gods of love and courtship such as the Greek Eros (Roman Cupid) and the Aztec Xochiquetzal, and goddesses of marriage and motherhood such as the Hindu Lakshmi and the Chinese Kuan-Yin, the goddess of mercy. The Domovoy of Russia and the Lares and Penates of ancient Rome are household spirits that safeguard the home and family. Deities of the arts and crafts include Benten,

the Japanese goddess of music; Wen Chang, the Chinese god of literature; Tane-Mahuta, the Maori god of woodcrafts and carving; and Hephaestus/Vulcan, the Greco-Roman blacksmith god. Abstract concepts such as wisdom, justice, truth and knowledge are also deified by figures such as Athena/Minerva, the Greco-Roman goddess of wisdom and warfare; Maat, the ancient Egyptian goddess of truth and justice; and Brigid, the Celtic goddess of learning.

GODS OF LOVE

The need for love and relationship is fundamental to humankind. It is a force for integration and the resolution of conflict; through trust and surrender to the love partner, opposites may be synthesized, leading to union and wholeness for each individual. When depraved, however, it becomes a principle of division and death. Love can take many different forms – from sexual love and passion at one end of the scale to spiritual love at the other – and in its many guises is represented by a multitude of gods and

goddesses. These include Kama, the Indian god of love; Aphrodite/Venus, the goddess of love in the Greco-Roman tradition, who was allegedly born from the foam of the sea; Iarilo, the Slavic god of love and regeneration; Freya, the Norse goddess of fertility, sensuality and erotic love; and Bastet, the ancient Egyptian goddess associated with pleasure and sexual love. Bastet loved music and dancing, and her sacred symbol was a sistrum or rattle. The spectacular annual festival held in her name attracted large crowds, and more wine was consumed then than during the whole of the rest of the year.

GODS OF WAR

Though war predominantly symbolizes aggression, destructive power and the triumph of brute force, warrior values such as courage and honour are upheld in many societies and sacred traditions. Even in Buddhism, a religion well known for its pacifism, the Buddha is referred to as a "warrior in shining armour". War can also be seen in symbolic terms as an internal struggle, a transitional stage in a

BELOW Lakshmi, the Hindu goddess of fortune, is associated with the elephant (a sign of royalty) and the lotus flower, a symbol of purity.

move from darkness to light, bondage to freedom. Examples of gods and goddesses of war include the Ahayuta Achi, the powerful twin gods of war of the North American Zuni Pueblo people, and the Morrigan, the war goddess of the Celts.

The Ahayuta Achi were children of the sun and displayed great courage when they stole rain-making implements from a ferocious warrior group. They were brave fighters and fiercely protective of the Zuni people, slaying monsters and wrongdoers on their behalf. They were also responsible for providing tools and knowledge of hunting to the people. The Morrigan, sometimes referred to as the Queen of Demons, often appeared as a triple goddess, her three aspects representing war, slaughter and death. Skilful in magic and prophecy, she appeared on the battlefield as crows or ravens (her symbols), feasting on the dead. She used her shape-shifting abilities to seduce men to satisfy her sexual appetite and engaged in a spectacular sexual tryst with Dagda, the Celtic supreme god.

Sometimes war gods are also associated with peace. The

THE MIMI TRICKSTER DEITIES

According to an Aboriginal myth from Arnhem Land, in the Northern Territory of Australia, the Mimi are said to inhabit gaps and cracks in the region's escarpments. They are sometimes depicted in bark paintings as slender, ghostly figures, and it is said they can be heard at night when they sing and beat on the rocks. The Mimi have a dual nature: on the one hand they are generous and helpful, teaching humans how to hunt, yet if disturbed they can wreak havoc, bringing illness and misfortune. Consequently bush hunters call out to warn the Mimi of their presence and avoid harming any wallaby that seems to be tame, as it might be a pet of the Mimi, who will inflict death on anyone who injures it.

Japanese deity Hachiman, though primarily a Shinto deity, is also acknowledged in Buddhism, where he is called Daibosatsu ("great bodhisattva"). His attributes are a staff and a dove, the latter symbolizing the peace that follows his actions. His function is to protect warriors and the community at large. Another protective peace-keeping god is the Chinese Guan-Di, a god of war, loyalty and justice.

TRICKSTER GODS

The trickster god is a rebellious, amoral and anarchic figure, an anti-hero who enjoys disrupting and upsetting the status quo – whether this be among gods or mortals. He is often of mixed nature with animal, human and divine characteristics. His mischief-making is viewed with ambivalence – sometimes he appears as a malevolent saboteur,

and sometimes his actions help humankind. The Norse Loki, for instance, was both a friend of the gods and a thief who stole their treasures, while the Native North American Coyote is both a hero and villain. Among the Navajo, Coyote is a co-creator with First Man and First Woman and comes up from the underworld bearing plant seeds, which he distributes to the different tribes; yet the Apache hold him responsible for the arrival of the Europeans, and the Maidu of California for bringing sickness, sorrow and death to humankind. Other examples of trickster gods include Eshu, of the West African Yoruba; the Polynesian Maui, bringer of fire to humanity; and the Australian Aboriginal Mimi.

FREYA

Norse goddess of fertility, sensuality and erotic love, Freya protected not only women in marriage and childbirth but also warriors and kings. She was an expert in magic and had the ability to shape-shift, wearing a cloak of feathers and transforming into a falcon to fly through the underworld.

BELOW This ancient carving shows a curly haired Loki, the Norse trickster god.

THE GOD TANE-MAHUTA

In the Maori tradition, Tane-Mahuta was the son of Rangi, the sky god, and Papa, the earth goddess. He was responsible for creating the realm of light by pushing his parents apart with his feet, thus separating earth and sky. Because his parents were naked, he created trees and plants to cover his mother and spangled his father with stars. Tane became lord of the forest and all the creatures that lived in it (including humans) and of all things made from trees. Consequently, he became the god of all those that work with wood. Canoe builders rest their axes in his temple and pray to him the night before they chop down a tree to make a canoe.

HEAVEN AND HELL

ABOVE The Bible says that souls will be divided on Judgement Day between the saved, who will go to Heaven, and the damned, who will go to Hell.

NINE HELLS

In Aztec mythology there were nine hells through which the souls of the dead were conducted by a dog, which was sacrificed as part of the funerary ritual. Their souls were literally returning to the land from which they originated. After passing the eighth hell, the soul was plunged into the ninth, the eternal house of the dead.

The division of the above and the below is a common mythical theme, symbolizing a fundamental duality in the universe. Different values and meanings have been ascribed to the two polarities, with the above associated predominantly with the abode of the immortals, a place of bliss, while the below is the abode of devils and divinities, where the souls of the dead are tormented. By way of contrast, in animist or shamanic traditions the above and below are seen as interdependent; a perspective that honours both life and death, and values the natural cycles of life.

In different cultures, and different times, Heaven and Hell have been understood both as literal places and as metaphors of various kinds.

SUMERIA

The earliest description of the underworld is in Sumerian mythology of around 2700 BC, when the goddess Inanna descends to the underworld and undergoes a symbolic transformation. She leaves the "great above" for the "great below" to face her twin sister Ereshkigal, the ruling goddess of the underworld. As Inanna descends she can pass through the seven gates of invisibility only by stripping away her life and fertility in the form of her sparkling clothes and jewels, until she arrives naked before Ereshkigal. She becomes a corpse, but the trickster god Enki finds a way for her to return to earth if she can find a substitute soul. Discovering that her lover

Dumuzi has not mourned for her, Inanna banishes him to the underworld in her place, while she returns to life for six months of each year.

Inanna is the goddess of fertility, and this story symbolizes the seasonal fertility cycle, in which plant life grows, matures and dies, and then is renewed. The story also represents the psychological journey in which a person faces their whole self by sacrificing their ego.

ANCIENT EGYPT

The Pyramid Texts are long columns of hieroglyphs inscribed on the walls of burial chambers. It is thought that they were written to aid the ascension of the pharaoh to the heavens in order to live eternally by the side of his father, Ra, the supreme god.

The first ruler of the Egyptian underworld was Anubis, depicted as a man with the head of a jackal. As the god of putrefaction and embalming, Anubis oversaw the judgement of the dead and protected them in the afterlife. Eventually Osiris, originally a god of vegetation, took over the role of judge of the dead. To reach the underworld, he himself died and was embalmed by Anubis: his mummification symbolized for the Egyptians a new and longstanding belief in the afterlife.

GREECE AND ROME

The ancient Greek underworld was called after its ruler, the god Hades, whose name means "unseen one". The Romans knew him as Pluto, the "rich one", and depicted him holding a horn of plenty, reflecting his command of the earth's resources.

Greek heroes, wise men and initiates went to a light and happy place in the underworld called the Elysian Fields, which Homer described as located at the most western point of the earth. Centuries later, the Roman poet Virgil (70–19 BC) portrayed the Elysian Fields as a place of perpetual spring, with its own solar system. The deepest part of Hades was Tartarus, the prison of the Titans and those condemned to eternal punishment.

JUDAISM

In Judaism there is no clear concept of a hell. Gehenna, which is described as a challenging and unpleasant place, can be understood to be a place in which the soul is purified or spiritually transformed in order that it can finally ascend to Gan Eden, or Heaven. Gehenna was originally the name of a rubbish tip just outside of the walls of Jerusalem, where fires were continually kept alight by adding brimstone to burn up the refuse. The bodies of criminals who had been executed were dumped there.

CHRISTIANITY

In the Christian tradition Heaven is a place associated with light, while Hell is dark, lacking the light of God's presence due to the sins of humanity. The early Christians believed Heaven to be a physical place above the clouds, but this notion was challenged by new ideas about the nature of the universe. Modern Christians do not see it as a physical place, but

may still believe in its physical existence in another dimension.

The original biblical depiction of Hell is of an underground cavern to which the souls of the dead, both good and bad, went for eternity. Later books of the Bible describe it as a place of annihilation or eternal punishment, and a more modern Christian image of Hell is of a state of great suffering.

ISLAM

The Qur'an describes Heaven and Hell in vivid detail. Heaven is seen as a paradise and Hell as a place of fiery torment, though there are divergent beliefs among Muslims as to whether these descriptions are to be considered literally or metaphorically. In Islamic belief, each person is judged according to whether they have lived life to their best abilities in accordance with the truth. Infidels who reject the truth of Islam are given no mercy, and will fall down into Jahannam, or Hell, while the good will live in Heaven.

BUDDHISM

In Buddhism there are six realms of existence, representing states of mind, which people continually pass through in cyclical reincarnations, until they attain liberation from the physical state. The deva, or heavenly realm, is a place of pleasant things, but it is also an impermanent state. The realm of humans is a place that can be both happy and sad. The realm of the asuras (jealous gods or demons) is a place of fighting. The world of the hungry-ghosts is

a place of dissatisfaction and discontent, where there is always hunger. The animal realm is a place in which there is no faculty of reason. Finally, the realm of Hell is a place of great suffering and pain. Someone who has become free from attachment and has seen into their true nature ultimately achieves the state of Buddhahood.

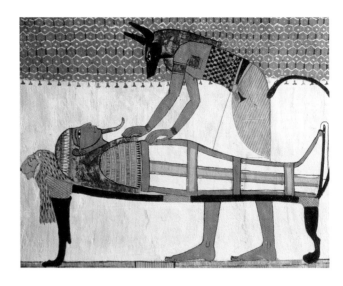

ABOVE The jackal-headed Anubis, first Egyptian ruler of the underworld, embalming a body on a lion-shaped couch.

BELOW Paradise (from the Old Persian word *pairidaeza*) is an enclosed or walled garden of pleasure where the righteous may live in the presence of God.

DEMONS AND ANGELS

THE IMP

A lesser or weaker demon associated with behaviour that is troublesome or mischievous rather than evil, imps are tiny, dark and shadowy creatures. They can shape-shift, becoming weasels or spiders, and are associated with minor misfortune.

BELOW RIGHT When illustrating John Milton's epic poem, *Paradise Lost*, William Blake said that, without realizing it, Milton had taken Satan's part and portrayed the Devil as having heroic status.

BELOW A more traditional image of the devil shows him as more beast than man.

Both angels and demons are beings with divine powers, existing somewhere between the gods and human beings. Angelic and demonic entities are predominantly characterized by qualities of light and shadow, and can also be associated with the light and shadow within the human unconscious. Jung noted that some religions split off the demonic aspect, focusing only upon the light, and pointed out that "divinity" is also symbolized within the realms of the shadow.

DEMONS

In Greek mythology, daimones were divine beings that carried out the will of the gods on human beings, in the forms of fate and destiny. A daimon was given to each person before birth, carrying their destiny as a set of images or patterns that must be lived out on earth. Destiny can be delayed and

avoided, but the daimon is irresistible and never goes away, demanding to be lived or else turning to possess the person, thus becoming their inner demon. With their ability to perceive someone's fate, daimones were thought to present flashes of intuition beyond rational thought, acting as inner guides.

The daimon is an individual's life calling, the equivalent of the Roman genius, the free-soul, animal-soul or breath-soul of the Inuit, the *nagual* of the Navajo, and the owl of the Kwakiutl of north-west Canada. In some cultures daimones are conceived of as particular animal species. They are often associated with fire, and a genius was described as a fiery nimbus or halo. For Jung, the term "daimonic" described a conscious relationship with the archetypal figures of the human psyche.

The origin of the concept of angels, and of angels and demons as embodiments of good and evil, lies in the interaction between Persian Zoroastrianism and Judaism. Zoroastrians describe the battle between two deities: Ahura Mazda, the "wise lord" and god of light, and Ahriman or Angra Mainyu, the "evil spirit" and god of darkness, in the midst of whose fiery battle the souls of humans are judged. Judaism, as a monotheistic religion, conceives of only one God. Thus the equivalent of the god of darkness, Satan, was symbolically cast out of Heaven.

Christianity inherited the idea of demons as angels who fell from Heaven when Satan rebelled

against God. Early Christians saw demons as vapour-like beings with no physical bodies, leading to great debate about whether or not they were divinities. In the 12th century, the Church conceded that demons, like angels, had spiritual bodies over which they were clothed with material bodies.

As pagan and polytheistic religions were increasingly taken over by monotheistic religions, daimones began to be portrayed as demons, and the hearing of inner voices came to suggest madness or the influence of the devil rather than divine guidance. The fallen angels, or demons, took on physical and mental deformities, and were portrayed with black hair, and human-like skin tinged with red, black or white. While angels had celestial wings and predominantly human characteristics, demons – in line

RIGHT A heavenly host of angels preparing for battle. Many religions tell of the battle between the angelic forces of good and the demonic forces of evil.

with the Judaeo-Christian attitude of superiority over animals and nature – embodied aberrant qualities of the animal kingdom, with bat wings, claws, horns and tails, associating their evil with pagan nature divinities.

THE DEVIL

Ahriman, the evil Zoroastrian deity, is himself a creator. In Christianity, however, the Devil is a being created by God. The name is derived from the Greek *diabolos*, meaning "slanderer", but the Devil is known by many other names, including Satan, Lucifer, Mephistopheles and Beelzebub, and titles such as The Antichrist or The Prince of Darkness. The name Satan comes from the Hebrew for "adversary" or "obstacle", as he is the adversary of God. Satan rebelled against God, and was exiled to Hell. In the Qur'an the Devil is known as Iblis or Shaitan.

During the early Middle Ages, Lucifer was seen as wicked but not frightening. As Christian imagery evolved, he was portrayed as a new, terror-provoking image of a beast with horns, cloven goats' hooves, wings and a spiked tail.

ANGELS

In one form or another, angels appear in most of the major religions as intermediaries between God and humans. They are invisible or semi-visible beings who act as guides to the soul, helping it to grow and evolve. They are also believed to organize the universe at its very foundations, keeping the planets on course, and controlling the growth of life on earth.

Early Christian images of angels were very similar to Greek and Mesopotamian deities. They had wings, reflecting their celestial quality. Angels are also central to Islam, and it is believed that the angel Gabriel dictated the Qur'an to the Prophet Mohammed.

ANGELIC HIERARCHY

Medieval theologians described a heavenly hierarchy of angels. In the first sphere are the heavenly counsellors: seraphim, cherubim and thrones. In the second sphere are the angels who work as heavenly governors: dominions, virtues and powers. And the lowest orders of angels, most familiar to humans, are the heavenly messengers, found in the third sphere: principalities, archangels and angels.

The seraphim, whose name means "to burn" in Hebrew, are angels who literally burn with passion for the creator, wrapping their wings around God and never revealing his presence. They continually sing his praises and regulate the heavens with the music of the spheres. The cherubim, whose name may come from an Assyrian word meaning "to be near", are the guardians of the light that shines down from the heavens and touches the lives of humans. After the Fall, God is said to have placed the cherubim east of the Garden of Eden, between it and the human realm, to protect the Tree of Life with flaming swords.

Called in ancient texts the "lords of the flame" because they are formed of pure light or energy, the archangels are the agents through which the creative will of God is executed. They bring loving guidance, protection and divine messages to humankind. The names of the archangels are Uriel, Tzadkiel, Khamel, Raphael, Haniel, Michael and Gabriel.

FAIRIES AND NATURE SPIRITS

The idea of a parallel universe occupied by sentient beings is at odds with the contemporary Western view of nature, and thus fairies and nature spirits have become relegated to the realms of the storybook. In popular belief, fairies have been on the decline since the 17th century due to urbanization and the supremacy of science, but there are still people who believe that the natural world is imbued with spiritual consciousness. Depending upon our perspective, fairies and nature spirits may either symbolize human aspects projected on to nature or be seen as independent beings with their own qualities and consciousness, living within their own reality.

Belief in nature spirits or fairies is most common where spirit is believed to animate nature. In Ireland, where there is still a connection to Celtic roots, and in Iceland, which is surrounded by wild nature, respect for the fairy peoples still thrives.

The Old French word "faerie" or "feyerie" originally referred to a state of enchantment, glamour or influence. Essentially amoral by nature, fairies or nature spirits often represent forces of fate that influence the human world for either malevolent or benign purposes. The fairy kingdom is often described as mirroring the human hierarchical structure, with the king and queen at the top, and also provides a picture of the structure of nature itself.

CHILDREN AND FAIRIES

Fairies are often connected with children, who are said to be more able to see them, and sometimes resemble them. Fairies are sometimes called "little people". In South America winged nature spirits, known as *jimaninos* and *jimaninas*, resemble well-fed children; they are said to be visible on the Mexican Days of the Dead. The tiny *abatwa*, from Africa, are said to live in anthills and are visible only to pregnant women and children.

A Christianized Icelandic legend tells that fairies were originally children of Eve. She was washing them when God called her, and she hid those who were not clean. God punished her for her deception, saying that what was hidden from God should be hidden from humans, and made the children invisible. This connects the separation of the fairy realm to a patriarchal culture in which women, children and nature have been devalued.

FALLEN ANGELS

Another Christianized view of fairies, this time Celtic, is that they were angels driven out of Heaven with Lucifer. As they fell to earth they became nature spirits of the earth, air, water, fire and plants. The *sidhe* of Scotland and Ireland are such spirits, known for their beauty and musical abilities. They are as tall as humans and live in underground fairy palaces.

The Tuatha de Danaan of Ireland are the fairy people of the mother goddess Dana. Legend has it that they built the Irish megaliths as gateways to the fairy world, and were the original guardians of the treasures of the Holy Grail. Finvarra, the king of the fairies, was obsessed by mortal women and enticed them to fairyland with his enchanting music. When someone is entranced by the music of a *sidhe*, they enter a trance – possibly the origin of the phrase "away with the fairies".

TREE SPIRITS

In the classical world, hamadryads (wood nymphs) were female spirits who lived within trees as their guardians, and who died if a tree was cut down. "Dryad" is a more general name for tree fairies found in enchanted groves. Often depicted as wisps of light, dryads are playful creatures, who may help, hinder or tease

humans, and become particularly active during the full moon.

In Japanese folklore Uku-No-Chi is a deity who lives in the trunks of trees, and Hamori is the protector of leaves. The elder mothers are Scandinavian tree fairies who live within elder trees, which are believed to possess a most potent magical power. The beautiful Swedish wood nymph Skogsra is the guardian of the woods and wild animals. Ghillie Dhu is a solitary tree fairy who lives in birch trees in Scotland.

THE ELEMENTALS

Elementals are spirits of the four elements, earth, water, air and fire, which, along with the moon, stars and sun, were the sources of all creation in ancient Greek mythology. The Swiss alchemist and philosopher Paracelsus (1493–1541) named them as gnomes (earth), salamanders (fire), sylphs (air) and undines (water) who inhabit a kingdom situated between the spiritual and material planes. They are said to govern natural and magical energies that influence human thoughts and desires.

Gnomes are spirits of the earth, appearing in the mythology and folklore of northern Europe. Depicted as dwarf-like beings who live underground, these elementals are associated with earth magic, herbal healing, protection, fertility and prosperity.

The Green Man is the archetypal earth spirit of green nature, commonly depicted entirely covered with green oak leaves. He appears as a symbol across most of Europe, where he

is associated with spring fertility festivals and the power to make rain. Stone and wood carvings of the Green Man were used to protect people against evil.

The elemental water spirits Paracelsus called undines inhabit caves beneath the ocean, lake shores, bogs, marshland and river banks. They possess the qualities of sunlit water, shimmering rhythmically. Nixies are water sprites of rivers, springs, lakes and marshes that often appear as beautiful maidens. They love music and dance and possess powers of prophecy. While they can bestow gifts upon humans, they can also be harmful, sometimes drowning people.

The water element is associated with the chalice, which symbolizes intuition and the emotions in the Western magical tradition, and with healing in such matters as love, sex, relationships and children. Water spirits can be consulted through "scrying", a form of divination that involves gazing into water in search of symbolic images.

The sylphs are ageless, winged elemental beings of the air, who live on mountaintops. They are commonly associated with logic, communication, learning and travel. Sylphs are invoked through the burning of incense or aromatic oils, and are connected to the ritual knife or sword, a magical tool of command.

Salamanders are elemental spirits of fire, originating from the fire lizard of the Middle Eastern deserts. Salamanders live in molten lakes, volcanoes and forest fires. They have flickering tongues

and change shape like fire itself. They are commonly associated with power, light, inspiration, purification and creativity.

In the Islamic tradition fire spirits are called "djinn". They inhabit the mountains that encircle the world and are known for their immense powers and their ability to shape-shift, sometimes appearing as gigantic men. The djinni (or genie) of Aladdin's lamp is such a spirit.

BIRTH FAIRIES

Birth fairies are said to be present when a baby is born, and bestow gifts or talents that will send the person on a particular life path. In the fairytale *Sleeping Beauty*, the 13th fairy bestows a curse instead of a blessing.

EARTH LIGHTS

Will-o'-the-wisps or Jack-o'-Lanterns were earth lights that floated in groups, thought to be fairies guarding lost treasure, with the intention of leading travellers astray. The light was actually that of burning marsh gas.

FANTASTIC CREATURES

ABOVE Giants appear in the mythologies of many cultures and are often viewed with terror, but in some creation myths they are symbols of the formation of the world.

ABOVE The flame-breathing chimera of classical myth had a lion's head, a goat's body and the tail of a serpent.

It seems likely that in early cultures, imagination and reality were not separated in the way that is habitual to the modern mind. Instead they represented two equally valid dimensions of existence, an inner and an outer world, each with its own wisdom. Fantastic creatures are inventions of the human imagination and occur in many traditions. They are attempts to explain the inexplicable, to catch hold of a dimension of experience that resists objective analysis and to explore important human issues through their symbolism.

ELEMENTAL BEASTS

Fantastic creatures usually inhabit a dimension that spans both the everyday world and other, magical worlds, acting as helpful messengers or teachers, or else as monstrous obstacles that must be overcome to reach a goal. Often they are hybrids – part-animal, part-human, or a combination of different animals, bringing together the symbolic properties represented by each to create something new. They are generally endowed with supernatural powers and linked to one of the four elements – earth, air, fire and water – although some are associated with more than one element: for instance, a mermaid is a fish with a human torso, linking her with both water and earth. As creatures of light or darkness, they also symbolize the struggle between good and evil and the spiritual journey of the soul as fears are confronted and transformed.

GIANTS

Named after the ancient Greek *gigantes*, who fought the Olympian gods and lost, giants are humanoid beings of enormous size. They are relics of a former age, existing at the beginning of the world or even, in some traditions, creating it, and may embody forces of nature. In China, trees and rivers appeared from the body of the giant P'an-Ku, and in Japan, natural features such as mountains and lakes were created by giants called *kyojin*. In the Norse tradition, the world was created from the body of the frost-giant Ymir, who was killed by Odin and his brother gods. Ymir's bones became mountains, his skull the dome of the heavens and his blood the seas that drowned all the other frost-giants except Bergelmir and his wife, who later bore a race forever opposed to the Norse gods.

Giants are usually the cruel enemies of gods and humans, as is the one-eyed Cyclops of the Greco-Roman tradition, although humans may outwit them – as in the Old Testament contest between David and Goliath. Sometimes giants use their superhuman powers to help people: the Dehotgohsgayeh of the Native American Iroquois offers protection against evil.

THE WILD MAN

Many traditions have stories of a wild man who is closely allied to nature. The Tibetan Yeti is a

---

CHIRON THE CENTAUR

Some mythical beasts have a positive symbolism. In Greek myth, the centaur Chiron was exceptionally gentle and wise. He was taught by Apollo and Artemis, and in turn mentored several heroes, including Achilles. Wounded by Heracles, he gave up his immortality rather than continuing to live in agonizing pain. He is an example of the "wounded healer" – embodying the idea that suffering is part of the human condition and that experience of it can be used to help others.

fearsome, gigantic creature made of snow and ice and in the Native American tradition, Big Foot or Sasquatch (derived from a Salish word meaning "wild man of the woods") is respected as a supernatural spiritual being. In European folklore the wild man who lives in the forest is typically hairy, with large teeth and sometimes with horns. During the Middle Ages he was known as the "woodwose" and, like the Celtic Green Man, represents the forces of nature.

The wild man has links with the Greco-Roman satyr – a creature of the woods and mountains that had the upper body of a man and the horns and hindquarters of a goat. Libidinous and mischievous, but generally benign, satyrs represented the carnal instincts of men; the fertility god Pan was the chief satyr. Later, in the Christian tradition, the satyr was identified with Satan.

TAMING THE BEAST

Mythical creatures often symbolize the tension between instinct and reason, nature and civilization that is part of human life. It seems that the more civilized humans become, the more fearful and suspicious they grow of their "animal" nature, which is seen as an out-of-control beast that must be tamed. This is symbolized, in Greco-Roman mythology, by the conflict between the centaurs and the Lapiths of Thessaly. The lascivious centaur had a human head and torso on a horse's body, and represented the wild, lawless and

instinctive side of human nature. At the marriage feast of the Lapith king, the centaurs tried to abduct the bride, raped the female guests and attacked their hosts with tree trunks and stones. In the ensuring battle, the Lapiths defeated the centaurs, symbolizing the victory of intellect and reason over instinct and animal passion – which in this story led to barbarous chaos.

The dark, bestial side of humanity is also represented in Greco-Roman myth by the minotaur, a man with a bull's head and tail. Imprisoned by King Minos of Crete in the labyrinth below his palace, each year it devoured seven virgins and seven boys sent in tribute from Athens. Theseus, who was part of this tribute, killed the monster and used a thread given to him by Minos's daughter Adriadne (a symbol of divine guidance) to guide him out of the labyrinth.

Classical myth provides many examples of terrifying creatures that are eventually confronted and killed by a hero. The hydra was a swamp-creature with the body of a snake and anywhere between seven and 100 heads. If one of its heads was chopped off, two grew to replace it. Eventually the hero Heracles killed the hydra by cauterizing each neck stump as he severed its heads.

Another fearful monster was the chimera, a fire-breathing creature with a lion's head, a goat's body and the tail of a dragon or snake; it was sometimes depicted with a head coming from each part. It was the offspring of the monsters Typhon

and Echidna and was a symbol of elemental chaos and natural disasters (especially storms and volcanic eruptions). The Greek hero Bellerophon killed the monster, swooping down on it astride the winged horse Pegasus and thrusting a lump of lead between its jaws. The beast's breath melted the lead, and it choked to death.

ABOVE The beautiful white, winged horse Pegasus and the courageous hero Bellerophon symbolize the triumph of good over evil, as together they kill the monstrous chimera.

THE BASILISK

Also known as the cockatrice, the desert-dwelling basilisk has the wings, triple crest and claws of a cock on the body of a snake. A guardian of treasure, a basilisk's poisonous breath was deadly and its glance could kill – the only way to overcome it was to force it to look at its own reflection in a mirror. It was said to have emerged from a yolkless egg laid in dung by a cock, and hatched by a toad or serpent. In the Christian tradition, the basilisk became a symbol of the Antichrist and during the Middle Ages was associated with sins such as lust, treachery and disease (especially syphilis).

RIGHT The harpies or "snatchers" of Greek myth were terrifying hags with bird's wings and talons who were symbols of death.

LEVIATHAN

Possibly based on the crocodile, the Leviathan of Mesopotamian folklore is a primordial sea monster, referred to in the Old Testament as the "crooked serpent". In Judaism it was considered the counterpart of the Behemoth, the primordial land monster (associated with the hippo) by whom it will be eventually destroyed. Its eyes lit up the dark seas, and its foul breath caused the waters to boil. In Christianity, the Leviathan represents worldly power, while its gaping jaws symbolize the gateway to Hell.

THE GORGONS

In Greek myth, the gorgons were three terrifying sisters – Medusa, Euryale and Stheno – who had scaly skin, fangs and snakes instead of hair. Like the basilisk, their power was in their eyes: they could turn humans to stone by looking at them.

RIGHT Here the Hindu god Vishnu is shown flying Garuda, a giant bird of power and a solar symbol.

RIGHT The harpies or "snatchers" of Greek myth were terrifying hags with bird's wings and talons who were symbols of death.

FEMALE HYBRIDS

There are many examples of female hybrids, all dangerous and destructive in some way. They represent male fears of the feminine principle, or anima, which is connected with instinct and irrationality. In classical myth, Scylla was a monstrous, six-headed creature with three rows of teeth in each mouth. She was named after the rock of Scylla where she lived, opposite the whirlpool Charybdis in the Medina Straits. She used her long necks to reach out and snatch sailors steering a course between the two obstacles.

The sirens were winged beasts with the heads and breasts of women and the bodies of snakes or birds. Similar to mermaids, they were known for the power of their singing, which they used to lure sailors to their death. Europeans once believed Amazonian manatees to be sirens.

In Greek legend the harpies were fierce and filthy flying hags, who could cause storms on land and whirlpools at sea; they were sent by the gods to inflict punishment on mortals. They symbolized sudden and early death and were also messengers of the underworld, to which they transported the souls of the dead. In common parlance, a "harpy" is a grasping or cruel woman.

MERPEOPLE

Mermaids and mermen appear in many mythologies. The Chaldean sea-god Ea was a man-goatfish, while the Philistine god Dagon, an ancient corn god, had a fish-like lower half. In Greek myth, merpeople inhabit Poseidon's underwater kingdom. Poseidon's son Triton, half man and half dolphin, directed the waters by sounding a horn or conch shell (heard by humans as the roar of the ocean) and was a positive symbol of power and control.

In European folklore, mermaids represented elusive feminine beauty as well as fickleness and vanity (symbolized by the mirror). They had magical and prophetic powers and loved music, they were often depicted holding a comb, which they used to control storms at sea. Usually dangerous to humans (especially men), mermaids such as the German Lorelei could lure mortals to death by drowning.

DIVINE CREATURES

As well as dangerous monsters, many fantastic creatures represent higher consciousness and offer protection. Pegasus, the winged horse of Greek myth, symbolizes the power for transforming evil into good. In China and Japan, lion-dogs are often placed outside temples and palaces to protect against evil forces and to signify the entrance to a holy or special place. In the Buddhist tradition, these creatures defend the Buddhist teachings, and male lion-dogs are sometimes depicted resting a paw on a globe, which signifies the *cintamani*, or Sacred Jewel, of Buddhism.

Popular among the Persians, Babylonians and Assyrians, the griffin has the head, wings and talons of an eagle (symbolizing vigilance and sharp-sightedness) and the body of a lion (symbol of strength). In ancient Greece it was sacred to Apollo (the sun god), Athene (the goddess of wisdom) and Nemesis (the goddess of vengeance). In medieval Europe the griffin represented strength, protection and solar power, and so became a symbol of Christ and the resurrection.

BIRDS OF POWER

Many traditions have examples of birds of power. In Hindu and Buddhist mythology, Garuda is the king of the birds and a symbol of spiritual power and victory. Half eagle and half man, Garuda is the emblem of the Hindu god Vishnu the preserver, who rides on his back. Garuda emerged fully formed from the cosmic egg and lives in the wish-fulfilling tree of life. He is the bitter enemy of the Naga – a legendary race of multi-headed serpents that inhabit the underworld and are symbols of water and fertility.

In the Native American tradition, the thunderbird is a powerful nature spirit. It is unimaginably vast (typically portrayed as an eagle) with lightning flashing from its eyes or beak and thunderclaps sounding when it beats its colossal wings. The Nootka of Vancouver Island believe it rules the heavenly realm, while tribes around the Great Lakes believe it is in continuous battle with the underwater panther, their battles causing storms that are dangerous to people in canoes.

THE PHOENIX

A mythical bird associated with fire and sun worship, the phoenix is one of the most important symbols of transformation, resurrection and immortality. It is often associated with the eagle and has fiery red or golden wings, suggesting the rising sun. In ancient Egypt it was known as the Bennu bird, and was said to return once every 1,400 years to

THE UNICORN

Usually white, with a single horn growing from its forehead, the unicorn is generally a symbol of purity. It has the body of a horse, the tail of a lion and the legs of an antelope, although it is sometimes depicted as a stag or goat. Unicorns were wild creatures that only virgins could capture, and so were associated with femininity and chastity. In Greek myth the unicorn was sacred to Artemis and Diana and was linked with the moon, while in Judaism the horn signifies unity of spirit. In the Christian tradition, the unicorn sometimes represented the Virgin Mary and also Christ – its horn was a symbol of the one gospel. In heraldry, its association with the moon makes it the counterpart of the sun-symbol lion. The unicorn also exists in China as the *qilin* (Japanese *kirin*), where it is depicted with a deer's body and white or yellow fur. This creature was so gentle that it would step on no living thing. Its appearance heralded times of peace and prosperity and it came to symbolize the wise rule of an emperor.

sit on the sacred *ben ben* stone at Heliopolis ("city of the sun"). In its most celebrated myth, the phoenix cremates itself on a wooden pyre set alight by the sun's rays, only to rise again from the ashes as a young bird. In Jewish tradition, the phoenix shrivels after 1,000 years, turning into an egg from which it re-emerges rejuvenated. In Persian mythology, it is called Simurg and is a symbol of divinity and of the mystical journey of the soul towards the light.

In China the phoenix is known as the Feng-huang; in its feng aspect it is a male, solar symbol, while as huang it is female and lunar, making it an embodiment of the union of yin and yang. It is depicted as a composite bird of colourful plumage, with the sun-like head of a cock and a swallow's back that suggests the crescent moon. Its wings signify the wind, its tails plant life and its feet the earth. Human qualities are also associated with the body parts of the phoenix, so that its breast signifies humanity and its head virtue. It is regarded as the emperor of birds and is one of the four sacred creatures (together

with the dragon, unicorn and tortoise) that bring peace and prosperity, its appearance heralding an auspicious emperor or prophet. Also known as the "scarlet bird", the phoenix is associated with summer, the south and red; it is also a Chinese bridal emblem, signifying unity through marriage.

In Japan the phoenix is called the Ho-O and is a popular symbol in Pure Land Buddhism, which emphasizes the reincarnation of the spirit. It is a popular motif on Shinto shrines (mikoshi) and, like the dragon, is a symbol of imperial authority.

ABOVE The phoenix is an archetypal symbol of transformation and immortality. As a solar symbol it is linked with death and rebirth in many cultures.

BELOW The griffin has the head, beak and wings of an eagle, the body of a lion and occasionally the tail of a serpent or scorpion. In Christian symbolism it is often used to personify Satan.

THE DRAGON

RIGHT Here, Saint George is depicted overpowering the dragon in a symbolic act of freedom from oppression.

ABOVE The Eastern dragon is a benevolent sacred or magical being with a serpentine body a lion-like head, and bird-like talons.

BELOW The western dragon, fire-breathing and often green in colour, represents a force to be reckoned with. It has none of the benign and auspicious symbolism of the Eastern dragon.

Dragons appear throughout the world as symbols of great power, with central significance to the cultures in which their legends are told. Their name derives from the Greek *drakon*, meaning "serpent". Dragon myths frequently deal with themes of chaos and disaster, fertility, rebirth and the cycles of the cosmos. Many ancient cultures have dragons or serpents with cosmological significance, such as the Greek Ouroboros, a serpent swallowing its own tail, which represents the destruction and eternal renewal of the universe.

Eastern dragons are more commonly symbolic of positive qualities, such as wisdom and strength, whereas in the West the dragon often embodies negative forces, or obstacles to be overcome by a hero on a quest. As a composite beast, the dragon combines different strengths and qualities of the animal kingdom.

CREATIVE AND DESTRUCTIVE DRAGONS

The earliest surviving dragon legend is that of Zu (or Asag), the Sumerian dragon who stole from the great god Enlin the Tablets of Law that maintained the order of the universe. Zu was killed by Ninurta the sun god, who thus prevented the universe from descending into chaos.

The Babylonian creation myth tells of a great beginning in which nothing existed except the two elemental forces: Apsu, the male spirit of fresh water and the abyss, and Tiamat, the female spirit of salt water and chaos. Tiamat was a dragon, with the

head of a lion, a scaly body, feathery wings, the legs of an eagle and a forked tongue. When she was killed by the god Marduk, her severed body became the sky and the earth, and Marduk created humans from her blood.

In the Bible the dragon is interchangeable with the serpent as a symbol of political opposition to God and his people. Representing the issue of evil, the essence of the devil and mankind's enemy, the dragon does not exist in the natural world, but remains a metaphor for evil in its many forms. Similarly in Persian myth the *azhi*, or dragon, had no regard for humanity, was in opposition to good and despised by the gods. Scandinavian myths tell of a

dragon that lurks in the pit Hvergelmir, gnawing at the roots of Yggdrasil, the World Tree that supports the universe, in a continual attempt to destroy it.

THE WESTERN DRAGON

In Western legend, battles with dragons often represent the fight between good and evil. Western dragons also represent greed, as they often guard hoards of treasure. In psychological terms, a fight with a dragon may represent an inner battle with a covetous nature or a resistance to development. The dragon can represent a huge psychological barrier to gaining access to the riches of the self.

A common mythical theme is that of the hero who leaves his familiar surroundings and meets

RIGHT Two dragons on a wall in China reflect how Eastern dragons are thought to be able to resolve the conflict of the opposites.

RIGHT Two dragons on a wall in China reflect how Eastern dragons are thought to be able to resolve the conflict of the opposites.

the monster or dragon at the edge of the known world. He faces the power of the dark forces and by killing the dragon is able to reconnect to life and the personal powers he has gained. The legend of St George tells of his fight with a mighty dragon that was wreaking havoc in Cappodocia (modern Turkey). The people had offered up a virgin princess in an effort to rid the area of the monster. George charged the dragon, killing it with his lance, saved the princess and freed the people from their oppressor. His example of bravery in defence of the weak chimed strongly with Christian values, and in the 14th century he was adopted as patron saint of England.

The red dragon is the emblem of the Welsh. The Mabinogion, a 12th-century collection of Welsh legends, includes the tale of the struggle between this red dragon and a white dragon, symbolizing the invading forces of the Saxons. The dragons were buried in a coffin of stone, representing the harnessing of the two powers: their containment was believed to protect Britain against invasion, and the story symbolizes the fusion of the fates of the Celts and the Saxons.

THE EASTERN DRAGON
Everything to do with dragons in the Far East is blessed. The year of the dragon, which occurs each twelve years in the Chinese calendar, is very auspicious and those born in it are destined to enjoy a long, healthy life and great wealth. Chinese people call themselves Lung Tik Chuan Ren,

"Descendants of the Dragon". The Chinese dragon, Lung, is a divine generative creature, the symbol of the emperor and imperial law and a key influence in Chinese culture. Lung symbolizes greatness, power, goodness and great blessings, and will overcome any obstacle to achieve success. He is intelligent, bold, noble, persevering and full of energy. The Taoist Chuang Tzu (399–295 BC) taught of the mysterious powers of the dragon to resolve the conflicts of opposites, making him a symbol of unity.

Dragons in the East are angelic in quality, beautiful, benevolent and wise. Temples are built for them, usually near the sea or rivers, as dragons live in and rule the waters. They create heavy clouds full of fertilizing rain, and are also associated with lightning and thunder, uniting the rain of Heaven with the Earth.

The royal family of Japan trace their ancestry back 125 generations to the daughter of a dragon king of the sea known as Princess Fruitful Jewel, and the emperors were believed to have the ability to transform themselves into dragons. Whether through ancestral lineage, or though a present relationship with a dragon figure, the dragon's qualities of power and wisdom are made accessible to the people.

DRAGONS OF THE AMERICAS
There are many different mythical creatures in the legends of the indigenous Native Americans. Some dragons of the Americas are benevolent figures with great

skills and wisdom to teach the people, while others are forces of destruction.

The Piasa, or "bird that eats men", of the Illini Indians resembled a dragon, being a large winged animal that ate flesh and lived in a cave by a river. It was greatly feared and attacked victims who came too close. The Piasa was eventually tricked from its cave by a chief called Quatonga, who killed it with poisoned arrows. The Chippewa and the Quillayute tell of a great thunderbird who created thunderclaps and winds with his wings, and whose eyes sparked lightning. His favourite food was the whale, who was forced to escape many times, eventually retreating to the ocean depths.

THE AZTEC DRAGON
Quetzalcoatl was a benevolent dragon god of the Aztecs and Toltecs. Creator of humankind, he civilized the people by teaching them to write and introducing them to agriculture. He also introduced the calendar, music and dance. He was known to the Maya as Kulkulkan, and to the Quiché of Peru as Gucumatz.

BELOW Quetzalcoatl (left), god of learning, battling Cuauhtli, the eagle-god of renewal.

CONNECTING WITH SPIRIT

SACRED OBJECTS

ABOVE Many sacred traditions use strings of beads as an aid to prayer or meditation.

BELOW A Buddhist prayer wheel is a rotating drum containing scriptures. Setting the wheel in motion is a symbolic act.

Every sacred tradition has its own ways of connecting with spirit and uses a variety of symbolic objects in its rituals and ceremonies. These are usually regarded as objects of power and are sometimes so sacred that they are unseen and untouchable.

PRAYER STRINGS

Common in many religions, the prayer string has beads or knots along its length and is a device to aid prayer or meditation. The number of beads usually has symbolic significance, and the string or chain is also symbolic: on one level it represents the connection between humans and the divine, but on another level a prayer string signifies the bondage of the human soul.

For Muslims, 99 beads symbolize the 99 names of Allah (the 100th being known only to Allah himself). Prayer strings are known as *misbaha* or *subha* and, as well as being used for the recitation of Allah's names and attributes, are a mnemonic device to aid the repetition of prayers. Hindus and Buddhists use a prayer string known as a *mala* when saying mantras, or sacred chants, in prayer and meditation. The 108 beads of a Buddhist string mirror the various stages of the world's development. A Catholic rosary usually has 165 beads, divided into 15 sets consisting of ten small beads and one large one. They are counted by saying prayers: each small bead represents an Ave Maria or Hail Mary and each large one the Lord's Prayer.

SACRED STICKS

Some cultures use sticks to connect with the divine. In the Native American tradition, special sticks for carrying prayers are made of painted wood and decorated with feathers, thread and other items. They are sometimes placed around the borders of a ceremonial site, or put into bundles and placed inside it. Maori priests use a god-stick to summon and hold the essence of a god or spirit. The stick, like a carved peg, is held by the priest or thrust into the earth. When people want to make a request, sacred strings are attached to the god-stick and pulled to grab the attention of the spirit residing in it.

PRAYER WHEELS, FLAGS AND STONES

Widely used in Tibetan Buddhism, the prayer wheel, or *khorlo*, is a rotating drum that is inscribed with and usually contains prayers, a passage from a holy book or a complete paper scroll. As the vehicle for a sacred force, setting the wheel in motion establishes contact between the person at prayer and the heavenly beings. It is rotated clockwise as prayers are recited. Large prayer wheels placed outside Buddhist shrines are rotated by pilgrims as they walk around the holy site.

Stones and flags are also used to carry prayers, and inscribed stones are a common sight along the pilgrimage routes of Tibet. Prayer flags originated in China and India, but have become a

RIGHT A *mani* stone tablet, in Tibet, inscribed with "All hail the jewel in the lotus", referring to the pristine consciousness.

colourful feature of the Tibetan landscape. People write their troubles on pieces of cloth and pin them to trees or suspend them on lines for the wind to blow the worries away.

As part of the natural landscape, stones are widely regarded as sacred objects and are often connected with myth and folklore: in China and Japan beautiful river stones were thought to hatch into dragons, and special stones were used to invoke rain and to bring a woman sons. In Nepal and Tibet *mani* stones, with prayers carved on to them, are put in temples and houses and alongside trails and passes, and probably number in their thousands.

In West Africa, the priests of the Yoruba god of thunder carry sacred stones that are thought to have been created by lightning. In the Celtic tradition, round stones with a central hole (known as "holey", or holy, stones) were used for healing and fertility rituals – it was thought that the hole would trap bad spirits.

MEDICINE BUNDLE

Native Americans use a special pouch to contain sacred objects such as stones, herbs and amulets. Known as a medicine bundle, it may be for personal use, or used by a shaman. Sometimes the bundle is a collective representation of the spiritual power and cohesiveness of the tribe. During the ceremonies of the Crow tribe the medicine bundle would be opened and the women would dance with the weasel skins to

obtain supernatural powers that ensured the fertility of the sacred tobacco, and so the growth of the Crow tribe as a whole.

CANDELABRA

Candlesticks and candelabra are sacred objects in many traditions. They illuminated Greek and Roman temples, appearing in classical art to represent piety and sacred ritual, and are used on Christian altars and in Buddhist ritual. In Mexico, "tree of life" candelabra combine pre-Christian symbolism with images of Adam and Eve and the serpent of knowledge, while death may appear as a skeleton in the "branches". The menorah is a seven-branched candelabrum that symbolizes the Jewish faith.

AMULETS AND TALISMANS

An amulet is a small object or piece of jewellery that is believed to possess magical or divine power; an object inscribed with a charm is known as a talisman. Both are thought to connect humans with the otherworldly powers they represent.

In ancient Egypt, mummies were covered in amulets made of gold, bronze or stone to ensure the immortality of the dead; the scarab beetle, the eye of Horus, the girdle of Isis and the ankh (the symbol of life) all featured on amulets used for protection or to gain qualities such as vitality or knowledge. A popular Hindu amulet is the *vishnupada*, the image of Vishnu's footprint. In the Native American tradition, animal amulets such as bears' claws are

thought to embody the spirit of the animal. In China, talismans are sometimes written in invisible ink or "ghost script", so that only the spirits can see them. In Japan, talismans known as *gofu*, designed to bring good fortune, are sold or given away at Shinto shrines: they are usually pieces of paper bearing the name of the deity. In the Islamic tradition, a common talisman is the *tawiz*, a stone or metal plaque bearing an inscription from the Qur'an.

ABOVE A Native American medicine bundle is a pouch containing sacred objects of power. This bundle contains tobacco.

THE MENORAH

The seven-branched menorah dates back to the Exodus of the Jews from Egypt. According to tradition it created itself from gold cast into the fire by Moses. Its seven branches symbolize the planets, the days of the week and the seven levels of Heaven.

ALTARS AND SACRED PLACES

ABOVE Salt can be used as an offering as a symbol of the earth, and also as a symbol of its life-preserving qualities.

TOP Burning incense is an ancient ritual act of consecration, the smoke often symbolizing the soul's journey heavenwards.

The word "altar" comes from the Latin *altus*, meaning "high", and describes a raised area that forms the focus of sacred ritual and worship. It is usually erected within a building or area dedicated to a deity, although some altars are not fixed but set up for particular ceremonies and then dismantled. Shrines also provide a focus for sacred activity, and vary from a small niche containing some kind of holy object (such as a statue) to a place of pilgrimage. All sacred sites, whether natural or constructed, symbolize ways of connecting with spirit and are places of meaning and power.

ALTAR SYMBOLISM

The altar reproduces on a small scale the entire sacred tradition it represents, and can even be seen as a microcosm of the universe. It has sometimes been thought of as the spiritual centre of the world, so its symbolic meaning is related to the world tree or the cosmic mountain. An altar may also symbolize the time and place where a person became holy or performed a holy act. Like the hearth at the centre of the home, the altar is the focal point of sacred activity: in the Christian tradition, transitional ceremonies

or celebrations such as weddings and funerals take place before it.

Traditionally altars were a place of sacrifice. The earliest altars were open to the sky, so that the smoke of burnt offerings rose up towards the gods; it was only later that they were enclosed in purpose-built temples in honour of specific deities, but the association with fire remains. In the Philippines, palm leaf prayer books are used as offerings, burnt on stone altars (*batong buhay*), while candles and incense are placed on altars in many traditions, symbols of the illuminating and otherworldly qualities of fire and smoke. Native Americans often use tobacco (which they believe to be a sacred herb), and sometimes salt, as an altar offering.

SHRINES

In many cultures shrines are an everyday part of life, appearing at the roadside, in the home, in shops and offices, as well as in holy buildings. In many Christian countries it is common to see roadside shrines dedicated to the Virgin Mary or to specific saints, while in India, China and Japan household shrines are dedicated to various deities to gain their blessings for the home. In a similar way, the lares and penates, the household gods of ancient Rome, were honoured with daily prayers and offerings.

A shrine may commemorate the dead: in China, ancestor deities appear on household shrines. A Christian grave, with its tombstone and offerings of flowers, is also a type of shrine.

TABLE OF THE GODS

For thousands of years it has been traditional to leave offerings of food and drink for the gods on the altar. Sometimes food and drink are blessed at the altar and then given to the people in an act of worship. In Christianity it is the bread and wine of Holy Communion, shared in a ceremony commemorating the Last Supper. In the Hindu faith the offering is known as *prasad* and is usually some kind of sweetmeat. Other traditions use items such as strings of flowers, money, lit candles, burning incense, or prayers.

THE SACRED IN NATURE

In traditional societies in which people are closely connected with nature, holy sites tend to be places in the landscape. Practically every feature of the natural landscape has been associated with some kind of sacred tradition. There are holy mountains, rivers and lakes, caves, canyons and craters, as well as trees and forests. Mount Fuji, a dormant volcano and Japan's largest mountain, is revered by both Buddhists and Shintoists and is the site of many temples and shrines – even at the bottom of its crater. The Nile was sacred in ancient Egypt and remains so today among traditional African peoples, while Lake Titicaca, the largest freshwater lake in South America, was sacred to the Incas, who believed the god Viracocha rose from it to create the sun, moon and stars.

ALTAR AND SHRINE DECORATION

Images or symbols of a deity are usually placed on or above the altar, and every item placed upon it has symbolic significance – candles, flowers and incense are typical examples. They may also hold personal items, such as perfumes and sweets. On the West African coast, shrines to Mama Wata, the water spirit, are painted a greenish blue and decorated with mirrors and items connected with water, such as fish and paddles.

For Australian Aboriginals,
Uluru – possibly the world's most
famous monolith – is the sacred
site of the Dreamtime. The
gigantic Serpent Mound of Ohio
is a sacred effigy built by Native
Americans; it is in the shape of a
snake and is possibly connected
with worship of the earth as a
divine mother.

In Europe, the site of Chartres
Cathedral was once a sacred
forest, as was the site of the
Temple of Apollo, at Delphi, in
Greece, and groves of oak trees
were sacred to the Druids. The
Ajanta Caves, in India, are rock
temples carved into almost
vertical cliffs above a wooded
ravine with cascading waterfalls;
the caves contain five Buddhist
temples and 24 monasteries. A
meteor crater near Flagstaff,
Arizona, which is deep enough to
hold a 50-storey building, is
regarded as a sacred site by the
Navajo, who believe it was made
by a flaming serpent god. Chaco
Canyon in New Mexico was the
dwelling place of the Anasazi, or
"ancient ones", ancestors of the
Hopi and Zuni peoples. It
contains circular chambers
known as *kivas*.

SACRED BUILDINGS

As societies became more
complex, people began to
construct sacred buildings and
towns and cities grew up around

them. Varanasi, on the banks of
the holy river Ganges, is India's
most holy city, with 6km/4 miles
of riverside temples and palaces.
In the central highlands of Java,
Borobudur (which means "temple
of the countless Buddhas") is the
largest Buddhist shrine in the
world. The way up to the summit
was designed as a clockwise path
of pilgrimage, with each tier
representing a progressively
higher level of spiritual
experience.

There are many examples of the
sacred sites of one culture being
adopted by another. Ephesus in
Turkey was once renowned as a
centre of magic and the occult
arts, and its temple to Artemis,
the moon goddess, was alleged to
be the greatest of the seven
wonders of the ancient world.
After Christians destroyed the
temple the site became associated
with the Virgin Mary; it has been
a shrine for many centuries.

The great golden-roofed Potala
Palace in Lhasa is the holy
residence of the (currently exiled)
Dalai Lama, and is a place of
pilgrimage for Tibetan Buddhists.

Its name, meaning "Pure Land",
comes from the mythical Mount
Potala, in India, a place roughly
equivalent to paradise and the
home of the Bodhisattva
Avalokiteshvara, of whom the
Dalai Lama is the incarnation.
The palace houses the tombs of
earlier Dalai Lamas, one of the
most splendid of which has a
massive golden stupa and a
beautiful mandala encrusted with
more than 20,000 pearls.

ABOVE The magnificent
Potala Palace in Lhasa,
Tibet, is a place of
pilgrimage for Tibetan
Buddhists and stands at
one of the highest points
of the world.

ABOVE LEFT This gigantic
meteor crater at Flagstaff
(Arizona) is a sacred site
for the Navajo.

ALCHEMICAL TRANSMUTATION

ABOVE Alchemists at work, in a 14th-century manuscript. The transformation processes they used in their scientific practices (here, distillation) have since become symbols of psychological and spiritual progress.

ABOVE The alchemy symbols for Mercury (top) and Sulphur (above).

Alchemy is a philosophy and practice that spans both science and mysticism. It has influenced the development of modern chemistry and even modern depth psychology. The alchemist sees direct relationships between matter and spirit and between organic and inorganic nature.

First conceived as a process similar to fermentation, in which common metals might be transmuted into gold or silver, the alchemical process became an analogy for psychological and spiritual transformation. The earliest references to alchemy are to be found in the records of ancient Egypt. The art was developed in ancient Greece and the Arab world, returning to Christian Europe via Moorish Spain during the 12th century. But alchemy – particularly the theoretical connection between

gold and longevity – was also known in ancient China and India. The process is described using a wealth of symbolism derived from astrology, astronomy, mythology and early science.

HERMETIC WISDOM

The philosophy behind alchemy is directly linked with the teachings of Hermes Trismegistus ("Hermes the Thrice-greatest"), who was described as a great teacher and imparter of wisdom. He appears to be a syncretization of the Greek god Hermes, who conducted souls to the underworld and carried the messages of the gods, with the Egyptian deity Thoth, patron of learning and magic. Hermes was represented wearing a winged cap and sandals and carrying the caduceus, a winged staff entwined with two snakes. His attributes symbolized the linking of the underworld with material reality and the transpersonal experience of "winged flight": he was essentially a mediator or guide between the worlds. Hermes Trismegistus was said to be the author of thousands of texts on science, philosophy, the occult and many other subjects that encapsulated all the wisdom of the ancient world.

Hermetic philosophy centres on the interrelationship of the microcosmic and macrocosmic worlds, contained within the idea "as above, so below", and that all things come from "the One". Applied to alchemy, this means that the human microcosm, where body, soul and spirit meet, is directly related to the elements,

the stars, planets, moon and sun, all of which are understood to be mirrored within each person as the "cosmic soul".

THE SYMBOLIC MAP

C.G. Jung considered alchemy to be a useful symbolic map for inner experiences. He related the different phases of the alchemical process to the stages a person goes through when receiving analytical therapy. Jung commonly used the term *unus mundus*, which he borrowed from the medieval alchemists. It is a description of a "one world" experience, in which the individual's body, soul and spirit are consciously reunited with the cosmic soul.

ALCHEMICAL TRANSFORMATION

The alchemical process, also known as the opus magnum or "great work", is essentially a process of change or transmutation, which may be physical, psychological or spiritual. The goal of alchemy is the transformation of a basic substance into a higher substance. This can be understood as changing base metals into gold, or as transforming the most basic of human awareness and experience into deep insight.

The result of the alchemist's dedication to the process was expressed as the *lapis philosophorum* or "philosopher's stone", an "inner treasure" or state of perfect harmony symbolized by the correct mixing of sulphur and mercury (which the alchemists believed were the principal materials of all metals). Alchemy is also associated with the process of prolonging life and striving for immortality by creating an "elixir of life" or "drinkable gold".

STAGES OF THE WORK

The *prima materia* is the raw material of the alchemical process, the prime matter that precedes the division into the four elements – water, air, earth and fire. In this raw state all the oppositions of life are present. The *prima materia* corresponds with the psychological state of minimum awareness.

The basic raw material is contained in an athanor, or oven, consisting of an egg-shaped glass vessel heated over a fire. The oven symbolizes the human, in which body, soul and cosmos are linked. It can also represent a ritualized space in which any transformative process is contained. The fire represents the generative force behind the process of transformation. Air from the alchemist's bellows is required to kindle the flames and amplify the process. The warmth within the vessel corresponds to a natural vital energy that is said to be within all things.

The *nigredo,* or "blackening", phase is the stage in which the raw material melts into a black liquid. This symbolizes the early awakening of awareness, and is also associated with the archetype of the wounded healer and the beginning of healing power. The *nigredo* can represent depression, through which a person begins to examine their life and face feelings of guilt, worthlessness

and powerlessness. As the elixir continues to be heated the next phase is the *albedo,* or "whitening", during which the molten metals begin to recombine in a purer form. In psychological terms this represents something like daybreak, during which depression shifts and life begins to return. The final phase of the great work is called the *rubedo,* or "reddening", and is analogous to sunrise. This is a point of great intensity in the work, in which the opposites begin to unite in the *coniunctio oppositorum,* or "sacred marriage", resulting in the the philosopher's stone.

SACRED MARRIAGE

The main symbol of alchemy is the uniting of the king and queen within the fire of love. The union is symbolized by the marriage of sulphur (masculine) and mercury (feminine) or of the sun (spirit) and moon (soul). Alchemy presupposes that humans are in a state of chaos and discord, having lost their connection with "Eden", the primordial state of contentedness. The image of the sacred marriage refers to the renewal of this integral nature through the coming together of the central forces within us.

The marriage of the king and queen also corresponds with a surrendering to our androgynous nature, represented by the half-male, half-female figure of the hermaphrodite. A hermaphrodite symbolizes the attainment of intuitive insight, as opposed to the one-sided power of rational knowledge and discourse. The term hermaphrodite is a

RIGHT Every tool, ingredient and scientific process in alchemy has its own sign or symbol.

combination of the names of two gods; Hermes, the god of the intellect and communication and Aphrodite, the goddess of sensuality and love. This androgynous unity represents a primordial state of humanity, before the fall into the world of opposites. It is embodied in the philosopher's stone, a kind of spiritual solidity.

BELOW The science of alchemy has a wealth of symbolism of its own, with every element and process given its own graphic sign, but it also has great thematic symbolism, rooted in the way the alchemists looked at the world and explored its possibilities for change.

LABYRINTHS AND MAZES

ABOVE The classic shape of the maze.

ABOVE The labrys, an axe whose double curved blades link it with the moon, and with the root of the word "labyrinth".

BELOW RIGHT This modern picture portrays modern cosmopolitan life as a maze (looking also like computer chip circuitry).

BELOW This classical Italian maze design is an example of a unicursal (one-path) maze.

The labyrinth is a symbol for life that has been interpreted in different ways to represent the central spiritual and psychological concerns of each culture that makes use of it. As a "walk-through" symbol, it is a creative or ritual space that reflects our sense of unknowingness and disorientation as we move through the challenges and obstacles of life. The labyrinth charts the connection between everyday life and the underworld, our conscious self and the unconscious or collective unconscious, and our waking consciousness and the dreaming process. This ancient symbol represents both the womb and the tomb, and the thread that helps us find a way through it represents the awareness needed to get through life.

The ancient root of "labyrinth" is "la", meaning "stone", referring to something firm and on the ground. The labrys is a double-headed axe from Crete, whose two curved blades symbolize the waxing and waning moon, in the centre of each blade is an image of the four-pointed cross. It is often shown held by a goddess who is guarding the entrance to the labyrinth or the underworld. The word "maze" is derived from the Old English *amasian* meaning "to confuse".

LABYRINTH FORMS
A labyrinth is "unicursal": it has only one path that twists and turns but eventually leads to the centre. A "multicursal" maze can have many pathways, and therefore dead ends. The first will disorientate, but the second can both disorientate and render you completely lost.

The simplest form of labyrinth is the "three-circuit" design, but the archetypal pattern is the classical, "Cretan" or "seven-circuit", labyrinth. It has only one entrance and one route to the centre. It may be either square or circular, and is found in Europe, North Africa, India, Indonesia, and North and South America. Almost every ancient labyrinth follows this design. Classical labyrinths with 11 or 15 circuits have been found, such as the 11-circuit labyrinth made from boulders at Visby, Sweden.

MEDIEVAL DESIGNS
The Romans elaborated the genre with meandering, spiralling and serpentine patterns, working them as mosaics on walls and floors. It was later adopted by the Church: the oldest known example dates from the 4th century and is in the pavement of the Basilica of Reparatus at Orleansville, Algeria. Church labyrinths became more common in the 9th century, and designs large enough to be walked as pilgrimage or penance were laid out in the naves of French cathedrals: the most famous was constructed at Chartres around 1230. A six-petalled flower at its centre represents the flowering and healing union of the masculine (Christ) and feminine (Mary) energies.

In the late Middle Ages a new form developed in the gardens and palaces of Europe. These mazes, constructed in topiary, included many wrong turns and dead-ends. The "simply connected" maze, although complex, has one continuous wall and it is possible to navigate by keeping one hand on the wall at all times. By the 19th century "multiple connected" mazes were formed with islands in them, which could not be solved by the "hand on the wall" method.

THE SACRED JOURNEY TO THE UNDERWORLD
Early labyrinths were maps to aid the passage of the soul to the underworld after death. Ancient labyrinth dances and rituals depicted the movement between life and death, through the

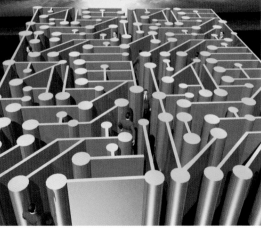

gateway of the tomb and into mother earth. The earliest recorded labyrinth was described by Herodotus in the 5th century BC, built by twelve Egyptian kings as their memorial beside a vast man-made lake. A pyramid rose from one wall of the labyrinth, which had an upper and an underground level. It enshrined the bodies of the twelve kings, and tombs of sacred crocodiles.

THE HEROIC JOURNEY

The most famous labyrinth is that of King Minos at Knossos in Crete, which is associated with the myth of Theseus and the bull-headed monster called the Minotaur. Theseus, King Aegeus of Athen's son, vowed to kill the creature to bring an end to Athen's enforced tribute to King Minos. Minos's daughter Ariadne fell in love with Theseus and gave him a ball of golden thread, the end of which she held as he descended into the labyrinth. Theseus met the Minotaur at the centre of the maze, killed him and returned to Ariadne by following the thread.

This myth has several important symbolic features: the "penetration" of the labyrinth, the experience of disorientation, the meeting and killing of an inner monster, and the resolution of the maze symbolized by the thread, which represents the cord of life joining the two worlds, upper and lower, with awareness. The relationship between male and female principles is another theme. The myth of Theseus and Ariadne describes a golden thread between man and woman. At the

Rad labyrinth in Hanover, Germany, and at the 300-year-old turf labyrinth at Saffron Waldon, in England, a ritual was enacted in which a girl stood in the centre and two young men raced to claim her.

PATHS TO SALVATION

The adoption of the labyrinth by Christians led to a change in symbolic meaning. The centre no longer meant an encounter with death or a monster but represented salvation, with the labyrinth as the path through the entanglements of sinful human nature. A symbolic pilgrimage or penitential journey through the labyrinth might be prescribed for sinners too frail to undertake a longer pilgrimage, and medieval monks might walk church labyrinths in contemplation.

FERTILIZATION AND BIRTH

The entrance to the labyrinth may represent the vulva, and the centre the ovum or the womb, suggesting a fertilizing journey of new hope, life and the potential for rebirth. This theme is connected to the journey into the earth mother and the underworld, thus linking the themes of life, death, fertility and birth.

A fivefold labyrinth with nine circuits is used as a motif on baskets woven by the Pima people of Arizona and also forms the great seal of the Piman tribal council. This design unusually features an entrance at the top, and is thought to depict a heroic journey into the womb.

The Chakravyuha labyrinth is an evolution of the classical form, and is found in India. It is based upon a threefold centre rather than the usual cross, displaying a spiral at its centre, and is thought to symbolize birth, mapping the way for the unborn child through the labyrinthine uterus. In the Indian epic the Mahabharatha, the Chakravyuha is an inescapable circular formation of standing warriors devised by the magician Drona.

Hopi labyrinths from the 12th century found in Arizona come in two forms. The Tapu'at form suggests a baby curled in the womb, or newly born nestling in its mother's arms; the entrance and exit paths suggest the umbilical cord and the birth canal. The second form is more rounded and symbolizes the sun father, who gives life. It represents the journey through life, and may also depict the boundaries of the Hopi territories.

ABOVE Theseus holds the thread, by which he maintained his link with the everyday world, given to him by Ariadne. This myth depicts Theseus as the symbolic hero-saviour, who overcomes the brutish aspects of his own nature as well as that of the Minotaur. The labyrinth, therefore, becomes a symbol of initiation and rebirth.

MULTIPLE DIMENSIONS

Adding a third dimension brings new levels of complexity to maze design, making it possible to move between levels by bridges or stairways. It is theoretically possible to keep adding dimensions to mazes, but this moves them out of the realm of the everyday world. Computer game designers use multi-dimensional mazes and labyrinths to create a "hero's journey" in the player's own home.

MANDALAS AND YANTRAS

ABOVE The ripples created when a stone is dropped in water form a type of mandala.

TOP Mandala patterns occur in nature, as the concentric circles on this tree trunk show.

BELOW Mandalas are meditation devices in spiritual traditions such as Buddhism. This one from Tibet is used in the Vajrayana Diamond or Thunderbolt vehicle.

The Sanskrit words "mandala" and "yantra" mean "circle" and "instrument" respectively, and describe schematic images designed to both represent and assist spiritual experience. Although rooted in the sacred traditions of the East, many aspects of their symbolism seem to be archetypal, and they appear in different guises all over the world. Mandala-like patterns occur in nature as well as in traditions as diverse as those of the Maya, Native Americans, Celts and Christians. They also feature in dreams and in spontaneous doodles and drawings, leading Jung to suggest that they are an attempt to preserve psychic order and a symbol of the individuation process.

THE TEACHINGS OF THE MANDALA

Just as a rainbow is created only when water droplets, light and the observer's sight come together, so the visual effects of a mandala are such that nothing exists except as an encounter between various fields and patterns of energy. The order of the cosmos is depicted through the balanced arrangement of geometric shapes (predominantly the circle, square and triangle), colour, and symbols such as deities or spiritual beings. Within an outer circle or square, concentric elements of the design radiate from and to the sacred space at the centre, symbolizing the divine presence. In Hinduism, this space is the *shunya* ("absolute void") and the *bindu* ("cosmic seed"), the creativity and spiritual fulfilment that emerge from

nothingness, the space from which all things are born and to which everything returns. Although the symbols used on the mandala are culture-specific, its overriding purpose is to bring the mind to a place of stillness and emptiness, disentangling it from the illusions of permanence in the everyday world in order to experience transcendence.

The traditional Hindu mandala is a square subdivided into smaller squares. As well as an image for contemplation, it is also a template for the ground plan of Hindu temples: the central square is the Place of Brahma and contains the womb-chamber, the holy area of the temple where the altar is situated.

Tibetan Buddhists create mandalas on rolled cloths called *thang-ka*. These are usually rectangular paintings showing the teachings of the Buddha, the wheel of life, the cosmic tree, saints and other spiritual guides in richly coloured images. Circular mandalas called *kyil-khor* are also used for meditation. Each symbol is considered in turn, moving from the edge inwards. Meditating Buddhas, protective and destructive creatures, clouds, mountains, flames and thunderbolts are all common icons on Tibetan mandalas, symbolizing the obstacles that must be faced before the centre can be reached.

MANDALAS IN NATURE

Many mandala-like patterns occur in nature, such as the concentric circles of a tree trunk, ripples on the surface of a pond, a spider's

web, a snowflake or a sunflower. Even natural formations in the landscape have been compared with mandalas. Mount Kailas, one of the tallest peaks in the Himalayas, has four distinct facades facing north, south, east and west, and is compared to an enormous diamond. Buddhists regard it as a mandala, a sacred circle from which four holy rivers (the Indus, Sutlej, Bramaputra and Ganges) flow like the spokes of an eternal wheel.

At the levels of both the macrocosm and microcosm, mandalas seem to be a universal pattern of life: the earth rotates around the Milky Way, while in the cells of every living creature electrons spin around a central nucleus. Even the human eye is a type of mandala.

SAND MANDALAS

Mandalas are not always painted. In Tibetan Buddhism, the *kalachakra,* or "wheel of time", a flat representation of all the cycles of the universe, is created in coloured sand as a symbolic ritual. It begins with a ceremony to call on the goddess of creation and consecrate the site. The mandala is then created from the centre outwards, symbolizing the growth of life from a single egg into the universe. One monk works at each of the four directions, pouring sand from a metal rod called a *chak-pur*. Once the mandala is finished, its role is complete, and a final ceremony is performed to release its healing powers into the world. The sands are swept up from the outside to the centre of the circle and placed

in an urn. This is carried in a ceremonial procession to a nearby river where it is emptied, carrying the healing sands out into the ocean to bring peace and harmony to the whole planet.

The Navajo also use sand paintings in healing rituals. The medicine man or woman performs a ceremony centred on a mandala sand painting called the *iikaah* ("the place where the spirits come and go") – a doorway through which helpful spirits will pass as they are called upon in the ritual. The ceremony begins at dawn and takes place in the hogan, a sacred lodge that has been blessed for the ceremony. The mandala is created using string and other markers, as the positions of the spirit figures must be precise to create a place of harmony. The base of the painting is built from sand, corn and pollen or crushed petals, then charcoal and ground stone are carefully poured to create outlines. The figures are solid shapes, with the image of their bodies, both back and front, poured into place to bring their complete presence into the circle.

At dusk, the person in need of healing comes to the hogan and sits in the centre of the mandala, with the images of the spirits in direct contact with his body to draw away the illness so that it falls into the mandala. The sand is then ritually disposed of.

YANTRAS

A variation of the mandala, the yantra is used in both Hinduism and Buddhism. It is a complex geometric figure that visually expresses a mantra or prayer. Sometimes the mantra is written to "fix" it, but predominantly geometric symbols are used in a mystical representation of creation and the interaction of cosmic forces. The powers inherent in the yantra are brought to life through ritual acts, such as smearing it with perfume and chanting the mantra over it.

The *shri-yantra*, considered one of the most potent yantra designs, is used in Hindu tantric ritual. It consists of a square, concentric circles and nine intersecting triangles. The external square functions like a city wall, with gateways to the four points of the compass. It represents the physical world and protects and encloses the interior. The concentric circles represent spiritual expansion and cosmic unity, while the triangles represent the joining of the linga (phallus), represented by the upward-pointing triangle) with the yoni (womb), represented by the downward-pointing triangle, or the sexual play of the divine couple, Shiva and Shakti.

The *shri-yantra* can be engraved only on eight surfaces: gold, silver, copper, crystal, birch, bone, hide (including paper) and a special "Vishnu" stone named after the preserver deity. Only these materials, in combination with the correct colours – red, to symbolize the female, or white, symbolizing the male – will create the necessary balance and harmony of energies.

ORACLES AND DIVINATION

ABOVE Tarot cards and a crystal ball are two methods of divination still used today.

RIGHT In a medieval illuminated manuscript classical Greek astronomers inspect the the stars from Mount Athos. They believed that reading these patterns would help them predict likely future events.

Speaking in a symbolic language, oracles and divination are a way of communing with the unseen influences beyond the reach of the everyday world. From a psychological perspective, they can be seen as a way of tapping into the deeper layers of the unconscious mind.

Above the entrance of perhaps the most enduringly famous oracle in the ancient world, the Greek oracle at Delphi, was carved the inscription, "Know thyself." Divination is not a method of predicting the future – this would imply that life is a fixed programme – but is best understood as something fluid, a process that involves an ongoing dialogue with the spiritual or mythical dimension. Through this relationship it is possible to read certain signs that would otherwise remain hidden, thereby increasing self-awareness.

ORACULAR DEVICES

Divination uses chance to create a doorway for the spirit to express itself through symbolic patterning. This can be anything from random patterns in tea-leaves, bones or sticks, cloud formations, weather patterns, the formations of the stars and the communications of plants and animals to sophisticated symbol systems such as the Tarot or the I Ching. To read these patterns and elicit meaning involves an intuitive leap of faith, as oracles will not be understood by the rational mind, which tends to reject or overlook the significance of information that comes through by chance.

THE I CHING

Paradoxically, the only certainty in life is change. In all change, however, there are patterns, and it is this predictability that the shamans of ancient China referred to when they were called upon to give advice on forthcoming events. Originally, the answer to a question was divined from the patterns on animal bones or tortoise shells. This developed into the I Ching, or "book of changes", which became much more than an oracular device: for the ancients it symbolized the workings of the whole universe.

The basis of the I Ching is the trigram, an arrangement of three lines that are either solid or broken. The solid line represents yang energy, and the broken line yin energy, yin and yang being the two opposing principles that underlie the whole of creation. Eight arrangements are possible, and the trigrams symbolize eight stages in the cycle of growth and decline, or ebb and flow, observable in all areas of life. Each has a name taken from nature: Heaven, earth, thunder, water, mountain, wind/wood, fire and lake. Trigrams once decorated the clothing of temporal and spiritual leaders and can be used as amulets. Combined in pairs, the trigrams make up the 64 hexagrams of the I Ching, with names such as "the creative", "decrease", "the receptive", "family", from which interpretations of human situations are made. These are further amplified by "changing lines", which increase the possible number of permutations to more than 10,000.

THE TAROT

The exact origins and purpose of the Tarot are unknown, but it was in use for gaming and divination in Italy, France and Germany by the late 14th century, though medieval churchmen denounced it as "the Devil's picture book". The Tarot is a card-deck illustrated with highly symbolic imagery. It may have been a way of disguising spiritual teachings that ran counter to the prevailing doctrines of the Church, but also seems likely to have formed part of a memory system. During the Renaissance, *ars memorativa* (pictorial memory systems) became linked with magical talismans or amulets for invoking a particular power.

The Tarot divides into two parts: the 22 cards of the Major Arcana and the 56 cards of the Minor Arcana. "Arcane" means mysterious or secret, and the Tarot is sometimes known as the Book of Secrets. The Major Arcana deals with archetypal themes that reflect turning points in life, symbolized by cards such as the Fool, the High Priestess, the Lovers, the Hanged Man and the World. The Minor Arcana is sub-divided into four suits, which are related to the four elements as well as everyday concerns: wands (fire and ambition), swords (air and ideas), cups (water and emotions) and pentacles (earth and material resources).

AUGURY

Today the term "augury" refers to all forms of divination. Originally, however, it meant interpreting oracular messages from birds,

often viewed as messengers to humans. Augury is one of the oldest forms of divination. Accounts from China, India, Persia and many other regions show that people paid careful attention to birds for divinatory purposes – their songs, movement, flight patterns, behaviour, even their eggs, as well as the particular species. For example, the Kakajarita, a 9th-century Tibetan text, gives detailed instructions for divining the meaning of crow cries.

Augury does not, however, require an organized system of signs. Originally it must have depended on an intimate rapport between birds and humans, with people entering into a mystical experience of bird-consciousness. The Roman state always referred to the augur before making an important decision, while by tradition, the site of the Aztec city Tenochtitlan was chosen when an eagle was seen on a cactus with a snake in its mouth, seen as an auspicious sign from the gods. The Bununs of Taiwan rely upon the chirping and the flight patterns of birds as hunting omens: a chirp on the left side is seen as a bad omen, and they invariably return home.

THE CLEDON TRADITION

Oracles can work in many different ways. In the classical world, words heard at random or out of context that struck a chord with the listener were regarded as oracular messages. Known as *cledon*, these symbolic fragments of speech that seemed to answer a

question or give advice were usually uttered unwittingly by strangers, children or passers-by. As with any other oracle, the success of the method depends as much upon the recipient's openness to the message and ability to comprehend it as on the oracle itself, divining being an interactive process.

THE DODONA OAK

One of the most revered oracles of antiquity was a great oak tree growing at Dodona, in north-west Greece. For centuries, pilgrims travelled to seek the tree's guidance. In the earliest stories about Dodona, oracles were delivered by the oak itself, but by the time of Homer, around 800 BC, a group of interpreters called the *selloi* – who, according to the Iliad, were "of unwashed feet and slept on the ground" – had established themselves at the site. Pieces of wood taken from the tree were said to have the same oracular power.

THE RAVEN

Often presaging death, the raven is usually seen as a bird of ill omen, but it may also augur well. In Genesis it was sent off by Noah to determine the extent of the flood, but never returned. The raven also appears in the flood stories of the Algonquin Indians. In Scandanavia ravens are thought to be the ghosts of murdered people, while according to a Chinese tradition, the soul of the sun takes the form of a crow or raven.

THE CYCLE OF LIFE

HOW HUMANS SEE THEIR BODIES, THEIR PHYSICAL POSITION IN THE WORLD, AND THEIR OWN LIFESPAN, GIVES RISE TO THE RICH SYMBOLISM THAT SURROUNDS BIRTH AND DEATH, LOVE AND RELATIONSHIPS, RITUAL AND CREATIVITY. ICONIC SYMBOLS SUCH AS THE HEART AND THE WHEEL ARE CENTRAL, BUT SO ARE THEMATIC SYMBOLS SUCH AS MARRIAGE AND SUNRISE.

THE HUMAN BODY

ABOVE The human body is a rich source of symbolic meaning. The female form can represent different aspects of woman, such as fertility and female sexuality.

ABOVE The head is associated with humans' thinking capacity. It can also be used to describe a person in charge.

Many ancient traditions saw the human body as a microcosm (literally a "little world"), containing in miniature all of the various stages of creation. The Chinese regarded the body as both yin and yang, and thus a symbol of perfect balance and wholeness. In some traditions the body is regarded as a "temple of the soul", which mediates between Heaven and earth, assisting each person to realize their divine purpose and unique potential. Other traditions have viewed it as an enemy that has to be overcome, the repository of the base instincts and passions that threaten to lower humanity to the level of the animal world. In addition to the symbolism of the body as a whole, practically every individual part has its own symbolic associations.

THE HEAD

Almost universally, the head is considered to be the seat of learning, the instrument of reason and of the spiritual and social capacities that raise humans above animals. Symbols of authority such as crowns are worn on the head, while bowing the head denotes submission to a higher being. In many African tribal cultures an elongated head is a sign of good character, wisdom and leadership, and elaborate hairstyles and headdresses are designed to accentuate this quality.

The head is sacred in Maori tradition, and the Celtic cult of the sacred head is illustrated by numerous myths. In many traditions, beheading an enemy is thought to humiliate the individual. The Hindu goddess Durga is often shown holding her own decapitated head, while Christian iconography has many instances of saints carrying their own heads, signifying the power of the spirit to conquer death.

THE HAIR

The hair often represents virility and strength, as in the Old Testament story of Samson, who lost his strength when Delilah cut his hair. The Khalsa community of Sikhs let their hair and beards grow because they believe it is a symbol of God's love. In China a shaved scalp was on a par with emasculation and could debar a person from public office. A shaved head can also indicate sacrifice or submission: monks and nuns in both Buddhist and Christian traditions may cut off their hair as they enter religious life. For the Gauls and other Celtic peoples long hair was a symbol of royal power, or of liberty and independence.

Long loose hair in women once indicated youth and virginity, while braided or bound hair could symbolize either a married woman or, conversely, a courtesan. In Christian art the redeemed and sanctified St Mary of Magdelene is often shown with very long, loose hair as a symbol of her chastity, love and humility.

Haircuts and hairstyles are frequently signifiers of social or religious difference, as with Rastafarian dreadlocks or the long ringlets of Hassidic Jews. In Hindu and Buddhist traditions, the topknot is believed to cover the area where the divine spirit enters the body at birth and leaves at death; it is associated with holy people. Body hair is associated with virility or animal tendencies: in Christian art it is used as a symbol of the devil.

LEFT An unlidded eye within a triangle is a Masonic symbol, shown here on a society apron. It symbolizes spiritual awareness.

THE EYES

As may be expected, the symbolism of the eye is connected with perception and vision, the ability to see beyond the purely physical to the realms of soul and spirit; consequently blindness is often used as a metaphor for the inability to see spiritual and moral truth. However, blindness can also be associated with wisdom and spiritual gifts.

In some traditions, including Hindu, Taoist and Shinto, the eyes are identified with the sun and moon, with the right eye corresponding to the active and the future (the sun) and the left to the passive and the past (the moon). To unify perception, some cultures believe in the existence of an invisible "third eye" in the middle of the forehead. Both the Hindu god Shiva and the Buddha are depicted with a third eye, the vehicle of perception that is directed inwards in meditation.

In ancient Greece the eye symbol had magical powers, and eyes painted on the prows of warships had the power to guide them. In ancient Egypt the wadjet, or eye of Horus, had a healing and protective function. One of the symbols of Freemasonry is a single, unlidded eye (a symbol of divine knowledge) enclosed within a triangle – an image that appears on the back of the US dollar bill. The phrase "eyes wide open" signifies a state of awareness.

THE MOUTH

As the organ of speech and breath, the mouth embodies the power of spirit and the inspiration of the soul, an elevated state of consciousness and the ability to reason and communicate. Through its association with eating the mouth is also linked with destruction, as with the mouth of a monster: in Christian iconography the entrance to hell is a fanged demon's mouth. Medieval artists depicted small demons flying from a person's mouth to signify evil words or lies.

The tongue and teeth have their own symbolism. In African sculptures, teeth can indicate a creature's terrifying power to consume, although they can also be associated with strength and growing wisdom. In Persian and European love poetry, teeth are frequently compared to pearls. The tongue is sometimes compared with flames and in the Christian tradition tongues of fire symbolize the Holy Spirit. It symbolizes speech but is also associated with ferocity: rolling tongues were depicted on ancient Chinese tombs to frighten away evil spirits. In Tibet, sticking out the tongue is seen as a friendly greeting, while in Maori culture it is a defiant, provocative (and also protective) gesture.

THE HEART

In the West the heart has been linked with romantic love since the Middle Ages. In the ancient world, however, it was a symbol of the centre and was often thought of as the site of the soul. In China the heart was also thought to be where the *shen*, or spirit, resides, and was considered the source of intelligence. The heart is also associated with moral courage and truth.

ABOVE The heart is not a symbol only for love but also for truth.

BELOW Mary of Magdelene is often portrayed with long, loose hair as a symbol of her chastity, and an allusion to the time she washed the feet of Jesus.

LEFT In the act of washing the feet
of his disciple Peter, Jesus
demonstrated his humility and
indicated that he was a servant of
humankind rather than its king.

as their servant, a gesture that was
later imitated by English kings
who washed the feet of the poor
to show their humility. In the Fon
Republic of Benin, the god of war
is usually shown with large feet,
symbolizing his ability to stamp
out his enemies.

BREATH AND BLOOD

Both breath and blood are
associated with the life force and
divine power. Native Americans
use the breath to pass power
between people, and it had
magical properties for the Celts:
the Druid Mog Ruith was able to
turn his enemies to stone by
breathing on them.

Many cultures consider blood
to be sacred because it embodies
the soul: in West African voodoo,
sacred statues are smeared with
chicken's blood to bring them to
life, and a similar practice was
performed by the Norse, who
smeared their sacred runes with
ox blood to activate them. Blood
has been used to seal oaths, and
14th-century Japanese warriors
stamped their fingerprints in
blood to assure a contract.
Christians ritually ingest the
blood of Christ, in the form of
wine, at the Eucharist ceremony.

However, in some traditions
blood also has the power to
contaminate. In the Shinto
religion, the word for blood (chi)
is taboo, while neither Jews nor
Muslims are permitted to eat meat
that contains any residue of
blood. Jews regard menstrual
blood as unclean, though it has
also been linked with fertility, as
in ancient Egypt.

THE NAVEL

As well as being a visual reminder
of the body's connection to life
through the umbilical cord, the
navel is often used as a symbol of
the centre of the world from
which creation emanated.
Muslims describe Mohammed's
birthplace as the "navel of the
world", and in ancient Greece
Delphi was the site of the sacred
omphalos, or "navel stone", a
cylindrical stone with a rounded
top that symbolized the
connection between the three
worlds (Heaven, earth and the
underworld).

The pole star is sometimes
referred to as the navel star,
around which the heavens seem
to rotate. In West Africa, the navel
is viewed as an ancestral
matriarchal symbol that relates to
fertility; scarification marks are
ritually made around a girl's navel
at puberty.

HANDS AND FEET

Traditionally the hand is a symbol
of active divine power.
Handprints frequently appear in
Australian Aboriginal cave art,
representing the artist's spiritual
imprint and signature. In
Hinduism and Buddhism, the
hand is a guardian and fragment
of the universal soul, and in India
handprints on walls, doors or
other objects signify protection.
In Christian iconography, a hand
represents God's blessing and
intervention, and the "laying on
of hands" is used in churches in
healing and ordination rituals.

The foot is the part of the body
that most closely relates to the
earth. It is associated with both
stability and movement. Bare feet
traditionally indicate humility,
and have also been a sign of
mourning. When Christ washed
the feet of his disciples, he was
using the act to symbolize his role

BELOW The symbolism of
the navel is connected
with the centre of the
world, life and creation.

SEXUAL ORGANS

The sexual and reproductive organs of both men and women carry a profound symbolism. As well as being linked with fertility, the womb is associated with protection and mysterious hidden powers. Vessels of transformation, such as the crucible and cauldron, are linked with womb symbolism, as are natural features in the landscape, such as caves. The womb is often linked with the mother goddess: Delphi in ancient Greece, the site of the oracle and sacred to the great mother of earth, sea and sky, was named from the Greek word *delphos*, meaning "womb".

The vulva is also usually associated with mother goddesses. In Hinduism it is symbolized by the yoni, represented as a vulva-shaped shallow basin and the graphic symbol of the triangle. The Bambara of Mali refer to it as "lovely big mother" and regard it as a gateway to hidden treasure and knowledge. The vulva symbolizes the dark, devouring aspect of the goddess, the jealous, possessive, over-protective mother who won't let go of her children, or the woman her lover. The concept of the vagina dentata ("toothed vagina") may be associated with this aspect and may also represent a man's castration anxieties – that once he enters a woman's body he will be unable to escape – and the fear of surrender to his instincts.

The phallus is a symbol of the masculine, active principle, the power of procreation and a channel for the life force. It is worshipped in many cultures as

the source of life. In Hinduism it is associated with the god Shiva and is symbolized by the linga, an upright stone that typically appears conjoined with the yoni, symbolizing the union of spirit and matter, of the male and female principles. Phallic objects were worshipped in ancient China, and the Japanese god of marriage is portrayed in a phallic shape. Fertility gods such as the Roman Priapus are often depicted with an erect phallus, and satyrs were shown with gigantic erections as symbols of their libidinous nature. In Kabbalistic thought, the phallus was responsible for maintaining equilibrium; through its hardening or softening in the presence or absence of energy it is a balancing agent whose role is to sustain the world.

THE ENERGY BODY

Many traditions believe in an animating force that runs through every living thing, including the human body. Known by various names (such as chi in China and prana in India), the life force runs along a web of energy pathways known as meridians (China) or *nadis* (India). Esoteric and healing systems, such as yoga, reflexology and accupuncture, are based on this system, associating physical and emotional distress with imbalances in the body's energy

field. In Hindu and Buddhist thought, subtle energy enters and leaves the body through chakras, or energy centres, which are gateways between the physical and the immaterial realm. The principal chakras are arranged along a central meridian running from the base of the spine to the crown of the head.

BELOW Hindu linga stones are shown nestling in round-shaped yoni carvings. The linga and yoni symbolize the male and female reproductive organs and the masculine and feminine principles.

BIRTH AND DEATH

Both birth and death are feared and welcomed in every culture, each representing both beginning and ending. Birth is the beginning of life, but may also be considered the ending of a previous life or soul journey, and the end of gestation. Death is an ending, but for some it is also the beginning of a significant new journey to the underworld, Heaven, or the next incarnation. Both are events of mysterious beauty, awe and terror, sources of inspiration and superstition for a huge body of symbolism informing religion, culture and science.

BIRTH AND DEATH FORETOLD

A great deal of symbolism surrounds the foretelling of birth or death, perhaps because these events are so mysterious, unpredictable and life-shaking. Astrology predicts likely times for births and deaths, and unusual heavenly signs have often been interpreted as pointing to the comings and goings of important people. In ancient times the sighting of a new star was the sign of a newborn king; thus the birth of Christ was predicted on this basis, possibly when Jupiter (known to the Jews as the "king's star") aligned with Saturn,

THE MIDWIFE

Traditionally, midwives had a similar status to shamans or priests. In modern society the midwife may no longer have such high status, but midwives protect and support the mother and child. In British Columbia, the word for midwife among the Nuu-chah-nulth people means "she can do everything" and for the Coast Salish people it means "to watch, to care". The Greek goddess Hecate was the divine midwife.

creating the "star of David".

Many signs and symbols in nature are taken as omens of birth or death. Perhaps because it is a symbol of transformation, the butterfly is variously taken to portend either. In the Orkney Islands a rainbow presages a birth, and an old English folk rhyme associates the sighting of magpies with birth: three for a girl and four for a boy. In Europe the death's head sphinx moth was commonly taken to predict death because of the outline of a skull on its back. The Samoans believed that if they captured a butterfly they would be struck down dead. The Celts believed that seeing a butterfly flying at night signified death, and in Christian art a chrysalis is a symbol of death.

The ancient Romans hated owls as they saw them as portents of death. Many carrion-eating birds, particularly ravens, are thought to be able to smell death before it occurs, and they are therefore a bad omen, but in African and Native American cultures the raven is also a helpful guide to the dead on their journey. The howling of a dog or the sighting of a ghostly black dog may both warn of death. Dogs also appear in shamanic lore as guardians and guides to the underworld.

BIRTH SYMBOLISM

Many cultures consider giving birth a powerful and natural initiation, and give great importance to the various stages for both mother and child. The birth process mirrors the process of initiation. Traditionally the

mother is removed from society – leaving her usual roles behind – to a sacred place for birth, and undergoes rites of purification and cleansing. Labour has strong associations with the "threshold" phase of initiation, in which there is often great pain and mystery, and in many cultures post-partum blood is considered powerful and unclean, possibly because it represents a strong link with the world of the spirits. During childbirth the gods and spirits are often deemed to have great influence. The Anglo-Saxons prayed to the goddess Freya during birth. Celtic cultures sometimes hid the birth from supernatural creatures that might otherwise have created mischief.

THE PLACENTA

The placenta is revered in many parts of the world, symbolizing life, spirit and individuality. It is often buried in the ancestral territory to provide a sacred link between the child and the land: the Maoris call the placenta *whenua*, which also means "land". The Aymara and Quecha people of Bolivia consider the placenta to have a spirit. It is washed and buried secretly by the husband, otherwise, they believe, the mother or baby may become ill. The Ibo of Nigeria and Ghana give the placenta a proper burial as they believe it to be the dead twin of the newborn, and the Hmong of South-east Asia consider it to be a "jacket" – the first clothing of the child. They bury it in the belief that after death the soul will travel back to find its clothing.

SECOND BIRTH

Water has always been symbolically important for birth rites. Christian baptism, which may involve total immersion of the child or adult in blessed water, symbolizes a "second birth", representing the death and rebirth of Christ, and the cleansing of sin. The ritual is thought to have originated in India, where priests still practise a similar rite today. An ancient Irish tradition was the immersion of the child in milk, based on the belief that its spirit was formed through being breastfed. The Catholic Church banned the practice in 1172.

DEATH SYMBOLISM

Death has many emblems, most of them alarming, although the symbolism of hope and that of fear sometimes appear simultaneously. In art the most familiar depiction of death is the Grim Reaper, a skeleton robed in black and carrying a scythe; other personifications carry a trident, sword or bow and arrows, and an hour glass, for measuring a life's span. Other symbols include the skull, or a tomb or gravestone and the plants poppy, asphodel and cypress. Death ships or barges symbolize a journey to the afterworld, particularly for the ancient Egyptians.

BURIAL AND CREMATION RITES

Funerary rites vary tremendously according to cultural attitudes and beliefs, and the combination of fear and celebration with which people approach death. The practice of burial is known to date back as far as 80,000 years, and is common in societies where doctrines of bodily resurrection are popular. At sites such as the Shanidar Cave in Iraq, Teshiq-Tash in Iran and the Grotte des Enfants in France, bodies have been found buried with tools and jewellery, and often decorated with red ochre, to symbolize the blood of the earth.

Australian Aboriginal death rites are complex and vary by clan and region. Essentially death is understood as a transformative event involving the parting of dual aspects of soul from the body. The spiritual being is thought to reintegrate with the ancestors in the Dreaming, in a sense returning home. After death the community sing songs containing symbols of death, such as a worm-eaten mangrove tree representing the dead body, or the tide marks of a "king tide", referring to a cleansing process and removal of the physical being. The coffin is a talisman painted to ask the spirits to help the deceased on his journey.

To ancient Indo-Iranian peoples and across Europe, from the Bronze Age onwards, cremation symbolized purification, sublimation and ascension. The fire itself signified the freeing of the soul, while the smoke symbolized its ascension. Roman funerals involved a procession to the tomb or pyre, with important relatives wearing masks of the deceased ancestor. Nine days later a feast was given, and the ashes were placed in a tomb.

ABOVE The black skeletal image of Death was a common medieval image.

ABOVE LEFT The first baptism, of Christ by John the Baptist. is used to symbolize divine grace and rebirth.

BELOW The gravestone, the Grim Reaper, and the hourglass symbolize the negative view of death.

SEX AND FERTILITY

ABOVE Water is a prime symbol of fertility, especially when in the form of rain.

TOP Sex and fertility have many symbolic associations, from the everyday to the sacred.

TOP RIGHT In this depiction of Love fighting Chastity, the symbols of chastity – her girdle and the arrow-deflecting shield – are in evidence.

ABOVE Grain is a symbol of the earth's fertility and is also used to symbolize human fertility.

Human beings are first and foremost sexual creatures, and to ensure the continuation of the species nature has ensured that sex is a pleasurable, health-promoting activity. Many traditions recognize a connection between sex and spirit, seeing sex as a vehicle for both bliss and transcendence.

FERTILITY RITES

In many traditions there is a connection between the fertility of the land and sexual symbolism. The Mongols and early Chinese saw rain as "seeds" sent from the sky to fertilize the earth; similar beliefs persist in parts of Africa and Australia, where women may lie down in the rain to help them get pregnant. In the myths of hunting societies, knowledge and power, and even human life itself, come from animals, and it is not uncommon for these gifts to have been obtained by sexual means. For instance, the survival of the Mandan of the North American plains depended on the bison. Human society was thought to descend from a sexual transfer of power between a bison and a woman, and the people's sacred buffalo dance mirrors this primordial act. In a ritual dance of the Blackfoot, a man decks himself with feathers and imitates the mating display of a prairie cock to ensure a good harvest.

Fertility and the attraction between male and female have been regarded as gifts of the goddess, associated with the Earth's seasonal cycles. In ancient Babylon, the king and the high priestess would perform ritual

intercourse as a fertility rite, symbolizing the mystical marriage of Tammuz, son and lover of the goddess Ishtar. The myth of Tammuz and Ishtar concerns the goddess's journey to the underworld to seek the release of her dead lover. While she is away, the earth is barren, but on her return, fertility returns to the land. This archetypal myth is echoed in the ancient Egyptian account of Isis and Osiris, or the ancient Greek story of Demeter and Persephone.

FERTILITY SYMBOLS

The bow, as a symbol of stored energy, is associated with dynamic sexual tension, and is an attribute of the god Apollo, a symbol of the sun's fertilizing power. Paintings of gods of love with bows often symbolize the tension of desire.

As the sacred tree of life, the fig tree also has sexual symbolism. For the Greeks the fig was an attribute of Priapus and Dionysus. In Egypt and in India it is linked

with procreative power, in particular that of Shiva and Vishnu. Graphic links between the fig leaf and the male genitals may have begun because of the milky juice that can be extracted from larger varieties. It was fig leaves that Adam and Eve used to hide themselves behind when they had eaten fruit from the tree of knowledge. The fruit of the fig is linked with female genitalia, but the fruit most commonly linked with sex and fertility is the apple, which appears almost everywhere in Europe as an emblem of love, marriage and fertility. The fish is a phallic symbol of sexual happiness and fecundity, linked with their prolific spawn, the fertility symbolism of water and analogies of the fish with the penis.

Corn dollies are traditional pagan fertility talismans made at harvest time. Sometimes they are decked with red ribbons, symbolizing blood and vitality, and set over the hearth until spring. The advent of spring is celebrated by a ritual dance around the maypole. The pole, decorated with ribbons, is both a phallic symbol and a representation of the world axis, or cosmic tree.

INFERTILITY

Just as crops are signs of the earth's abundance, so children are the "fruits" of a couple's sexual union. Traditionally the inability to have children was attributed to a woman's "barrenness", and divine assistance was often invoked. This involved petitioning fertility goddesses such as the Sumerian Inanna or the Greek Artemis, or ithyphallic (perpetually aroused) gods such as Legba, a deity of the Fon of West Africa. Phallic emblems are also common fertility charms.

ABSTINENCE, RESTRAINT, CHASTITY

While some cultures believe that expending sexual energy can inspire similar activity in nature, others think it may interfere with the earth's fertility: the Akan of Ghana believe that if a couple have sex outside they will be struck by madness and the earth goddess will make the ground where they lie infertile. Another belief is that by abstaining from sexual activity, a store of energy will be built up that will help the earth replenish its resources.

Chastity is often personified as the foe of erotic love, often a woman carrying a shield as a defence against the arrows of love or desire. Another common personification of chastity is the unicorn, while other symbols include the colours blue and white, bees, chestnuts, doves, girdles, hawthorns, irises and lilies. Ermine was associated with chastity because its white winter coat linked it to purity.

TANTRA

Sometimes referred to as "the technique of ecstasy", tantra is a Sanskrit word meaning "web" or "weaving". Although the philosophy has many different schools, a common theme is that the everyday world (samsara) contains seeds of that which is eternal and unchanging (nirvana or enlightenment); similarly, the body-mind is a mirror of the universe. Hence enlightenment may be achieved through conscious participation in everyday life rather than through denial, and the body is a vehicle for transcendence.

A common tantric theme is the idea of cosmic sexuality. Through the desire and interplay of the primal couple, Shiva and Shakti, an all-encompassing creation arises; the couple are sometimes depicted in Hindu iconography as the hermaphrodite Ardhanarishvara. Through ritualized sexual intercourse, the divine fusion of the male and female principle is re-enacted, with each partner aiming to activate the energy of the opposite sex to achieve energetic and psychic wholeness. Sexual energy is symbolized by a coiled serpent (or kundalini), which lies dormant at the first chakra, at the base of the spine. Through sexual practice it is awakened and

CORNUCOPIA

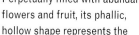

The cornucopia, or horn of plenty, is a classical symbol of inexhaustible fecundity. Perpetually filled with abundant flowers and fruit, its phallic, hollow shape represents the fertile union of male and female. Zeus/Jupiter was said to have created the cornucopia from the broken horn of Amalthea, the nanny goat who had suckled him, so that it represented divine and unasked-for bounty. Over time, it came to mean generosity, prosperity and good fortune, as well as the harvest season.

refined into increasingly subtle levels until it finally merges with cosmic energy and a state of blissful euphoria occurs.

Tantrikas (followers of tantra) were often found living in graveyards, a symbolic reminder of the impermanence of the world and the desire for sublimation that transcends death. The teachings of tantra were often considered shocking and a threat to the social order, as its practice was specifically designed to break caste barriers and taboos.

BELOW Ardhanarishvara, the Hindu hermaphrodite figure of Shiva and Parvati conjoined, symbolizes the reconciliation of opposites, and the achivement of union.

LOVE AND KINSHIP

The bonds that draw us together may be sexual attraction, a sense of common purpose or meaning, a marriage commitment or family and community. Since love does not always accommodate itself to social forms and conventions, the symbolic systems and rituals of love and kinship are diverse and changeable, as are the meanings associated with them.

Eros, who originated as a primeval creative force, became the Greek god of love and the son of Aphrodite, goddess of love. His Roman counterpart was Cupid (or Amor), the son of Venus, a cherubic winged boy shooting arrows of desire from his bow. His equivalent in Hindu mythology is Kama, who shoots sweet but painful arrows of desire into people and gods, suggesting the pain involved in love – his five arrows of flowers can make the heart glad, lead to great attraction, cause infatuation, weaken, or kill in a pleasurable way. In psychology the term "eros" refers to the libido and the urge for life, but to the Greeks it was a passionate and impersonal kind of love. Plato understood eros as desire that seeks a deep quality of beauty, an ideal of which the person before us is a reminder, hence the term "platonic love".

The Greek term "agape" refers to a kind of spiritual or selfless love, the love of God for humanity and of humanity for God, which also includes a love for fellow humans. Agape was not passionate but compassionate love. Agape feasts were rituals in which early Christians celebrated the Eucharist and the Jews celebrated Passover. Another Greek term, "philia", refers to a fondness and appreciation for the other, and is closer to what we understand as platonic love, meaning friendship and loyalty.

"Amor", derived from a name for the Roman god of love, described a new approach to love as a high spiritual experience: the courtly love celebrated by the troubadours, the poet-musicians of medieval Europe.

ROMANTIC LOVE

Courtly love was a personal and romantic form that involved two people falling in love with one another's virtues, rather than with an ideal. A knight was expected to show deep respect to the lady with whom he was in love, and had to be willing to suffer for his love. Much Renaissance literature refers to common motifs of love as a "torment" or "disease", with lovers becoming sick or unable to sleep and eat. Women took on an almost divine symbolism: their eyes became centrally important as channels of emotion, while their feet, ideally white and narrow, with a high arch, became a powerful sexual symbol.

LOVE SYMBOLS

Flowers frequently symbolize love. For Hindus it is the white flowering jasmine, in China the peony; to the Romans red roses were the flower of Venus, and have remained a strong love symbol in the West. In Iran wild olives and apples both symbolize love. A pair of mandarin ducks represents enduring and committed love to the Chinese, and doves and pigeons commonly represent lovers, either because they mate for life or because they coo while looking into each other's eyes. Lovebirds, colourful small parrots from Africa, also represent lovers because they sit close together in pairs.

ADINKRA LOVE SYMBOL

The people of Ghana weave symbolic designs into brocade called adinkra. The love symbol is called *osram ne nsoroma*, and it features a star "woman", above a moon "man"; it is used to symbolize a faithful, harmonious and fond love.

ABOVE Red roses are a well-used modern symbol of love, courtship and romance.

ABOVE The indestructible quality of the diamond makes it a symbol of enduring love.

ABOVE Heart-shaped items are used endlessly, and across cultures, as a symbol of romance.

ABOVE Rings symbolize eternity and are perhaps the ultimate love symbol.

Precious stones are significant emblems of love, first because they are "precious", and second because of their individual qualities. The diamond, because it is indestructible, represents enduring love. The red ruby symbolizes passion, sexual desire and power. Lace became a symbol of romance because a woman might drop her lace handkerchief so that the right man could pick it up for her. But the most enduring and cross-cultural of love symbols is the human heart: whole, bleeding, or pierced by arrows of love, the heart feels the passions and pain of love. It also represents warmth and openness to the "other".

Each culture uses its own symbol system to designate relationship status. Traditional Mennonites paint their door green if their daughter is eligible for marriage, and the Zulus of South Africa use beads of seven colours to depict a person's status: for example, a white bead (representing purity and spiritual love) next to a blue bead (representing faithfulness) is commonly used to show engagement, while blue, white and black beads show marriage.

The wedding ring dates back to Egyptian times, when brides were given circles of hemp or rush. The Anglo-Saxons used a ring as a token of the promise of love, and the gold wedding ring has become a symbol of eternal love and unity. The Egyptians and Romans believed that the vein in the third finger (*vena amoris*) was connected with the heart; so wearing a wedding ring on that finger symbolizes the linking of the couples' hearts. Christian priests would count the Holy Trinity from the thumb, and end up at the ring finger, using powerful unifying symbolism. The Irish wedding ring is the *claddagh*, with two hands holding a heart and crown to symbolize love, loyalty and friendship.

MARRIAGE AND KINSHIP
Kinship is a "family-like" relationship that is essential to the effective functioning of societies. Its structure and rules vary from culture to culture, but kinship systems are often built on the institution of marriage. Though this is usually the formalized bond between a man and a woman, other successful forms also exist, such as same sex marriage, polygamy and marriages of convenience. Marriage serves as a foundation for living, working and surviving together, for reproduction and sustaining a family.

For most traditional cultures, the predominant form is the arranged marriage, in which the parents or elders determine who will marry whom. In the Western world after the Middle Ages it became increasingly acceptable to marry as a consequence of falling in love. Marriage itself is a symbolic act in which the partners become two halves of a symbolic whole or "we". It is depicted in the symbolism of rings, "tying the knot", and the sharing of property and dowry.

CELTIC CLANS

The word "clann" in Gaelic means family or children. A clan is another word for a descent group; if the clan's ancestor is considered to be an animal, it is a totemic clan. In Welsh medieval society, the number nine symbolized the whole, and therefore the ninth generation was considered to be the limit of the kin relationship. In Ireland kinship was recognized until the 16th or 17th generation.

LEFT One of the Hindu symbols of love is white flowering jasmine, given by lovers to each other as a sign of their commitment.

IBHEQE

A Zulu token like a Valentine, called an *ibheqe*, is worn around the neck. The downward-pointing blue triangle inside a red band, inside a white, worn by a girl, means something like "Will you be my love?" A boy's request to a girl would be the same, but the triangle would be pointing upward as the symbol for "girl".

VALENTINE'S DAY

The origins of Valentine's Day probably lie in a pagan ritual in honour of Juno, Roman goddess of women and marriage. The feast of Lupercalia was celebrated on 15 February. On its eve, girls' names were written on paper and drawn like a lottery by young men, establishing their partnership for the period of the festival. Common Valentine symbols are pictures of Cupid, love arrows and bleeding hearts – all symbols of being love-struck.

RITES OF PASSAGE

ABOVE A Muslim woman hands out sceptres to three boys in white costumes preparing for their circumcisions at an Istanbul mosque. On the day of their circumcision, Muslim boys become a prince for the day.

THE BIRTHDAY

Much symbolism associated with birthdays has ancient origins. The birthday cake may have originated in moon-shaped cakes given as temple offerings to Artemis. The candles may suggest the glowing of the moon, while in Germany a large central candle represents the "light of life".

Formalized rituals symbolically mark the passage of an individual or group through major life transitions, such as birth, puberty, marriage and death. Others mark important societal transitions and the celebration of nature. All are powerful symbolic processes.

INITIATION RITUALS

Many cultures value initiation ceremonies as part of the movement through life transitions. They all involve recognizing the role or status a person is moving into, and throwing off the old one. Most initiation ceremonies are grounded in cultural stories and symbolism. The French anthropologist Arnold van Gennep (1873–1957) saw the rite of passage as an essential process in cultural rejuvenation and described the phases of initiation as separation, transition and incorporation.

Separation involves removing a person (or sacred object) from a previous situation or status. It may involve the removal of identity, such as the removal or changing of clothes, hair or teeth, or scarification and tattooing. Another important factor is the preparation of ritual space, by drawing a circle, erecting a building or travelling to a different location such as a cave or mountain. The church, the mosque, and the medicine wheel are all examples of ritual spaces that allow people to separate from their everyday reality to connect with the divine. The registry office, where people are legally married, is an example of a legal ritual space.

Transition, the "threshold" or "liminal phase", involves undergoing certain trials, tests, ordeals or ritual actions, which essentially involve a metaphorical death and rebirth. The previous identity is broken down, making the way for a new identity to come forth. Taking an oath is an example of this phase, as when a person becoming a citizen of the United States pledges allegiance to the national symbols of the American flag.

Incorporation means returning to the "body" of the community, or else reconstituting the person, with new roles, awareness and responsibilities. The ringing of bells after the coronation of a monarch symbolically celebrates their new role. After a major sports tournament, such as the Olympic Games or the World Cup, the successful teams often return to their homeland and parade the streets victoriously. Eating and feasting is common symbolism for the incorporation phase. The Christian holy sacrament involves symbolically incorporating or swallowing the body and blood of Christ in the form of bread and wine.

PUBERTY

The time of puberty marks the transition from childhood to adulthood, involving dramatic physical and emotional changes, as well as changes in roles and responsibilities. Ritual initiation at puberty varies from culture to culture, but fundamentally honours and marks this major life transition In the Muslim tradition, boys of 10 to 12 who undergo circumcision are paraded as princes for the day, sometimes on a horse, and often showered with gifts. The Luiseño people of southern California proudly celebrate the onset of menstruation in their daughters, who are partially buried in warm sand, possibly to symbolize their strong connection with the earth.

A Jewish boy becomes bar mitzvah ("a son of the commandment") at the age of 13. On the first Saturday following his birthday he reads from the Torah in the synagogue and may lead part of the service. In preparation he must study Jewish history, ancient Hebrew and his spiritual roots, discussing his learning with the rabbi and his family in relation to his own life and oncoming adulthood.

BAPTISM

The Jewish and Christian practice of initiating people into the faith by dipping them in water represents the purification and cleansing of the spirit. Early

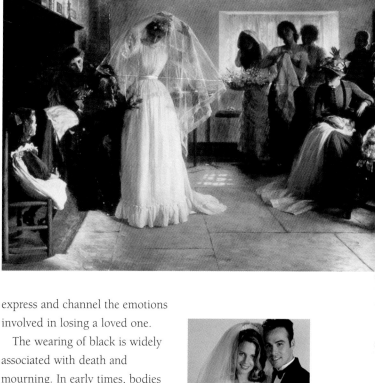

Christian writings describe a meal of milk and honey accompanying baptism, representing the entry of the Israelites into the promised land of Canaan. Roman Catholic baptism also involves the exorcism of the devil and anointing with olive oil, a symbol of the gifts of the Holy Spirit.

MARRIAGE

The meaning and symbolism of marriage reflects the underlying beliefs of the culture, but most are redolent with the ancient symbolism of a couple attaining a semi-divine state of wholeness necessary to create and protect new life. This idea of the union of the human and divine is echoed in the Christian tradition of calling its nuns "brides of Christ".

One of the most significant symbols of marriage still in use is the ring, a circular symbol of eternity, union and completeness. This is echoed in the Christian ceremony when the couple's hands are joined together by the priest, and in the Hindu ceremony when the bridegroom ties a ribbon around the neck of his bride. Other symbols of

marriage include bells, as a means of proclaiming good news, and peach blossom, which is believed by the Chinese to be linked with immortality, longevity, spring, youth and marriage and is also an emblem of virginity.

Symbols of fertility were once central to wedding ceremonies, and are echoed in modern times by the rice (or confetti made of rice paper) thrown over the couple. The wedding cake was once a symbol of fertility, food being a sexual symbol and its formal sharing during the feast a symbol of the two families coming together. Bridesmaids are symbols of sympathetic fertility magic, while the flowers they carry are further symbols of femininity and fruitfulness.

DEATH RITES

A person's death represents a considerable transition, for both the individual and the family and community around them. The deceased is ritually prepared to move on, possibly as part of a journey into another reality, and the mourning process employs a great deal of symbolic ritual to

express and channel the emotions involved in losing a loved one.

The wearing of black is widely associated with death and mourning. In early times, bodies of the dead were stained with red ochre to symbolize blood and the connection with the earth. Another common symbol of mourning is the shaving or dishevelling of the hair. Cultural values are clearly mirrored in funeral rites. Even the expressing of emotion reflects cultural attitudes: in some cultures, such as Sikh, wailing is discouraged, whereas in others it is expected.

The deceased are often treated as if they are undergoing a journey: they are dressed in special clothes and accompanied by personal and religious objects or talismans. Burying the body may symbolize the person's return to Mother Earth or to the dead ancestors. Cremation represents the liberation of spirit and release from Earth. For the Hindus, the flames symbolize Brahma.

ABOVE A bell is one of the symbols of a wedding, and is often used as a motif on the invitations, orders or service and menus, and silver bell-shaped ornaments might be carried by the bride and bridesmaids.

TOP The Romans would break the cake over the bride's head, but in modern ceremonies the cutting of the cake symbolizes the first task in the couple's life.

LEFT In a Hindu funeral the colour of mourning is white, and coffin, deceased and mourners are all dressed in it.

THE WHEEL

ABOVE The traditionally shaped wheel, as in this representation of the Buddhist eight-spoked wheel, holds the symbolism of the sun and the cosmos. The wheel is also an enduring symbol of human endeavour and advancement.

The symbolism of the wheel relates to the passage of time, the world, and the unity that exists at the heart of diversity. It is associated with the zodiac and with life's ups and downs (as the wheel of fortune); as the Native American medicine wheel it provides a blueprint for living. As an archetypal motif, the wheel's significance relates to its shape – a circle containing spokes radiating from a central hub – and its mobility. It combines the symbolism of the circle with movement, representing the cosmos as an eternal round of creation and dissolution. In many cultures it appears as a sun symbol, with countless beliefs associating it with solar myths, although some have argued that it was pre-eminently a lunar symbol, signifying the continuous cycle of the moon.

SOLAR AND LUNAR SYMBOLISM

The wheel has both solar and lunar associations. The simplest form has four spokes, which may reflect the four directions and four seasons (as in the medicine wheel), as well as the four-stage lunar cycle: waxing, full, waning and dark. Arianrhod, the Welsh goddess of weaving and spinning, was connected with the moon; her name means "silver wheel".

Wheels with 12 spokes appear frequently in Indian literature and art, suggesting the movement of the sun through the zodiac, while the traditional Chinese wheel has 30 spokes, signifying the lunar cycle. In classical antiquity, the wheel was linked with the god Apollo (and so with the sun), as well as to thunderbolts and the lighting of fires.

The wheel as a solar symbol persists in European folklore. It was traditional to carry blazing wheels by torchlit procession to a hilltop at the summer solstice and roll the wheel down the hillside at the winter solstice.

SACRED TRADITION

The wheel, or chakra, is an important symbol in both Hindu and Buddhist traditions. In Hinduism, the wheel represents the unity of time and space and is a symbol of completion: a six-spoked wheel is one of the symbols of the preserver deity, Vishnu. In Buddhism, the eight-spoked dharmachakra is the wheel of the law or truth (dharma). It often appears on carvings representing the footprints of the Buddha and symbolizes the power of his teachings to roll over and stamp out lies. Like human fate, once the wheel is set in motion there is no power that can stop it or reverse its direction. The eight spokes represent the eightfold path of Buddhism, the hub the moral anchor of the Buddha's teachings, while at the motionless centre stands the *chakravarti* ("he who makes the wheel revolve"), the Buddha himself. His Celtic equivalent is Mag Ruith, the mythic druid who was an incarnation of the supreme god, the Dagda. Mag Ruith was the *magus rotarum,* or "wizard of the wheels", and it was with the help of wheels that he spoke his druidic oracles.

In the Old Testament, Ezekiel compares the throne of God to a chariot with four wheels, each wheel representing one of the Four Living Creatures and the seasons, while in Daniel's vision flaming wheels appear around God's head. On early Christian gravestones, the wheel is sometimes found as a symbol of God and of eternity.

THE CATHERINE WHEEL

As the emblem of St Catherine of Alexandria, the wheel is associated with torment. She was said to have been a Christian convert of the early 4th century, who was mystically married to Christ in a vision. The Roman emperor Maxentius desired to marry her, and when she refused him he ordered her to be tortured on a spiked wheel. The wheel miraculously broke when she touched it, but she was eventually martyred with a sword. She is usually depicted with the wheel, which subsequently gave its name to a spinning firework.

THE WHEEL OF LIFE

In Hindu philosophy, the symbolism of the wheel is used to refer to samsara, the continuous cycle of life, death and rebirth. In Chinese symbolism, the hub relates to Heaven and the rim to Earth, with humankind represented by the spokes that link the two. The Chinese noria (waterwheel), and the Taoist sage Chuang Tzu's potter's wheel both represent the ceaseless whirlpool of creation and the never-ending life–death cycle. The point of liberation is at the hub, pointing to the spiritual journey as a movement from the periphery to the centre, from activity to stillness, which is the purpose of meditation. In the Celtic tradition, the year is seen as a wheel, with the summer and winter solstices and the spring and autumn equinoxes marking four points of transition as the sun's power rises and decreases with the changing seasons.

WHEEL OF FORTUNE

Its turning nature means that the wheel has often been associated with chance and fortune, both fickle and fortuitous. It frequently appears as a motif in medieval European art and was an attribute of Fortuna, the Roman goddess of fate (Tyche was the Greek equivalent). Fortuna represents each moment's potential for luck or ill, with the turning of her wheel bringing happiness and success to some, and ruin and

RIGHT A blindfolded Fortuna, goddess of fate, rolls her wheel at random and without mercy over crowned kings.

misery to others, in a seemingly random way. She is often depicted as blind or blindfolded, because fate is morally blind. Her wheel teaches that what goes up must come down and vice versa – so that success and failure follow on each other's heels, just as life and death cycle and circle. In the Tarot, the Wheel of Fortune is the tenth card of the Major Arcana and represents an important turning point.

THE MEDICINE WHEEL

In many traditions, the wheel is a symbol of the world. This forms the basis of the Native American medicine wheel – a cross within a circle emanating from a central hub. The wheel is drawn on the ground, and the four spokes represent the four seasons, the four elements and the four directions. The seasons symbolize time, and the compass points, space. The fifth and sixth directions (above and below the wheel) represent father sky and mother earth. Each place on the wheel is associated with a particular colour, an animal totem and a quality, and the whole wheel represents the journey through life.

RIGHT The Native American symbol of the medicine wheel, a circle segmented by a cross, is reproduced here in stone.

FLORA AND FAUNA

THE SYMBOLISM OF TREES, PLANTS, FLOWERS AND ANIMALS HAVE BEEN CENTRAL TO SYMBOLIC CONCEPTUALISATION SINCE PREHISTORIC DAYS. ANIMALS HAVE BEEN PARTICULARLY IMPORTANT, WORSHIPPED AS GODS OR PROTECTIVE SPIRITS, AND, LIKE FRUIT AND VEGETABLES, VITAL FOR LIFE IN THE FOOD THEY PROVIDE.

TREES

LEFT In ancient times sacred groves of trees were places of sanctuary and worship.

ABOVE The banyan tree is sacred to the Hindu gods: watering its roots and placing offerings is thought to bring happiness and fertility.

The tree is a central and archetypal symbol in most parts of the world. In the West, trees are deeply associated with time and historical continuity. Elsewhere they tend to have stronger associations with life, health and potency. Ancient peoples worshipped in sacred groves, with their trunks and canopies of branches, which were later echoed in the design of churches. The words "truth" and "trust" are derived from the Old English word for "tree".

THE WORLD TREE
The cosmic tree, symbolizing the ultimate reservoir for the forces of life continually regenerating the world, is central to many creation myths. It frequently represents the axis of the universe, connecting a number of realms: its branches hold up the heavens, its trunk stands in the earthly realm and its roots descend into the underworld. Other commonly associated symbols are reptiles crawling in the roots and birds in the branches symbolizing shamanic flight.

The world tree is usually represented by a species that is particularly important in a geographical region. Norse mythology tells of the ash tree Yggdrasil, which grew between Asgard, the realm of the gods, Midgard, the realm of humanity, and Hel, the underworld. The ancient Egyptians believed a holy sycamore grew at the threshold between life and death; in Mesopotamia the world axis passed through a palm tree. Hindus hold the banyan tree as sacred, while the Maya believed in Yaxche, the sacred tree whose branches supported the heavens. The Chinese sacred tree was thought to grow from the centre of the world, emitting no echo and casting no shadow. The sakaki tree is venerated as the "heaven-tree" of Japanese mythology, and a branch is stuck in the ground as a sacred centre around which a wooden Shinto shrine is built.

ABOVE The European oak is a symbol of strength, stability, firmness and an enduring nature.

THE MAYPOLE
In Europe, on 1 May, the spring fertility ritual of the maypole dance symbolizes the marriage of the vegetation god to the May queen. The pole, representing the spirit of the tree (and with obvious phallic symbolism), was erected and decorated, and danced around with abandon.

Trees are also powerful symbols of the interconnectedness and ecology of life. The Native American elder Black Elk saw in a vision the "sacred hoop" of his people combining with many others to create a larger hoop, within which grew a mighty and holy tree of protection. The world tree of the Amazon region is the ceiba, or yuchan: the Huaorani creation myth tells of the giant ceiba tree Bobehuè, which contains all forms of life. It thus represents an entire ecosystem central to life on earth, which may be not far from the truth.

TREES AND THE ORIGINS OF HUMANITY

The world tree is commonly associated with the origins of humankind. The Yakut of Siberia believe in a tree with eight branches, which stands within the golden navel of the earth, growing into a primordial paradise where the first man was born and suckled on the milk of the woman, who was herself part of the tree. The first man in ancient Indian mythology, Yama, drank with the gods beside a magnificent tree.

A common Indo-European mythical theme describes an apocalypse during which tempests, fire or floods devastate the earth, leaving as the only survivors the ancestors of humanity, who are made of wood.

TREES OF LIFE AND IMMORTALITY

In one of its aspects, the world tree is the tree of life or immortality. It is often associated with a nourishing and protective universe from which the elixir or bounties of life may be received – a state of grace from which humans may fall. The Egyptian sky goddess Nut was depicted emerging from a sycamore fig to offer the bread and water of eternity to the dead.

Seraphim wielding swords of fire guard the biblical tree of life. In Taoist tradition it is the divine peach that confers the gift of immortality, while the apples of the goddess Idun are the source of the powers of the Norse gods.

The Qur'an describes the prophet Mohammed coming across the tree of Tuba standing in the heart of paradise, glowing with emeralds, rubies and sapphires; milk, honey and wine sprang from its roots.

THE INVERTED TREE

The symbol of the inverted tree is found in the Jewish Kabbalah and in the Hindu yogic Bhagavad Gita. This tree of life has its roots in the heavens and its branches below, representing God in Heaven as the origin of all things. The inverted tree image can be related to the human nervous or chakral system, underlining the connection between the human microcosm and the macrocosm.

TREE DRESSING

The practice of tree dressing is found throughout the world. The Karan is a Hindu ritual in which a tree in the centre of a village is covered with butter, and decorated with vermillion, turmeric and garlands, after which women dance with marigolds in their hair. In Africa trees are revered as the centre of life and fertility, and are dressed as a way of connecting with the ancestral spirits. Evergreens are dressed at Christmas in Christian cultures as a symbol of life.

TREES OF DEATH

Evergreen trees are ancient symbols of death and the potential for eternal life, but the cypress tree symbolizes the finality of death because, once cut, it will never again sprout from its stump. Images of tree stumps or trunks are found in heraldic emblems representing death and rebirth.

In Britain, the yew tree is most closely associated with death. It was considered immortal by the Druids, and is commonly found in graveyards and at ancient sacred sites. Its roots were believed to soak up the spirits of the dead, releasing them to the winds from its branches.

THE MULBERRY

In China the mulberry tree represents the cycles of life. Its berries start white, representing youth, then turn red for the middle years, and finally ripen to black, suggesting wisdom, old age and death.

CHRISTMAS TREE

The modern variation of decorated trees at Christmas originated in 16th-century Germany, where fir trees were dressed with apples and coloured paper. The tradition has become a Christian ritual, perhaps refering to the tree of paradise, but its roots are older, an emblem of rebirth dating back to at least Roman times when the celebrants at the feast of Saturnalia used evergreens to celebrate the birth of the new year.

PLANTS, HERBS AND SPICES

ABOVE In European folklore, the mandrake was associated with death, insanity, witchcraft and magic. When picked it was said to utter a piercing human-like scream.

ABOVE Saffron, the stamen of a type of crocus, is a sacred herb in Buddhism. In Europe it is associated with royalty.

The symbolism of plants is closely related to their perceived magical properties and power to influence humans on many different levels – physical, mental, emotional and spiritual. In symbolic terms, they are associated with ideas of balance and cosmological order, which have often been reflected in sophisticated theories of the nature of health and disease.

THE DOCTRINE OF SIGNATURES

According to the "doctrine of signatures", everything in nature is marked with a pattern or sign that indicates its potential properties. The name evolved from the Signatura Rerum (The Signature of All Things) by Jakob Böhme (1575–1624), a German shoemaker whose philosophy was informed by a mystical vision in which he saw the relationship between God and humans. The doctrine was applied to the powers of plants for medical application. For example, the heart-shaped leaves of the purple foxglove were used as a heart medicine (digitalis), while the purple veins and yellow fleck of the eyebright flower, which suggest an unhealthy-looking eye, designated the plant as a remedy for eye ailments.

Because of its resemblance to the human form, the mandrake was credited with human and superhuman powers in European folklore. It was said to thrive around the gallows, fed by the faeces and urine falling from those hanged, and to scream when it was pulled up or disturbed: the sound led to deafness and insanity in those unfortunate enough to hear it. The mandrake was associated with witchcraft and used in love magic, and a mandrake root doll was said to have the power to

BELOW In European plant lore, rosemary is a symbol of remembrance, love and fidelity.

make its owner invisible. Medicinally, it was also used to treat arthritis, ulcers and inflammation, to induce menstruation, ease delivery in childbirth and aid conception. In the Jewish tradition the mandrake is associated with fertility and love – its Hebrew name means "love plant".

HERBS

A great variety of symbolic meanings are attached to common herbs. In ancient Greece, students wore sprigs of rosemary to improve memory and concentration, and the plant came to symbolize remembrance. It was also associated with love and fidelity and became a symbol of immortality in funeral rites. Sage was also associated with immortality and was thought by the ancient Greeks to promote wisdom. It takes its name from the Latin *salvare,* meaning "to save" and in European herbal medicine was thought of as a cure-all. Native Americans consider sage a healing and cleansing herb, especially the variety known as white sage; its

BELOW Sage is a sacred herb in Native American traditions, used for cleansing and purifying.

dry leaves are often formed into smudge bundles for burning, the smoke being ritually smudged, or wafted, to purify the atmosphere. In ancient Rome, peppermint was associated with clear thoughts and inspiration and was used as a brain tonic, while in the Arab world it was widely believed to stimulate virility and has been drunk as a refreshing tea for centuries, offered to guests as a symbol of hospitality.

In India, *tulsi*, or sweet basil, is sacred to Vishnu, and the funeral custom of laying a basil leaf on the chest of the dead was thought to open the gates of Heaven for the departed; in Tudor England departing guests were given a miniature pot of basil to help them on their journey. In the central Congo, basil leaves protect against evil spirits and bad luck, while in ancient Greece they were an antidote to the deadly venom of the basilisk, a fabulous creature whose glance was fatal. The plant takes its name from the Greek *basilikon*, meaning "royal".

SPICES

Many spices are similarly rich in symbolism. Black pepper, one of the earliest known spices, was widely regarded as an aphrodisiac in antiquity. Saffron is a species of crocus (*Crocus sativus*) whose stamens yield a deep yellow dye. Traditionally it was used to dye the robes of Buddhist monks, and the colour became associated with the Buddhist paradise and with wisdom. In Europe, saffron was linked with royalty and gold because of its costliness as well as its colour. In ancient China,

coriander seeds were believed to contain the power of immortality, and cardamom pods share a similar symbolism in India and the Middle East. In China and Japan, cloves represent sweetness and health, and in Japanese art they were one of the objects associated with the Seven Deities of Good Fortune.

TOBACCO

The tobacco plant is indigenous to North America, and the Native Americans are said to have been the first people to use it. They regard it as sacred, and it has widespread ritual and ceremonial use. The Machiguenga of Peru use the term *seripegari*, meaning "he who uses tobacco", to describe a shaman; roasted tobacco leaves (*seri*) are used in shamanic rituals. To many Pueblo people, tobacco was the gift of the hummingbird, who brought smoke to the shamans so that they could purify the Earth.

In Europe, smoking tobacco was originally associated with dissolute young men and soldiers, so that when women first began to smoke in public in the late 19th century it was regarded as shocking. Today the symbolic associations surrounding tobacco are ambiguous. On the one hand it has become synonymous with deadly illnesses such as cancer and heart disease, yet on the other it retains an element of sophistication and rebellion.

MISTLETOE

The Celts associated mistletoe (*Viscum album*) with magic and medicine. To the Druids it was a

CANNABIS

Rastafarians, who know it as ganja, regard cannabis as a holy herb mentioned in the Bible, where it performs a sacramental function, producing an altered state of consciousness through which it is possible to attain a glimpse of the divine. The cannabis leaf became a symbol of Rastafarianism, as well as representing a protest against the dominant social order, which had deemed its use illegal. In the Western world today, many teenagers see the cannabis leaf as a symbol of rebellion against adult authority and mainstream society.

GARLIC

An ancient Egyptian medical papyrus includes more than 200 prescriptions for garlic. It was used to treat headaches, physical debility and infections, and raw garlic was included in the diet of Egyptian workers to keep them strong. In ancient Greece and Rome garlic was a symbol of strength, and athletes chewed it to maximize their chances of winning races. In many traditions, garlic is believed to offer not only physical but also metaphysical protection, hence the popular belief in European folklore that garlic cloves can keep werewolves and vampires at bay, or in ancient China that it could ward off the evil eye.

symbol of immortality and the soul of their sacred tree, the oak, on which it grew. The Celts believed that mistletoe was created when a lightning bolt struck an oak tree, giving it magical properties, and ritual demanded that a white-robed Druid cut mistletoe after the winter solstice using a golden sickle (both a solar and a lunar symbol). The plant had to be caught in a white cloth, as it was believed that it should never touch the ground. Mistletoe was used to treat many different health conditions and was also a fertility symbol. The custom of kissing under the mistletoe at Christmas has its roots in the plant's ancient associations.

BELOW Mistletoe is a symbol of immortality and was associated with magic and medicine for the Celts.

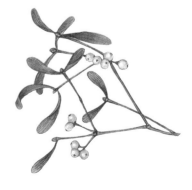

FLOWERS

ABOVE Cultures all over the world have used bouquets of flowers at funerals as a way of honouring the dead.

BELOW The Hindu goddess Lakshmi sits on the lotus, symbol of enlightenment and elevation of the spirit. Hindu deities are often pictured with this flower.

While the aesthetic beauty of flowers has inspired poets and artists through the ages, they also have a long tradition of use in healing and ritual – more than 100,000 years ago, the Neanderthals made flower offerings to their dead. To this day, flowers are given as tokens of love or thanks, to acknowledge achievement, honour the dead and to mark transitions of all kinds. They have become symbols of a wide range of human experiences and are woven into myth and sacred tradition.

In general, flowers represent the culmination of a growth cycle and a crowning achievement. Growing from the earth and receptive to the sun and rain, they are related to the power of the passive, feminine principle, manifesting beauty literally and physically as well as spiritually and metaphorically. In Hindu ritual, the flower corresponds to the element ether (or spirit); in the Taoist text The Secret of the Golden Flower it represents the attainment of a spiritual state.

SAY IT WITH FLOWERS

Many different cultures, including those of China, Egypt and India, have evolved their own "language of flowers". Contemporary audiences of the plays of William Shakespeare (1564–1616) would have been familiar with the hidden meanings contained in his floral references: for instance, thyme symbolized sweetness, oxlips meant comeliness, the violet meant "love in idleness", eglantine or honeysuckle meant "united in love", and pansies stood for thoughts. The Victorians developed this language into a popular art, instilling meaning in the colour, arrangement and presentation of flowers as well as the species.

IKEBANA

Practitioners of ikebana, the Japanese art of flower arranging, have developed a complex symbolism to reflect the precepts of Zen Buddhism. The Zen ideal of *wabi* (deliberate understatement), for instance, is reflected in the minimalist form of the arrangement. Traditional ikebana arrangements follow a ternary plan, with the upper spray representing Heaven, the central one humanity, and the lower one earth – a symbolic pattern of all that lives, with humans as the intermediaries between Heaven and earth. In the "flowing" style, the sprays hang down, suggesting the decline and flow into the abyss, while the "standing", or *rikka*, style reaches up, symbolizing loyalty – between husband and wife, to the emperor and to the divine. Rikka arrangements are asymmetrical and are intended to suggest an aspect of nature, such as the interplay of light and shade.

LOTUS

In the East, the lotus is the flower most commonly associated with the elevation of the spirit. Brahma, the Hindu creator god, was born from a golden lotus sprouting from Vishnu's navel (a symbol of the centre of the world). A thousand-petalled lotus is a symbol of spiritual enlightenment. The Sanskrit names for lotus are *padma* or *kamala*, which also describe the vagina, and lotus blossom also represents the vagina in China.

LILLIES

In the Christian tradition, the lily is associated with repentance: it is said to have grown from the tears of Eve as she left the Garden of Eden. It is the flower of the Virgin Mary: the white Madonna lily symbolizes purity and chastity; it also represents purity in alchemy. In Australia, the Gymea lily is linked with courage and steadfastness: in an Aboriginal dreaming story the young man Kai'mia rescued members of his tribe even though he was wounded, and lilies grew where his blood fell. In China and Japan, the day lily (*Hemerocallis*) was believed to have the power to dispel grief, and women wore them in their belts to forget the sorrow of a lost love.

ROSES

In classical antiquity it was said that the first rose was created by Chloris, the goddess of flowers (whose Roman equivalent is Flora), from the body of a beautiful nymph. It was sacred to Aphrodite/Venus, the goddess of love. In the Arab tradition, the first rose was brought to life by the rays of the rising sun in the Great Garden of Persia, spreading its seeds to all other lands, and was a symbol of fertility, beauty and purity. A nightingale sang when the first white roses bloomed, but was so overcome by their perfume that it dropped to Earth, its blood staining their petals red.

In Islam, the rose is sacred to Mohammed; for the mystic Sufi sect, the rose is associated with pleasure, but because of its thorns, it is also linked with pain.

In Christianity, red roses symbolize the blood of martyrs and life after death, while white roses are associated with the Virgin Mary. The Rosicrucian Brotherhood, a Christian sect founded in Europe in the 15th century, combined the symbol of a rose with the cross to form the emblem of their society.

TULIPS

In ancient Persia, the tulip was a symbol of perfect love, exalted in poetry as one of the blooms found in the gardens of paradise. During the Ottoman period, the Turkish word for tulip was spelled using the same letters that form the word "Allah", so the flower came to symbolize divinity, and the tulip became the emblem of the Ottoman rulers. Tulips were exported from Turkey to Europe in the mid-16th century, and were hybridized to produce rare and distinctive flowers. Their value rose to fantastic heights in The Netherlands during the 1630s, when they became symbols of wealth and beauty. The tulip is the symbol of The Netherlands.

CHRYSANTHEMUMS

In China and Japan, the chrysanthemum is linked with autumn and is a symbol of long life, good luck, happiness and wealth. Its radiating petals make it a sun symbol, leading to its use as the emblem of the Japanese imperial family and Japan's national flower. With the plum, orchid and bamboo, the chrysanthemum is one of a group called the Four Gentlemen, believed to represent the virtues of a Confucian in their simplicity, uprightness and hardiness. In the West the chrysanthemum is associated with autumn and is used in art to represent decadence and death.

POPPIES

Because it produces the narcotic opium, the poppy was associated with sleep and death in ancient Greece, where it was dedicated to Hypnos and Morpheus, the gods of sleep and dreaming. It was also linked to the myth of Demeter and Persephone – the latter was picking poppies when Hades abducted her – in which it came to represent the annual death of nature. Since World War I, red poppies have commemorated fallen soldiers: the flowers grew on the battlefields of Flanders. In Britain red poppies mark Remembrance Sunday, the day when the sacrifice of soldiers in all wars is remembered.

SUNFLOWERS

The sunflower arrived in Europe from the Americas, where the Spanish called it *girasol*, or "turn to the sun" because of the way it turned to face the sun. In China the sunflower was linked with immortality, and eating its seeds was said to promote longevity.

RIGHT In the Western world, white roses are associated with purity and spirituality, and are a favourite flower at weddings.

BELOW In Japan, the art of ikebana has developed its own symbolic language and ritual and reflects the simplicity of Zen Buddhism.

VICTORIAN LANGUAGE OF FLOWERS

Some of the symbolic associations for flowers were:
broom: ardour
carnation: pure love
camellia: perfection
candytuft: indifference
clover: happiness
daffodil: kind regard
gentian: you are unjust
hawthorn: hope
hollyhock: ambition
passionflower: faith
wallflower: always true

FRUIT

ABOVE In this allegory of the Earth, the artist uses an abundance of fruit to symbolize wealth and prosperity, the cornucopia suggests plenty, and the beautiful, curvaceous young woman reinforces the symbolism of fertility.

ABOVE In addition to its role as the "fruit of knowledge", the apple has also been used as a symbol of love, marriage, youth, fertility and longevity.

Most of the symbolism of fruit appeals directly and powerfully to the senses. The eating of fruit easily conjures up associations with eroticism and sensuality, and this imagery has been much used in art. Fruit also suggests abundance and fertility: it spills out of the cornucopia in classical mythology, representing the generosity of the gods and a good harvest. The fruit of the tree of life is food for the immortals, and contains seeds for reproduction and growth.

APPLES

The apple is identified as the "fruit of knowledge", whether of good and evil, as in the Garden of Eden, or of life, wisdom and immortality, as in the Greek myth of the golden apples of the Hesperides. The Celts saw the apple tree as the "otherworld" tree, the doorway to the fairy world. Celtic kings and heroes such as King Arthur took refuge on the legendary Isle of Avalon, the "apple orchard".

In China, apple blossom symbolizes feminine beauty, and apples are symbols of peace. But as the Chinese word for "apple" is very similar to the word for "illness" it is thought inauspicious to give an apple to an invalid.

New symbolism evolved around the apple in the early 19th century, when Johnny Appleseed pursued his dream of a land of blossoming trees where no one went hungry, by planting apple seeds throughout America. The great metropolis New York City is known as the "Big Apple".

FIGS

The fig tree and its many-seeded fruit are symbols of plenty and fertility often associated with feminine qualities. The Ruminal fig in the Palatine temple in Rome was said to be the tree beneath which Romulus and Remus were suckled by a wolf. Romans considered figs lucky or unlucky according to whether they were light or dark.

In the Book of Genesis, Adam and Eve used fig leaves to cover themselves when they became shamefully aware of their nakedness, and the forbidden fruit they ate may have been a fig rather than an apple. In Africa, the Kotoko people of Chad connect the fig with childbearing, and its milky sap is thought to increase lactation.

BANANAS

The banana plant's botanical name, *Musa sapientum*, means "fruit of the wise men" and was given by Linnaeus, a Swedish botanist, who had heard that Alexander the Great encountered sages in India who lived entirely on bananas. According to the Qur'an and in Islamic stories, the banana was the forbidden fruit in paradise. For the Buddha, the banana tree symbolized the transient nature and weakness of matter and mental constructions. In the Hindu tradition it is a symbol of fertility and prosperity, due to its tendency to fruit regularly, and thus bananas may be left in front of houses where a wedding is taking place.

CHERRIES

A cherry colour in the lips of a Chinese woman is considered a quality of great beauty, and the phrase "eating cherries" is a euphemism for sexual intercourse. In the West the cherry is associated with the hymen, and the phrase "losing one's cherry" refers to the loss of virginity. Cherry blossom is the national flower of Japan. Samurai warriors would meditate upon life and death beneath a cherry tree, as at the height of its flowering the blossom would gracefully fall to the ground and die, paralleling the Samurai's willingness to face death in his prime.

PLUMS

In the Far East the plum tree is a common symbol for the spring, and also for the end of winter: as it blossoms at the threshold

RIGHT This picture of the god Dionysus deploys the sexual symbolism of apple, fig and vine to accentuate its eroticism.

between the two seasons, it represents the renewal of youthfulness. It was also thought that the immortals fed from plum blossoms, so the tree was connected with immortality. In both the Japanese and Christian traditions it is a symbol of fidelity.

PEACHES

The peach tree originated in China, where it was considered the holy tree of life, producing an elixir of immortality. The Taoists associated peach blossom with virginity and with the female genitalia. ("Tao" is the Chinese word for "peach".) In early Europe the peach was called the "fruit of Venus" and was sacred to Hymen, the Roman god of marriage. In Christian imagery a peach in the hand of the infant Christ symbolizes salvation.

APRICOTS

In China the apricot is associated with a woman's beauty and sexuality. Red apricots symbolize a married woman who has taken a lover, and the eyes of a beautiful woman are often compared to the stones of apricots. It has also been used to symbolize female genitals.

POMEGRANATES

Growing in Mediterranean climates, by the end of the summer pomegranates swell to become red-orange spheres glistening inside with juicy red, jewel-like seeds. Their name means "apple of many seeds". It was one of the gifts of Allah in the Qur'an, and for the Israelites it represented the charm of their land and the wisdom of its

people. The pomegranate has often been associated with fertility – symbolizing the womb – but also with death. Pomegranates were left as food in Egyptian tombs to accompany the dead on their journey. In Greece, at weddings and on New Year, a pomegranate is broken on the ground as a symbol of fertility and abundance.

DATES

The date palm originated near the Persian Gulf, and has always grown prolifically in Iraq. To the Egyptians the fruit was a fertility symbol. The date palm is referred to as the "king of the oasis" and a "tree of life" by the Arabs, who state that the tree is at its best when its feet are in water and its head is in the fires of the heavens.

LICHEES AND MANGOES

The lichee is a small fruit from southern China with a rough reddish brown skin and a large shiny brown stone. Placing lichees under the bed of a married couple expresses the hope that they will be blessed with children.

Mangoes, with their succulent orange flesh, are native to eastern India, and Burma. In India they are considered sacred, representing fertility and good fortune. Legend has it that the Buddha was given a mango grove in which he could seek repose.

ORANGES

The orange tree's Latin name, *Fructus aurantia*, refers to the golden colour of the orange, whereas *naranja*, the Spanish

word for the fruit, comes from the Persian *narang*, meaning "interior perfume". The orange suggests both virginity and fruitfulness, as the flowers and fruit appear simultaneously. Orange blossom featured in ancient marriage ceremonies because of its association with fertility, a tradition that has continued to the present day. In Christian imagery, an orange in the hand of the infant Christ represents fertility and good fortune; for the witches of Europe, the fruit represented the heart. In China the orange is still eaten as a symbol of good fortune on the second day of the New Year.

GRAPES

Vines and grapes often appear in Roman art, suggesting wealth and pleasure, and are associated with Bacchus, the Roman equivalent of the Greek Dionysus, god of the vine, sexuality, fertility, and the liberation of passion and expression. Grapes from the Promised Land represented the possibility of new life for the Israelites. For Christians, wine is a symbol of the blood of Christ.

BOTTOM In modern Judaism an orange placed on a *seder* plate came to symbolise the leadership of Jewish women.

BELOW Pomegranates and their seeds often symbolized fertility. Pomegranate juice was used as a remedy for infertility by the Romans, while in Christian art it is a symbol of hope.

ANIMALS

ABOVE Cats were sacred to the ancient Egyptians and appeared throughout the culture in sculpture and in paintings.

ABOVE The wolf is at times associated with courage and victory, and at others with cruelty, cunning and greed.

TOP In China, the tiger (and also the leopard) is king of beasts and guards the gates of Heaven.

Throughout history, animals have played an important part in the symbolic language of many different cultures. They have been worshipped as gods and seen as sources of wisdom and power, as harbingers of good or bad fortune, as protective spirits and guides to other worlds, as well as symbolic representations of human characteristics. Animals have been used in ritual sacrifice and hunted to provide food, medicine, clothing and cosmetics, as well as to satisfy human vanity. Symbolically, they touch on all levels of the universe – Heaven, Earth and the underworld.

DOGS AND WOLVES

The dog is probably humankind's oldest domesticated animal, and signifies loyalty, protection and companionship. Dogs are widely connected with death and the spirit world: the Ainu people of Japan believed their dogs had the psychic power to detect ghosts; for the Incas, the howling of a dog could signal the death of a relative; and in Greek myth, Cerberus the watchdog guarded the underworld. The Maya buried dogs with their masters so that they could guide them through the afterlife.

Along the north-west coast of America the wolf is a powerful spirit animal that can endow the shaman with supernatural abilities, and many shamanistic cultures speak of sorcerers obtaining their powers from a woman disguised as a wolf. In Christian tradition, the wolf is usually contrasted with the lamb, the latter symbolizing the faithful and the wolf the powers that threaten to destroy them. The colloquial expression "a wolf in sheep's clothing" refers to feigned innocence, while the American Plains tribes regard the prairie wolf, or coyote, as a trickster and figure of deceit. This idea also appears in European folklore in the story of Little Red Riding Hood, in which the wolf symbolizes a predatory male.

THE BIG CATS

Because of its mane, golden coat and regal bearing, the lion is an ancient solar symbol and the embodiment of earthly power. In ancient Egypt, the pharaoh was often depicted as a lion, and African kings used images of lions as personal symbols. In alchemy, the lion represented sexual passion, while a green lion was linked with the wild forces of nature. The lion was also associated with the mother goddess – it was one of the symbols of the Babylonian goddess Ishtar. In the classical world, it was a guardian of the underworld and a symbol of divine protection. Both the Buddha and Christ have been associated with the lion, making it a symbol of spiritual zeal and enlightenment.

For the Chinese, the tiger, rather than the lion, is the king of beasts. A guardian spirit, initially of hunting and later of farming, it is the third sign of the Chinese zodiac. The white tiger is associated with the moon and, because it can see in the dark, it symbolizes illumination. In Hinduism, the tiger represents unbridled passion and loss of control – the deities Shiva and Durga ride tigers when destroying demons, demonstrating their ferocity and fearlessness.

Among the pre-Columbian civilizations of Central and South America, the jaguar was king of the jungle and was said to have given humans the gift of fire and hunting. The Maya considered it a creature of the underworld that knows the mysteries of the earth; by gazing into its eyes it was thought possible to see the future. Today, many Amazonian tribes continue to revere the jaguar as a *nagual* (spirit guardian) and a source of healing, associating it with fertility, water and rainfall; the Matses people believe that jaguars eat the souls of the dead.

DOMESTIC CATS

The ancient Egyptians venerated and mummified cats, and it was a capital offence to kill or injure one. Conversely, in Buddhism, cats and snakes were cursed because they did not weep when the Buddha died – although from a different perspective this may be perceived as a sign of spiritual wisdom. The early Jews reviled cats as unclean, while medieval Christians associated black cats with witchcraft.

RABBITS AND HARES
Both the rabbit and the hare have lunar associations and are fertility symbols in many cultures. Eostre, the hare-headed Saxon goddess of spring, brought dawn and new life. In China the hare represents reproductive power and longevity. The hare and rabbit both appear as trickster figures, most notably in the Brer Rabbit stories, traditional African stories taken to American plantations by slaves.

ELEPHANTS
Both Africa and India are often symbolized by the elephant. It is a symbol of strength, longevity, wisdom and good luck; ridden by rulers, it also represents power and authority. In the mythology of India and Tibet, the elephant holds up the world and symbolizes unchanging stability. Ganesh, the Hindu elephant-headed god, is the remover of obstacles. In Buddhism, the white elephant is sacred: the Buddha's mother dreamt of one at his conception. In Thailand, Laos and Cambodia it is said to grant rainfall and bounteous harvests.

BULLS AND COWS
Traditionally the bull is a symbol of virility, the cow of motherhood and fertility. Because its curved horns resemble the crescent moon, the cow is a celestial symbol of mother goddesses (such as the ancient Egyptian deities Isis and Hathor). In Norse mythology, the primordial cow – the Nourisher – licked the ice to create the first human. For the Hindus, the cow is a sacred animal and may not be killed; the animals wander the streets of India freely.

Unlike the cow, which has rarely been sacrificed, the bull's use as a ritual animal is widespread. In ancient Rome, a bull was sacrificed annually as its blood was believed to fertilize the earth and confer virility; echoes of such beliefs survive today in Spanish bullfighting. Because of its roar, the bull was the animal of thunder gods such as the Norse Thor. The Apis bull in ancient Egypt was a symbol of creation and was often shown carrying the sun disc of Ra between its horns, yet it was also sacred to Osiris, god of the underworld.

BISONS AND BUFFALO
Evidence from cave art (such as in Lascaux, France) reveals the central role played by bison in the physical and spiritual life of early hunter societies. Related to and at times synonymous with the bison, buffalo were also revered.

The Zulus believe the buffalo is able to possess the soul of a human, while the Dakota Sioux see it instead as a manifestation of the supreme creator, and it plays a central role in vision-quest ceremonies.

BEARS
In many shamanic traditions, the bear is associated with medicine, healing and magical wisdom. In northern Europe, the bear is king of the animals and is associated with warriors: the feared Norse "berserkers" went into battle dressed only in bearskins. In Christian symbolism, the bear was regarded as cruel and vicious and a devilish image of carnality.

ABOVE A Mughal emperor is shown riding a white elephant, a symbol of royalty, power and wisdom in India.

MONKEYS
The baboon god Thoth of Egypt was credited with the invention of numbers and writing. The Maya believed that the monkey created art, numbers and writing.

THE HORSE
An ancient animal symbol, the horse is linked to sun and sky gods. It represents the elemental power of wind, storm, fire, waves and running water. Death is shown riding a black horse, while the white horse is a symbol of light, life and spiritual illumination. The Buddha is said to have left his earthly life on a white horse. Horses drew the sun chariot in classical, Iranian, Indian, Nordic and Babylonian myths.

BIRDS

ABOVE The Seal of the President of the United States of America, changed by President Truman in 1945 from the original 1880 version; the turning of the eagle's head from right to left (towards the olive branch, symbol of peace) was thought at the time to signify a move from war to peace.

BELOW In Greek myth the markings on a peacock's tail feathers were said to be the eyes of the slain giant Argos.

BELOW RIGHT In Western folklore, the stork is said to bring babies to their mothers, while in many parts of the world it is the bearer of good news.

Because they can fly, birds are often seen as mediators between Heaven and Earth, acting as messengers of higher or otherworldly powers. They are also widely regarded as embodiments of the spirit or soul, because flight symbolizes freedom from the physical restrictions of the earthbound world and is frequently used as a metaphor for mystical experience.

BIRDS OF PREY

Warriors and nobles have been associated with birds of prey, especially the eagle, hawk and falcon. Falcons, used for hunting by the aristocracy of China, Japan and Europe, have come to symbolize nobility; in China, the banners of high-ranking lords bore falcon-headed images. In ancient Egypt, the falcon was the king of birds, and the hieroglyph for falcon meant "god"; it was also the symbol for the sky god Horus. Native American tribes regard the hawk as a messenger of the ancestors, while in Polynesia the bird is connected with the powers of healing and prophecy. In China, the hawk denotes war, as well as being a solar symbol. For the early Christian Church, the hawk signified evil, but a tamed

hawk represented a converted pagan and a hooded hawk hope for illumination.

The eagle is widely associated with power and leadership and has been adopted in various guises by ambitious, expansionist civilizations (including ancient Rome and the USA) as a symbol of national identity and sovereignty. In China, the eagle symbolizes strength, while in Celtic folklore it is a symbol of longevity and rejuvenation. For Christians the eagle symbolizes the omnipotence and omniscience of God, as well as Christ and St John the apostle. In many Christian churches, the Bible is placed on an eagle-shaped lectern, symbolizing the power and inspiration of God's word.

RAVENS AND CROWS

Many cultures do not distinguish between the raven and the crow, and the birds share a similar symbolism. Both are widely seen as birds of ill omen, war, death and the supernatural. In the Judaeo-Christian tradition, the raven is the dark counterpart of

the dove; it was also believed to be the spirit familiar of witches. In the Greco-Roman tradition, crows were sacred to Athene/Minerva, goddess of war, but they were prevented from landing on the roofs of her temples as this foretold a death. The name of the ancient Welsh king Bran means "raven"; his head is said to be buried beneath the Tower of London, and ravens are kept there in line with the popular myth that if they should ever depart the English would fall.

Some Native American tribes believed that the raven brought light and fire to the world. The Inuit of Siberia and Alaska share a similar belief – that the bird came from the primeval darkness and stayed to teach the first humans how to survive. Consequently the raven represented the creator god, and it was said that killing one would bring misfortune and bad weather. The crow is a bird of prophecy in China.

DOVES

Today the dove is widely used as an emblem for world peace. In the Old Testament, it was the bird that returned to Noah's ark bearing an olive leaf, indicating reconciliation between God and humankind, while in Japan a dove bearing a sword announced the end of war. The dove is also a symbol of purity and the soul; in the Christian tradition, it represents the Holy Spirit; in Arthurian legend it is associated with the Grail. For Romans, the dove was sacred to Venus, and in China it was associated with fertility and longevity.

PEACOCKS

Because of its grandeur, the peacock represents divinity, royalty, love and beauty. In Persia, it dwelt in the gardens of paradise, and the court revolved around the "peacock throne". In Hindu tradition, the bird is the cosmic mount of Kama, the god of love, and sacred to Sarasvati, goddess of wisdom and the arts. The peacock's distinctive tail markings have long been identified with eyes, and likened to the stars, as well as to solar symbols. In Buddhism it denotes compassionate watchfulness.

STORKS

In many cultures, the stork is the herald of good news. As a migratory bird, it is the emblem of the traveller, and in the land to which it migrates it represents the arrival of spring and hence new life. In ancient Greece the bird was sacred to Hera, goddess of marriage and protector of childbirth. The Western saying that the stork brings babies relates to the idea that the souls of unborn children live in marshes and ponds – the stork's natural habitat – and are discovered by the stork as it searches for fish.

SWANS AND GEESE

Both the goose and the swan are large, web-footed water birds that have otherworldly associations in many cultures. In Siberia, the swan symbolizes the shaman's immersion in the underworld, and according to the Tungu it was the guiding spirit of the first shaman. The migrating goose is also regarded as a spirit-helper, carrying the shaman on celestial adventures.

In Hinduism, the two birds are mythically interchangeable, so that the Hamsa – one bird made of two – can appear as either a goose or swan, and symbolizes perfect union and balance. Because swans often mate for life, they are associated with fidelity in Western traditions.

OWLS

With its night excursions, haunting call and intense eyes, the owl is widely associated with supernatural powers. It was the bird of death in ancient Egypt, India, China and Japan: in China, its hooting was thought to sound like the word for "dig dig", predicting that someone was about to die and a grave should be prepared. The owl's superb night vision may account for its traditional link with prophecy. Among the American Plains tribes owl feathers are worn as magic talismans, while for the Pawnee tribes of Nebraska, the owl is a nocturnal protector. In ancient Athens, the bird was sacred to Athene, goddess of wisdom; similarly, in alchemy, the owl is considered to be the wisest of the birds and also a symbol of the true alchemist.

MAGPIES

In Australian Aboriginal lore, magpies are associated with happiness and enthusiasm, while in China the bird's name means "bird of joy". When shown carrying a Chinese coin, they represent the desire for world peace. However, in European folklore, magpies are regarded as thieves and birds of ill omen.

ABOVE LEFT In the Greco-Roman tradition, the swan was sacred to Aphrodite/Venus; it also appears in the myth of Leda, who is seduced by Zeus when he takes the shape of a swan.

ABOVE In many traditions, the owl is associated with magic, the otherworld, wisdom and prophecy.

CRANES

In China and Japan, cranes are traditional symbols of longevity, wisdom and fidelity. In Western art they personify vigilance.

AQUATIC CREATURES

ABOVE The ancient Greeks revered dolphins as symbols of wisdom and prophecy.

BELOW Ancient Egypt's crocodile-headed god, Sobek, linked with evil, is a symbol of destruction.

The symbolism of aquatic creatures relates partly to their habitat, partly to their appearance and behaviour and partly to the significance they have for human society. Water creatures have been variously revered as deities, feared as monsters and hunted for their flesh, oils, eggs, skin and bones. They play a significant role in myth, folklore and religion.

FISH

Many traditions use the fish as a symbol of spiritual wisdom. In Christianity it is a symbol of Christ, and in Hinduism, Vishnu appeared as the fish Matsya to save humankind from the flood and reveal the Vedas, or holy scriptures. Because of the vast number of eggs they lay, fish are also widely linked with life and fertility. In China they are symbols of good luck.

Particular species have been singled out for their symbolic properties. For example, in Japan, the carp symbolizes love, courage, dignity and good fortune, while the Celts associated the salmon with wisdom, prophecy and inspiration.

WHALES, SHARKS AND DOLPHINS

In Japan, the whale was one of the Seven Deities of Good Fortune and was worshipped as a god of fishing and food. In Maori tradition, it symbolizes plenty and abundance; the *pakake* figure – a stylized whale with large spirals for its jaws – is a popular motif.

In the Judaeo-Christian tradition, the Old Testament account of Jonah and the whale associated it with death and rebirth. It is sometimes claimed that the story relates to a man-eating shark rather than a whale, and the Hindu god Vishnu is at times portrayed as emerging from the mouth of a shark. They are symbols of the dangers of nature.

In ancient Greece dolphins were linked with Apollo and his gifts of wisdom and prophecy, and with the water-born goddess of love, Aphrodite, signifying a union of the masculine, solar world and the feminine, watery realm; the dolphin's Greek name, *delphis*, is related to *delphys*, "womb", after which the sacred site of Delphi is named. In many Native American cultures, the dolphin is both a divine messenger and a form of the Great Spirit, while the seafaring Nabataean Arabs believed that dolphins accompanied the souls of the dead to the underworld.

CROCODILES AND ALLIGATORS

Crocodilians inhabit two worlds – land and water – making them symbols of fundamental contradictions. Some African tribes revere crocodiles as intermediaries between the everyday and the spirit world and as oracles for water deities. In many parts of West Africa the crocodile's liver and entrails are credited with powerful magic and are sometimes used by shamans to cast destructive spells.

In ancient Egypt, crocodiles were sacred and were sometimes mummified. A cult centre existed at Crocodilopolis, where tame crocodiles were adorned with golden earrings and ritually fed in order to honour the crocodile god, Sobek. Sobek was linked both to the evil and destructive powers of Set, god of the underworld, who took crocodile form after the murder of his brother, Osiris, and also to Ra, the benevolent solar deity.

For the Aborigines of Australia's Northern Territory, large crocodiles embody the spirits of important people and are associated with wisdom, while the Madarrpa peoples of north-east Arnhem Land believe that Crocodile Man created fire. In China, the alligator or crocodile was the inventor of singing and the drum, and plays a part in the rhythm of the world. In early Christian belief, being eaten by a crocodile indicated that a person had gone to Hell.

FROGS AND TOADS

Traditionally both frogs and toads were lunar animals, and their radical growth stages were linked with the changing phases of the moon. Both creatures are also linked with fertility, the watery processes of birth and rainfall and with transformation and

ABOVE In the fairy story, the frog is changed into a prince when kissed by the princess, symbolizing transformation.

ABOVE The turtle is a sacred animal in many traditions. In Native American traditions it is a symbol of the earth.

SHELLS

Because it is a structure that shelters life, the symbolism of the shell is often connected with the womb, birth and creation. In Greco-Roman myth, Aphrodite/Venus emerged from a huge scallop shell, and in Hinduism, the conch shell symbolizes the origin of existence, its shape forming a multiple spiral evolving from one central point. Conch shells have been used as ceremonial horns by the Maya and Aztecs and are also one of the emblems of Buddhism. In Benin, cowrie shells were once used as currency and are associated with wealth, royalty and prestige. In Christian iconography, the Virgin Mary is sometimes compared to an oyster shell, and Christ to the pearl.

immortality – hence the theme of frogs changing into princes in Western folklore. To the Celts, the frog was lord of the earth and the curative powers of water, and for the Maya and Aztecs it was a water deity whose croaking predicted and made rain. In ancient Egypt, Heket the frog goddess was associated with magic and childbirth, and in China and Japan both frogs and toads were associated with magic. In Japan, the toad was associated with lunar eclipses and in China with wealth and longevity. Both frogs and toads were linked with magic and witchcraft in medieval Europe. In the Bible, frogs were one of the ten plagues of Egypt.

TURTLES

Because of the sturdiness and shape of its shell, the turtle (or tortoise) is a symbol of the world in many cultures. It is the oldest Native American symbol for the Earth or earth mother – while earthquakes and thunder are the cosmic turtle shaking its earthly shell. The Maya also envisaged the Earth as a huge turtle, as did the Chinese, who regarded the marks on the turtle's shell as a map of the constellations and used them in divination. Of

China's four sacred creatures, the turtle was the only real animal (the others being the dragon, the phoenix and the unicorn), and it was a symbol of longevity.

In Hindu myth, the turtle Chukwa is one of the ten incarnations of Vishnu. It is a symbol of meditation and spiritual wisdom. In Australian Aboriginal myth, the turtle was said to arise from the creative waters that were melted from the primeval mountain of ice by the sun goddess, while in Polynesia, the turtle embodies the power of the ocean deities. Among African tribes, turtles are often sacred to water gods.

SEALS AND WALRUSES

In some Inuit stories, these creatures figure as primordial ancestors, capable of assuming human form and teaching people to swim and hunt fish; they are also messengers, moving between the world of spirit (water) and matter (land). Inuit custom dictates that, when the animals are killed in a hunt, their bladders are thrown back into the sea, as it is believed they will then be reborn as living seals or walruses. The walrus is also known as the sea elephant.

CRABS

Because its movement is governed by the lunar tides (hunting as the tide comes in, retreating as the tide goes out), the crab is often associated with the moon. In Inca tradition, it was an aspect of the great mother, who devoured both time and the waning moon.

OCTOPUSES

In classical antiquity, the octopus was seen as a monster that would attack shipwrecked sailors by pulling them apart. Like the crab, it was associated with the moon and the summer solstice. The octopus was much used in the art of the Minoan and Mycenean civilizations in the Mediterranean, where it sometimes occurs in conjunction with the spiral or swastika. Its tentacles associate it with the unfolding of creation from the centre.

CORAL

According to an ancient Chinese belief, coral came from a tree growing at the bottom of the sea. In alchemy it was known as the tree of life, filled with a blood-like substance (because of its colour). In Buddhism, coral trees are said to grow in paradise.

BELOW Seals play a prominent role in the myth and custom of the Inuit, where they are often seen as primordial ancestral figures.

INSECTS

ABOVE This portrait of Napoleon makes use of the motif of the bee, embroidered not only on the emperor's robes but also on the podium on which he stands. It is a symbol of equals under one leader.

BELOW RIGHT The butterfly is a symbol of spiritual growth and transformation. In Latin America it is also used to describe a prostitute, flitting from one man to the next.

From a perspective that sees the universe as an interconnected web of being, every part of nature is significant, no matter how small or ordinary. Consequently even the tiniest insects are rich in symbolic associations, frequently associated with the gods, spirits and the otherworld. For instance, in the mythology of Central America, small flying insects were regarded as the souls of the dead revisiting earth, and a similar

belief endures in Guatemala, where they are linked with the stars. As with other animals, the symbolic associations of insects are based on their behaviour and physical characteristics and are rooted in culture and time.

FLIES

The name of Beelzebub, the chief devil mentioned in the Bible, comes from a Hebrew word meaning "lord of the flies", pointing to the fairly common belief that flies are harbingers of disease and devilish misfortune; they were the third of the ten plagues of Egypt. However, in the ancient Egyptian New Kingdom (1550–1100 BC), flies were noted for their persistence and bravery and were adopted as warrior symbols: magic wands decorated with fly amulets have been discovered from this period. Among the Navajo, Dontso ("big fly") is a spiritual messenger associated with healing.

BEES

Because of their diligence, social organization and collaborative labour, bees are often used as models of human society. The beehive became a metaphor for

the ordered and charitable life of Christian monastic communities. Bees have also long been valued for their honeycombs, a source not only of sugar but also of wax, used in the making of candles. Thus they are associated with both sweetness and light. In ancient Egypt they were a solar symbol, born from the tears of the sun god Ra.

As the hive is organized around the queen bee, the bee was a regal symbol: it was adopted by the medieval kings of France and revived by Napoleon as an emblem of equals under a single leader. In Chinese art, a bee or butterfly hovering around a flower (symbolizing a woman) suggested buzzing desire. In ancient Greece, honey was

THE ANTHILL

In the cosmologies of many African peoples (notably the Dogon and Bambara of Mali) the anthill plays a significant role. It is linked with language and the art of weaving, the female sexual organs and creation: it is a traditional fertility custom for a woman to sit on an anthill. The traditional pattern of Dogon huts is based on the anthill design, and the belief that ants know the location of underground streams means that wells are often sunk near an anthill. In Tibetan Buddhism, the anthill is a symbol of an industrious life.

associated with eloquence, while in the Celtic world, mead (a fermented drink made from honey and water) was regarded as the drink of the gods.

BUTTERFLIES

Because of its metamorphic life cycle, the butterfly is an archetypal symbol of transformation, mystical rebirth and the transcendent soul. Some Australian Aboriginals regard butterflies as the returning spirits of the dead, while in Greek myth, Psyche (the soul) is often represented as a butterfly. The creature's grace and beauty make it an emblem of woman in Japan, where two butterflies dancing together symbolize marital happiness, and in China it is associated with the pleasures of life and high spirits. Someone who flits from one thing to another and is never satisfied may be described as a butterfly, while in Latin America, the Spanish word for butterfly (*mariposa*) can refer to a prostitute, moving from one man to the next. The Aztecs associated the butterfly with women who had died in childbirth, while for the Mexicans it was a symbol of the "black sun" passing through the underworld during its nightly journey.

SPIDERS

In Australian Aboriginal cultures the great spider is a solar hero, but in other traditions it is a female force, a personification of the Great Mother in both her creative and devouring aspects. Among the Amazonian Tukano people, for instance, the spider's web is likened to the placenta, while Ixchel, the Mayan goddess of midwifery, appears as a spider. In Japan, spider-women are thought to ensnare travellers, while in the West predatory women are sometimes likened to spiders, using their feminine wiles to lure men into their web. Among the Ashanti of West Africa spiders are associated with Anansi, the trickster god, who taught humans the art of weaving. In some Native American myths the spider is said to have taught humans the alphabet, tracing the shapes of the letters in its web.

Because of the web's strength and near invisibility, Native American warriors decorated themselves with web designs. For the Celts, the web is the invisible structure that holds the pattern of life in a grand design. For Hindus and Buddhists, the web stands for the illusions of the world, while in Christianity it represents Satan's snare. In European folklore, however, it is unlucky to kill a spider, which is linked with money and good fortune.

SCORPIONS

Because of its poisonous sting, permanently unsheathed and ready to strike, the scorpion is associated with death and destruction: in Africa, many people use a euphemism for the creature since even uttering its name would release evil into the world. The scorpion has many links with the underworld: the zodiac sign of Scorpio is ruled by Pluto, lord of the underworld, while the ancient Egyptian scorpion goddess Selket (a sorcerer-healer) was one of four goddesses who protected the dead Osiris. Through its association with the desert, the scorpion can represent drought and desolation. Some Amazonian peoples believe it was sent by a jealous god to punish men for having sex with women whom he himself desired. In one version of the Greco-Roman myth of Orion the hunter, he died when he was stung in the heel by a scorpion, and both were turned into constellations, placed on opposite sides of the sky.

WORMS

The symbolism of the worm links new life with corruption and death. According to Chinese myth, the human race has its origins in the worms that fed on the corpse of the primordial being, and a similar belief exists in Icelandic tradition, where the worms feeding on the frost giant Ymir (from whose body the earth was created) assume human form. The legendary Irish Celtic hero Cúchulainn was said to have been born from a worm. In psychological terms, worms may be associated with destructive processes that erode personality.

ABOVE The scorpion is widely linked with death and destruction. In parts of Africa, many people refuse to say its name in the belief that this would bring evil into the world.

CRICKETS AND LOCUSTS

In Japan, crickets are linked with the moon and in China they are symbols of death and resurrection. Finding a cricket in the home is thought to bring good luck in China and in some Mediterranean countries. Because of their ability to destroy crops, locusts are usually connected with voracity and destruction.

THE SNAKE OR SERPENT

ABOVE The goddess of the snakes is a Cretan Earth Mother, shown here holding the snakes of death and rebirth.

Of all animal symbols, the snake is probably the most significant and complex. From very early times, snakes seem to have been linked with eternity, as creators and destroyers of the universe, and associated with both healing and wisdom; they have also been demonized and aligned with temptation, immorality and Satan.

SNAKES AND THE FEMININE

The snake was often associated with deities, particularly mother goddesses and Mother Earth. The ancient Phoenician fertility goddess Tanith, who is linked with Eve and Lilith, was associated with snakes. In Egyptian mythology Buto was a snake goddess, often depicted as a cobra. Her image on the Pharaoh's forehead protected him from his enemies. The matriarchal cult at Delphi was symbolically dissolved when the god Apollo killed the female serpent Python, and the Iliad tells of Calcas interpreting an eagle carrying a wounded snake in its talons as a sign that the patriarchal Greeks would overcome the matriarchal traditions of Asia.

FROM PRIMARY GOD TO EVIL SERPENT

In many parts of the world snakes, with other reptiles and fish, have been used to represent nature in its most primordial or fundamental aspects. Because the snake sheds its skin and then starts life anew, it embodies the cycle of death and resurrection. The serpent was a primary god, existing at the roots of life, and has a strong chthonic or underworld connection, arising from the depths of Mother Earth, and psychologically from the collective unconscious. He was the lord of the tree of life, where time and eternity meet. Sumerian seals from 3500 BC show the serpent with the tree and the goddess giving the fruit of life to a visiting male figure.

The Canaanite deity was a mother goddess who was strongly associated with the serpent and represented the mysteries of life. When the Hebrews introduced a male god into Canaan, the female deity and the snake were

NAGAS AND WISDOM

In Indian mythology, nagas (from the Sanskrit word for "snake") are divine water-serpents, benevolent and wise, portrayed with a human face and the hood of the cobra. Indian alchemy, *nagayuna*, aims to unify the body's energies in a journey of self-realization to preserve the elixir of life.

relegated and associated with evil. The snake in the story of the Garden of Eden has Satanic characteristics, tempting Eve into the sin of disobedience against God, whereas the Nassene Gnostics (*nass* means "snake") honoured the serpent in the form of the Sumerian god Enki, a liberating influence who helped to make Adam and Eve fully human by introducing them to the tree of knowledge.

For Jung, snakes symbolized that which is totally unconscious and instinctual, nevertheless possessing an almost supernatural and unique wisdom, which can come into conflict with conscious

LEFT Eve pictured with the devil-serpent, and the forbidden fruit that it uses to tempt her to sin.

attitudes. The snake can therefore symbolize both evil and wisdom, easily overriding human morality. To dream of a snake suggests that there is a large gulf between the conscious and unconscious, and that the unconscious is making itself known in a compulsive and reflexive way. A snake in our dreams might also suggest that we have strayed from the serpentine path of our individuation.

THE SNAKE AS CREATOR AND DESTROYER

Serpents appear as the source of life in many creation myths, though they can also be figures of destruction. The Sumerians and Akkadians of Mesopotamia described the mingling of the waters of Apsu and Tiamat, from which emerged Lakhmu and Lakhamu, two monstrous serpents who gave birth to Heaven and Earth. The Rainbow Serpent appears in Aboriginal rock art in Arnhem Land from between 6,000 and 8,000 years ago. This Dreamtime ancestor is a life-giving creature associated with fertility, abundance and rainfall, as well as often being the creator of human beings. Its destructive side involves punishing those who go against the natural law by swallowing them in great floods and regurgitating their bones.

Ancient Germanic mythology associates the serpent with death and the continual undermining of the roots of the world tree. Norse tradition foretold a deluge that would destroy the world when Jormangand, the Midgard serpent, was awoken.

HEALING AND DEATH

Serpents have long been associated with healing and mediation between life and death. In Greek mythology, Asklepios, the son of Apollo and the mortal Coronis, was able to metamorphose into a snake and could bring the dead back to life, thus angering Hades, god of the underworld. One tale tells that he became a serpent to end a plague in Rome, and the Romans came to worship him as the god of medicine and healing. The Asklepian healing process, called incubation, involved the patient spending the night in a sacred place. They would be visited by the god in a dream, and its message was interpreted by a priest, resulting in a remedy.

The Asklepian symbol of a tree snake wrapped around a staff represents healing and is today used as a medical symbol. It is often confused with the caduceus, or "winged staff", of Mercury, on which two snakes were twined. These snakes were involved in a fight in which Mercury intervened, revealing his nature as a psychopomp, or conductor of souls between worlds.

The serpent's association with healing, life and death is found in the pagan-Christian Slavonic story of Bogatyr Potok, who when his young bride died, had himself buried with her, fully armed and on horseback, in a deep tomb. At midnight many monstrous reptiles appeared, including a great fire-breathing serpent. Potok cut off its head and brought his wife back to life by anointing her body with it. The homeopathic

principle that "like cures like" is essential to the poisonous/healing nature of the snake.

THE TUKANO ANACONDA

The Tukano people of the Amazon ascribe a complex and contextual symbolism to the anaconda. They believe that monstrous anacondas live in forest lagoons and deep pools beneath waterfalls. They also compare the motion of the Milky Way to the intertwining of two copulating anacondas, reflecting seasonal periods of insemination, germination and fertility. The anaconda is the path that twists through the forest like the river, and when travelling upstream it represents a journey of initiation.

ABOVE Two snakes entwined upon Mercury's "winged staff" represent the transformative power to change male to female and vice versa. The Asclepian staff with its single snake was the original medical symbol; however, possibly mistakenly, this caduceus is also used for this purpose.

BELOW The art of the Australian Aboriginals often depicts the snake, and its association with fertility and abundance.

THE LIVING PLANET

INEVITABLY, MUCH CULTURAL SYMBOLISM STEMS FROM THE EARTH AND HOW WE LIVE OUT OUR LIVES ON OUR PLANET. SEASONS AND CYCLES, TIME, DISTANCE, THE ELEMENTS AND THE LAND ITSELF HAVE ALL GIVEN RISE TO HUMANITY'S MOST ANCIENT SIGNS AND SYMBOLS, WHICH REMAIN CONSTANT DESPITE THE WAY SCIENCE HAS INCREASED OUR KNOWLEDGE OF THE PLANET WE LIVE ON.

SEASONS AND TIME

RIGHT The 22,000-year-old stone carving known as the Venus of Laussel. The horn she holds is thought to be marked with a year of thirteen lunar cycles.

Humankind has always used symbolism and ritual to relate to the rhythms and cycles of life. Nature punctuates existence with life events – the moments of conception, birth and death – and life goes on in interdependent cycles. The phases of life have always preoccupied us, and have been given their own universal symbolic language.

CALENDARS AND TIME

Early calendars were based on the phases of the moon. Cave paintings at Lascaux, in France, show that they were counted around 17,000 years ago, and the carving of the Venus of Laussel, which is about 22,000 years old, shows her holding a horn with thirteen markings, representing a year of lunar cycles. The lunar calendar is associated with the menstrual cycle, and predominates in civilizations that

PLEIADES

The constellation of the Pleiades has many symbolic associations. The stars represented the mother goddess Net in ancient Egypt, and in China they were the blossom or flower stars. The Khoikhoi tribe of South Africa call them Khuseti, the rain-bearing stars. In Hindu tradition they are the flames of Agni, the god of fire.

THE TYRANNICAL CLOCK

In Charles Dickens's 1848 novel Dombey and Son the clock is a tyrannical figure that makes itself heard and felt everywhere. Mr Dombey, an emotionless character, does everything by the clock. It is used as a symbol of a mechanistic way of life, showing how time had come to dominate the consciousness of industrial society.

worship The Goddess. Britain's Stonehenge is a symbolic monument aligned with the movements of both sun and moon. Lunisolar and solar calendars emerged with the shift from female to male values.

To this day Jews and Muslims continue to use lunar calendars. The Chinese calendar, another example of a lunisolar calendar, is still used to establish the timing of holidays and festivals, and is important to Chinese farmers who still plant by the moon.

Whereas time was originally associated with rhythm, rebirth and renewal in nature,

symbolized by the circle and the yoni, the influence of Judaeo-Christianity led to the foundation of linear time. In the 14th century, Europeans conceived the universe in terms of clockwork, and in the 17th century, Isaac Newton characterized time as being absolute and uniform.

Technological advances have enabled us to ignore or colonize "nature's time", growing crops out of season and literally extending daytime into the night. It is only in recent years, since Einstein's theories of relativity, that time, along with space, has again been thought to bend.

THE CELTIC WHEEL OF THE YEAR

In the Celtic tradition, a symbolic circle of time represents transitional points during the year: Samhain, winter solstice; Imbolc, spring equinox; Beltane, summer solstice; Lughnasada, autumn equinox. The wheel of the year describes the cycles of death, birth, youth, maturity and renewal of life, and each point is marked by seasonal celebrations.

Samhain (31 October–1 November) is also the Festival of the Dead, when the veil between the living and the dead is thought to be at its thinnest. The year begins in the dying and decaying part of the wheel, reflecting the Celtic understanding of the importance of ageing and death in order for life to thrive. This time is symbolized by the figure of the old woman, who is also an elder. Youth, beauty, growth and productivity are symbolized later in the Celtic year by the maiden and the mother, the other two aspects of the triple goddess.

SEASONAL SYMBOLISM

Early measurements of time were based on the appearances and disappearances, and the changing paths of the sun and the moon. The main phases of the day had their own symbolism that still has resonance today. Dawn was a universal symbol of hope, joy and youth, while noon was the hour of revelation in Jewish and Islamic tradition. Twilight was often linked with the shadowy and uncertain time of decline and therefore with death.

Again inspired by the cycles of the moon, and the rising and setting of the sun, the four seasons were universal symbols of birth, growth, death and rebirth. In Western art, spring is depicted as a young woman, at times a child, sometimes linked with blossom, the lamb or kid and with the Greek goddess Aphrodite. Summer is again a woman, this time in the full beauty of maturity, crowned with ears of corn and sometimes carrying a sickle. Autumn is associated with Dionysus and with harvest, and also with the hare. Winter is at times depicted as an old man or woman; the blacksmith god Hephaestus is associated with this season, as are the salamander and the duck.

HARVEST FESTIVALS

Festivals of thanksgiving at harvest time are common to all agrarian cultures. They are times to appreciate the forces of nature and the ancestors, bringing the community together to share ideas and experiences, tell stories and strengthen social bonds.

The harvest moon festival in Korea, called Chusok, takes place on the 15th day of the eighth lunar month. The same day in China and Vietnam is Chung Ch'ui, considered the birthday of the moon and celebrated with a feast and special "moon cakes", symbols of togetherness.

Pongal is the southern Indian Hindu harvest festival, which starts on 14 January. Its name means "boiling over" – a reference both to the bounties of nature and to a sweet rice dish. The festival lasts three days, and offerings are made to the rain and sun gods, who watered and ripened the rice, and to the cattle, which are essential to a prosperous community.

The Sikh festival of Baisakhi is a northern Indian harvest festival celebrated on 13 April, the first day of the Sikh solar year, in which dancers and drummers re-enact scenes of the sowing, harvesting, winnowing and gathering of crops.

GOD OF TIME

The Greeks conceived of two types of time: Chronos (shown above, the snake around him symbolizing eternity), was the god of absolute, linear and quantifiable time, whereas Kairos was the god of timing, opportunity and chance.

BELOW A procession of Sikhs at the festival of Baisakhi, which celebrates the beginning of the corn harvest, and takes place on the first day of the solar year.

THE EARTH

RIGHT The view of the planet Earth from space changed the way we view our world, and symbolizes the wholeness and inter-connectedness of life.

BELOW The Psalter Map, with Jerusalem in the middle, is the earliest surviving map symbolizing Christ's role as overseer of the world.

What the Earth means to us has changed markedly over time. Its symbolism is strongly linked to our collective state of mind or consciousness, and reflects changes in human values and our relationship with nature.

THE FLAT EARTH

Most early societies conceived of the Earth as flat, as a huge wheel or disc. The ancient Chinese described the Earth as a flat square on top of a truncated, four-sided pyramid, below the circular heavens. In India, the Rig Veda described the Earth and sky as two wheels at either end of an axle. Classical, Hindu, Buddhist and Jain texts agreed that the Earth was in fact a flat disc, though some Indian myths saw it as spherical.

The ancient Hebrews, Egyptians and Babylonians all had flat Earth cosmologies. According to the Hebrew book of Enoch, the angel Uriel guided Enoch to the ends of the Earth, where he saw huge beasts and birds, and beyond which he saw Heaven resting on the edge of the Earth. The Egyptians envisaged a rectangular Earth, with the sky goddess Nut stretching her body like an enclosing dome over the land. The Babylonians imagined a flat land surrounded by ocean, with the vault of the sky resting either on the ocean or on pillars. In the West, the earliest description of the Earth is in the Iliad, where Homer described the sky as a bowl-like hemisphere, covering a flat, circular Earth.

THE ROUND EARTH

Although most early people thought the Earth was flat, there were exceptions. Japan's indigenous people, the Ainu, thought of it as a ball floating in the ocean, but their word for Earth means "floating land", suggesting that this was the localized perception of an island people. In 375 BC Plato described the Earth as a globe, in the context of an Earth-centred universe, and Aristotle (384–322 BC) suggested it was a sphere based upon his observations of circular shadows cast on the moon during a lunar eclipse. In 200 BC, the Egyptian Eratosthenes calculated the Earth's diameter using trigonometry, by measuring the length of the shadow of a vertical tower in Alexandria, when the sun was directly above Aswan, 800km/500 miles away.

However, the paradigmatic shift from a flat to a round Earth took place over many hundreds of years. In 1492 Christopher Columbus, by sailing partly around the world, proved by experience what, until then, had been surmised through calculation: that the Earth was indeed a sphere. It seems likely that Galileo and Copernicus were greatly encouraged by Columbus's experience, and dramatic new theories concerning a universe centred on the sun, around which the spherical Earth and moon orbited, rapidly followed.

EARTH AS A DEITY

The Earth was worshipped in ancient times as the supreme mother goddess and was believed to be both alive and divine. Mother Earth was a figure of great compassion and the source of all life and fertility. Paleolithic images of the mother goddess, dating from around 22,000-18,000 BC, include the Venus of Laussel, a rock carving from the Dordogne in France, and the statuettes

known as the Goddess of Lespugue, found in Haute-Garonne, France, and the Goddess of Willendorf, found in Austria. Each depicts a female form with pendulous breasts and a full, rounded womb.

In the West, the last Earth Goddess was Gaia, no longer the supreme mother but nevertheless a conscious and living deity. In Greek her name means "land" or "earth". She was a triple goddess, differentiated as the maiden, or Persephone, the mother, or Demeter, and the crone or Hecate. During the Classical period there was a shift in emphasis from Gaia to her great-grandson Zeus, reflecting the replacement of the image of the divine mother with a far more remote male god, which swept across Europe, the Middle East, North Africa and India, gaining particular prominence in the Judaeo-Christian God.

In Christian times Mary, the mother of Christ, embodies or echoes some of the qualities of the ancient mother goddesses, and acts as an intermediary between Heaven and Earth. Meanwhile, the male God exists in Heaven, outside the earthly sphere, symbolizing a separation between Earth and deity.

THE HIERARCHY OF HEAVEN AND EARTH

The Judaeo-Christian worldview stresses a hierarchical relationship between Heaven and Earth, placing humanity closer to God than other living creatures, with the responsibility to assume dominion over the Earth and nature. This has been interpreted

RIGHT The Virgin in her role as quasi-earth mother, interceding with God on behalf of humankind.

by many to justify an image of the Earth as a resource for human use. With the divine no longer synonymous with nature, the Earth could easily become an object of interest and exploitation. Francis Bacon (1561–1626) spoke of nature in feminine terms, and advocated its domination for human benefit. He suggested that nature should be "bound into service", "moulded" by the machine and made into a "slave" – simultaneously representing prevailing attitudes towards both women and nature.

THE LIVING EARTH

When in 1969 the scientist James Lovelock conceived his Gaia hypothesis, he described feeling like an astronaut looking at the Earth while standing on the moon, and that at times he has felt that the whole planet is partaking in something like a "sacred ceremony". His vision of the Earth as a complex and self-regulating closed system, which operates as if it were a living being – a pragmatic and scientific view – has aroused a great deal of speculation concerning its potential as a modern religious symbol. Using the name of the Greek Earth goddess Gaia may well have furthered the power of this scientific model and symbolic imagery. For many, Gaia has come to represent the idea of the "living Earth", despite the theory's stress that the Earth acts only "like" a living system. For Lovelock, Gaia is something that humans can reconnect to by maintaining a sense of wonder for nature.

To the Kono people of Sierra Leone, the Earth is indeed a living being: she is God's wife and is hugely productive and fertile. The emphasis of the Kono lifestyle, like that of many indigenous peoples, lies in maintaining the harmony of nature, through human relationships and community, and relationships with the land and unseen forces.

NEW SYMBOLISM

The image of Earth as seen from space offers a meaningful symbolism for contemporary humans. It is Earth as seen from the "heavens", and this changed view shows us that the separations we perceive between different cultures, and between us and nature, are immaterial when viewed from a distance. Earth seen from space offers the symbol of a renewed relationship between humankind and nature.

MAPS AND DIRECTION

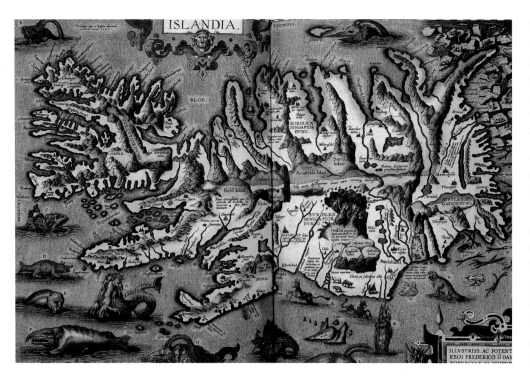

ABOVE A map of Islandia (Iceland), charted by Abraham Ortelius in the late 16th century, displays a wide array of sea monsters, polar bears, icebergs and the erupting volcano Mount Hekla.

BELOW A stone disc containing an Australian Aboriginal songline design. The Aborginals believe that the songlines draw together diverse groups into one common dreaming relationship with the land.

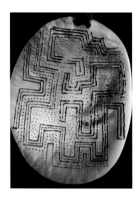

The symbolism of orientation and direction focuses on how people move through life and the world, what it means to be in a certain place at a certain time, and the relationship with places beyond our everyday experience.

MAPPING THE WORLD

How a map is drawn depends upon the worldview and beliefs of the cartographer, and what is considered central or peripheral, what is known, mysterious or threatening to the culture. The early *mappa mundi*, or world map, was a symbolic representation of the known world infused with the *imago mundi*, or the image of the world as an ordered cosmos. Early maps were as much cosmological and mythical as they were tools for practical orientation. The Beatus map, drawn by a Benedictine monk in AD 787, charts the world in a rectangle encircled by a world

sea. This form, called a "T-map" was common until the late Middle Ages. T-maps divide the world into three, the number of the Holy Trinity: Jerusalem usually lies at the intersection, with Eden either at the top or to the east, and the rest of the world divided into Asia, Africa and Europe. As the medieval worldview receded during the Renaissance, Jerusalem and Eden were no longer charted as central features and the edges of maps began to display unexplored regions, with strange hybrid creatures at the edges of the known world. The Carta Marina, by the Swedish Archbishop Olaus Magnus, first printed in Venice in 1539, showed the North Sea around Scandinavia filled with threatening sea creatures. It was the first map to chart the Nordic regions, which had previously been considered terra incognita (unknown lands).

CHARTING BY SONGLINE AND STORY

Australian Aboriginals believe that the topography of their land was created by the journeys, or "songlines", of the Ancestors. These songlines criss-cross Australia, and are sung by Aboriginals as they follow the sacred pathways.

In a hunting culture such as the Alaskan Nunamiut, a young man must learn the details of the hunting terrain before he can join the hunt. He builds up a symbolic map of the local topography by listening to the myths of spirits and heroes who populate the hunting grounds.

THE COMPASS

For some people the compass is a neutral symbol that unifies the people of the Earth, since we all share the directions north, south, east and west. However, it is also a symbol of exploration, orientation, expansion and even the conquering of nature. The phrase "moral compass" is now commonly used in the United States to refer to morally "straight" actions.

Practitioners of the geomantic art of feng shui (which means "wind and water") use a special circular magnetic compass known as the *luo pan* to locate houses and tombs where the energies are in harmonious balance for good fortune. Dragon lines, or dragon currents, which are thought to run through the land, consist of a negative yin current, symbolized by a white tiger, and a positive yang current, symbolized by the blue dragon. A yin countryside will have gently undulating feminine features, and a yang landscape will have sharp or mountainous male features.

ORIENTATION

Travellers and explorers on land and sea have, since ancient times, orientated themselves according to the positions of the stars in the night sky. Orientation is necessary both in everyday reality, to know where we are and where we are going, and for our personal and cultural sense of meaning and identity. Many cultures consider a place sacred to them to be the centre of the world, this might be represented by a holy mountain, world tree or sacred site; the people will "centre" themselves in relation to it in an act of renewal or balancing of nature and spirit.

Places of worship such as mosques, temples and churches, and graves and burial grounds, often align with the east-west axis, the directions of the rising and setting sun. Wherever they are in the world, Muslims face their sacred centre, Mecca, in daily prayer. Native Americans offer prayers to the four cosmic directions, often beginning with the east, where the sun rises.

THE HORIZON

An important orientation symbol, the horizon represents the furthest point the eye can see on the earthly plane. It is the place of vision, exploration and new discoveries. The sun on the horizon signals the dawn of a new day, world or era, and points to the potential for new beginnings and bright futures.

SACRED JOURNEYS

Myths and legend are filled with stories of journeys. Tales of migration, exploration, conquest, heroic quests and pilgrimage serve to focus or renew a people's identity, commune with the gods and spirits, and justify or honour their relationship with the land.

The Hebrew story of the Exodus describes how Moses led the Israelites out of servitude to a land promised to them by God. The Aztec migration of the 12th century was a journey of cultural renewal, in which the Mexica people were guided by the god Huitzilopochtli in their travels from the island of Aztlan to Tenochtitlan, their future capital.

A pilgrimage is a symbolic journey – representing spiritual reorientation, religious devotion, healing and renewal – through a sacred or meaningful landscape. A physical pilgrimage is a liminal act, meaning that at some point the pilgrim crosses a threshold, leaving their everyday life behind them and travelling towards a sacred destination.

In Islam the hajj is a pilgrimage to the holy city of Mecca. The ancient Greeks would travel to receive guidance from the oracle at Delphi, or healing from the shrine of Asklepios at Epidaurus. In 9th-century Europe many pilgrims journeyed to Santiago de Compostela in north-west Spain, at the outer edge of the known world, to visit the miracle-making relics of St James.

Hindus make a pilgrimage to Mount Kailas, the physical manifestation of the mystical Mount Meru, the centre of the world. The journey to Mount Sinai, where Moses received the tablets of the law, like many pilgrimages, reflects the spiritual, as well as physical, journey of Moses himself.

ABOVE The luo pan, or feng shui compass, was used as a source of guidance by ancient Chinese emperors and sages. The encircling symbols, such as 24 mountain stars, 64 hexagrams, 60 stems and branches and 12 mountain dragons, were used in helping to site and orient buildings, and for divination.

LEFT A Muslim prayer involves standing and then bowing or prostrating in the direction of Mecca.

BELOW The horizon often symbolizes our earthly limits, the end and the beginning of new possibilities and exploration.

THE LAND

THE PLOUGH

In ancient times ploughing was considered a spiritual act, as it made the land fruitful. The plough came also to represent the male active principle in relationship to the passive female principle of the Earth: ploughing thus symbolized the act of coitus.

Whether we think we own the land, or whether we borrow it or share it with the gods, it features prominently in world symbolism. From a perspective of ownership, the claiming of land is a symbolic act of power, wealth, nationhood or individual identity. The "discovery", conquest and colonization of other lands is often symbolized by setting foot on the soil, planting a national flag, or writing legal deeds conferring ownership.

For many indigenous peoples land is not owned by individuals but is understood as a living entity or divine gift, which warrants respect and relationship. The indigenous peoples of the Philippines, for example, consider the land as God's gift, and its ownership is assigned to their ancestors and the nature spirits. The land is held by them in trust and guardianship.

EARTHQUAKES

Understandably, the shock and turmoil of earthquakes have often been associated with the anger of the gods in reaction to the degeneracy of the people. The Japanese considered seismic activity to come from the storm god Susano-O, and the Greeks believed that the storm god Poseidon, also known as Enosicthon ("earth shaker"), was the cause of earthquakes. According to Plato, earthquakes and floods consumed the legendary civilization of Atlantis in a single day.

Earthquakes may be taken as omens predicting a huge change in religion or politics: the New Testament describes the quaking of the Earth at the time of Christ's death. Like other natural disasters, earthquakes frequently symbolize the vulnerable qualities of humanity in relation to the natural forces of the Earth.

THE SOIL

Fundamental to food production, soil is seen as "black gold" by agrarian societies. The Burmese consider it to be as valuable as metals such as gold, silver, iron, copper, lead and tin. Many creation myths tell of humans being shaped from clay, and we all share a dependence on the life-sustaining fertility of the soil.

Soil from a particular field or region may possess special qualities or essences. The Finno-Ugric people known as the Chuvash practise a ritual in which they "steal" a clod of earth from a productive field nearby to improve the fertility of their own land. Modern biodynamic growers make special preparations such as burying herbs in a cow horn during an astrologically significant time, then homoeopathically potentizing the mixture by stirring it in water and spreading it on the land. This is said to concentrate cosmic forces in the soil, so raising the vitality of the plants and those who eat them.

The fertility ritual of performing sexual intercourse in a field is common in pagan traditions. It is also found in a Greek myth about Demeter, goddess of the soil. She and the Cretan youth Iasion had sex in a thrice-ploughed field, as a result of which she bore a son, Ploutos ("wealth").

MOUNTAINS

A natural symbolic significance of mountains is that they are the part of Earth closest to the heavens, where humans may communicate with the gods. A high peak is frequently held sacred by the local culture as it is considered to be the world axis, linking Earth with Heaven. Moses climbed to the peak of Mount Sinai to receive the Ten Commandments, and Jesus made his ascent to Heaven from the

LEFT In antiquity, earthquakes were seen as a sign of a deity's wrath, and early Christianity was no exception: here it is angelic trumpets that shake the Earth.

Mount of Olives. For Hindus, Jains and Tibetan Buddhists, the mythical Mount Meru is the centre of the universe, with its roots in the underworld and its peaks in the heavens. Its earthly manifestation is Mount Kailash in the Himalayas.

Sometimes mountains are literally thought to be the bodies of divinities. In Shinto tradition, Japan's Mount Fuji is a physical manifestation of the gods. The Navaho of North America believe particular mountains embody important male and female nature spirits. A male spirit stretches across the Chuska and Carrizo chains, with his head lying at Chuska Peak, while the female spirit spans the valley with her head on Navaho Mountain.

STONE AND ROCK

Rocks are symbols of eternity and immovability, and are often associated with divinity – many are thought to be inhabited by particular gods and spirits. Rocks store heat, cold and water, and crystals reflect and refract light – all qualities that lend themselves to symbolism – and astrology associates many precious stones with planetary influences.

The Sami of north-eastern Russia believe that certain stones are inhabited by the spirits that control the surrounding animal

life, and rituals are performed at these rocks to ensure good hunting. The Tungu people believe that the forest master, a fearsome woodland spirit, may take on the form of a rock, and thus they avoid rocks that have an animal or human shape. In Vietnam, stone is endowed with living qualities, and is thought to bleed when it is struck.

Unlike the symbol of the tree, which embodies the cycles of life, stone signifies the eternal and unchanging. The Greek omphalos, or navel stone, represented the birthplace of the cosmos. Ancient standing stones in northern France and the British Isles are thought to have been used by early agrarian societies to pin and harness the powerful energies of the earth, and were commonly aligned with cyclical movements of the cosmos. Stonehenge became the main

ritual centre in the south of England in around 2,100 BC and was probably used for sun worship. The phallic stones of Brittany have been associated with orgiastic rituals and were approached by women wishing to conceive a child, who would rub their bellies with dust and water from the stones' surface. Rocks with holes through them are also believed to have fertilizing qualities, and to pass through the hole can symbolize regeneration through the feminine principle. In parts of Africa, large stones are thought to hold ancestral souls.

ABOVE Tibetan Buddhist pilgrims circle the base of Mount Kailash, sacred mountain to both Buddhists and Hindus, and believed to be the home of the gods.

TOP LEFT Stonehenge is the most famous of England's stone circles, thought to have been built to link in with the movement of the planets.

THE DESERT

Symbolically, the desert may be understood in two different ways. It represents the primordial state before the emergence of life, but may also depict the superficiality of life, beneath which reality lies. The desert is barren and sterile, yet in Christian thought it may also symbolize the most divine grace when infused with the presence of God, and it was the chosen home of the earliest Christian monks, the "desert fathers".

WATER

EL DORADO

The idea of a spring or fountain that can confer eternal youth occurs in various legends and myths. When the Spaniards landed in what is now Florida they were seeking a city called El Dorado (the gilded one) with a fountain from which flowed the elixir of life.

Like the other fundamental elements of life, water plays an important part in world symbolism and creation myth. It often represents the source of life, but also inevitably leads to death or the underworld. Water moves downward from above, always taking the easiest course, and for this reason it is a powerful shape-shifting symbol. Water is both dynamic and chaotic, moving in waves and spirals and never taking a straight path. Water's sacred powers are universal; as a psychological symbol it is linked with the unconscious, the soul, feelings and the flow of life.

POSEIDON

The Greek god Poseidon was the ruler of waters and earthquakes. He was a raging and stormy god who provoked intense fear and possessed powers to stir up life, using his trident to create surges of thunder, rolling waves and lightning. Poseidon had affairs with both goddesses and mortal women, who gave birth to monsters, heroes, and even the legendary ram with the golden fleece. His sacred animals were the horse, a symbol of gushing springs, and the bull, representing Poseidon's fertilizing power.

THE OCEAN

The vastness of the oceans of the world explains how a limitless body of water was often the precondition for creation in many mythologies. As bearers of all life, oceans have been endowed with maternal and life-giving qualities, nourishing those who live from her fruits. But seas are also unpredictable, representing sudden danger, lurking monsters, storms and the underworld.

For early Jewish writers the sea was a creation symbol. Conversely, the Dead Sea, which is saturated with salt, is lifeless and is described in Hebrew symbolism as a spiritual wilderness. The iniquitous cities of Sodom and Gomorrah are thought to have been on the southern shore of the Dead Sea.

RIVERS

A flowing river commonly represents time, history or the span of a human life. Its source can represent conception and birth, while its outlet into the sea often symbolizes death and the afterlife. Islamic, Jewish, Christian, Hindu and Buddhist traditions tell of four rivers of life that flow from paradise towards the four directions, symbolically dividing the earth into quarters. They are associated with enlightenment, spiritual power, nourishment and death.

The life-giving nature of rivers probably relates to the fertility of their banks, which led early civilizations to grow up around the Nile in Egypt, the Indus in India, and the Tigris and Euphrates in Mesopotamia. Rivers are also natural boundaries, and mythical rivers often separate the dead from the living, such as the sacred Styx that bounded Hades, and the Japanese Sanzunokawa.

The Yoruba of West Africa believe that the goddess Yemoja transformed into the river Ogun. In Russia, the Votjak throw offerings into the river to appease the water spirit after the festivities of Twelfth Night. The river Ganges is also revered as the goddess Ganga. Pilgrims take water from her *shakti*, or female

RIGHT This painting of a deluge powerfully illustrates the symbolism of floods as bringers of destruction, but also the possibility of cleansing and regeneration.

source, in the Himalayas and pour it over a lingam (phallus) at a village called Ramesvaram, 3,200km/2,000 miles away, uniting the river goddess with Shiva, the male god of fertility.

SPRINGS, WELLS AND WATERFALLS

Water emerging from the ground has a special connection with the underworld and the source of life. Wells and springs are commonly associated with the womb of the earth and were thought to have powers to fulfil wishes, foretell the future and confer healing. In Europe, holy wells sprang up in sacred places where saints had been martyred, dragons had been defeated or the Virgin Mary had appeared. Those known as "granny wells" were believed to aid fertility and childbirth, and a closed well symbolized virginity.

Prophecies were often read in wells or pools by observing movements in the water surface, patterns made by floating leaves, or fish and eels swimming in their depths. At Glastonbury, in Somerset, England, the waters of the Chalice Well were said to be tinged red by the blood of Christ, which was carried to England in the Holy Grail.

Springs and wells commonly symbolize the source of life. The Zuñi people of New Mexico believe that the first humans emerged via springs from the underworld, and also tell of a plumed serpent living in the waters of their sacred springs. The Zuñi therefore avoid killing snakes to protect their water supply.

WHIRLPOOLS

The interaction of opposing currents in large bodies of water leads to vortices, which at their most powerful can suck a boat into the depths. In the Odyssey, the whirlpool that tries to suck Odysseus' boat into the sea is personified as the monster Charybdis, offspring of the gods Gaia and Poseidon. Odysseus survives only by clinging to the branch of an overhanging tree. In his poem The Wasteland, which explores the theme of loss, T.S. Eliot uses a whirlpool to symbolize death and annihilation.

FLOODS

All flood stories can be understood as symbolizing the chaos that arises when humanity is out of alignment with the spiritual laws of nature. The biblical stories of the flood that wiped out the human race probably originated in southern Mesopotamia (now Iraq), where the Tigris and Euphrates meet – a fertile area prone to severe floods, which may also have been the origin of the Garden of Eden. The biblical story of Noah

describes the Flood as God's punishment of human sinfulness. Noah, the virtuous man, builds an ark and survives the flood, eventually repopulating the world. In the Babylonian epic of Gilgamesh, Utnapishtim tells Gilgamesh of a seven-day flood, which he survived by building a ship for his family, servants and animals; it finally came to rest upon a mountaintop, whereupon the gods granted Utnapishtim and his wife immortality.

Flood stories are told in many other cultures. The Kimberley people of Western Australia have a place called Wullunggnari, where three stones represent a Dreamtime flood that devastated all, except for a boy and a girl, who grabbed the tail of a kangaroo that took them to higher ground. The two became the ancestors of all human beings.

A SIP OF WISDOM

The Norse God Odin sacrificed one of his eyes in exchange for sipping the water from the wisdom-giving fountain of the nature spirit Mimir.

ABOVE Whirlpools can represent the change from one state to another, for example life to death. Many animistic cultures believed that spirits dwelled within whirlpools.

WATER AND ISLAM

In the Islamic tradition water features centrally as the source and sustenance of life and for purification. Rain, rivers and fountains are symbolic of the benevolence and mercy of Allah, who is said to love those who purify themselves with water.

AIR AND SKY

ABOVE In mystical Islam, clouds are a symbol of the primordial, unknowable state of Allah before creation.

ABOVE RIGHT In many cultures, thunder and lightning are symbols of divine power.

The skies are the dwelling place of the gods, who control the elemental forces that impact on human life on earth, inspiring both fear and wonder. Hence clouds, wind and storm, thunder and lightning have all been seen as divine manifestations and imbued with symbolic associations. Air fills the space between earth and sky and in symbolic terms is linked with the wind, the breath and spirit. It is an invisible, animating force that links the individual with the cosmos, and very often is the medium by which the gods communicate with humankind. Air is usually related to the masculine archetype.

WEATHER VANE

The wind is a symbol of change – a new wind direction signals changing weather conditions. On churches, the traditional design for a weathervane is a cockerel perched on top of a cross indicating the four directions. The bird symbolizes watchfulness against evil, which could be "blown in" by the wind.

THE WIND

Typically, the wind is associated with the four compass directions. Each is represented by different deities or qualities, and is the harbinger of different weather conditions according to the local climate. Along the north-west coast of America, the native Tsimshian believe that the four great winds were the great chiefs of the four corners of the world; after deliberating how their powers should be balanced, the four seasons were established. For the ancient Greeks, the four winds were viewed as boisterous and rebellious gods imprisoned in the caverns of Aeolus, chief god of the winds; their names were Boreas (the north wind), Auster (the south wind), Eureus (the east and morning wind) and Zephyr (the west and evening wind).

Knowledge of air currents and their effects is central to the Chinese art of feng shui. The Chinese identify eight rather than four winds, corresponding to the eight trigrams that form the basis of the I Ching. According to one legend, the wind was the creation of the White Tiger of the West, while in another story the winds were let out of a sack. The Japanese god Fujin was also said to keep the wind in a sack. The Celts used their knowledge of the winds to predict the weather, while the supernatural "Druid's wind", created at will by the exhalations of a Druid, signified power over the elements and allied the breath with the wind as a vehicle for magic.

Among the Native American Apache, the whorls on the fingertips are said to show the path of the wind entering the body at the time of creation, while the whorls on the soles of the feet show how the wind (or soul) will leave the body at death. The wind is widely thought to communicate with humans: among the Navajo, Wind's Child whispers to the heroes of their stories. Alternatively, the wind may "speak" through an instrument: examples include the bull roarer used by Australian Aboriginals and Native American shamans, and the Aeolian harp of the ancient Greeks. The wind's many "moods" are described in vocal terms such as "roaring", "sighing" or "whispering".

CLOUDS

Because of their cloaking character and their connection with the heavens, clouds are associated with the mysteries of the divine in many traditions. In the Judaeo-Christian tradition, clouds sometimes indicate the presence of God: in the Old Testament he appeared as a pillar of cloud to lead his people through the desert during the Exodus, and in Christian iconography he is sometimes represented as a hand emerging from a cloud, while Christ is said to have ascended to Heaven on a cloud. The Taoist immortals rose up to Heaven on clouds and, in Norse mythology, the Valkyries (female spirits and servants of Odin) rode on clouds.

As bringers of rain, clouds are connected with fertility and nature's abundance. In China, the word for cloud is a homonym for

RIGHT The Norse god of thunder, Thor, wields his mighty hammer, Mjölnir, in a fight against giants.

WIND OF THE SOUL

In some traditions, it is thought that the vital energy of the cosmos is carried in the air, so that when people breathe, they are breathing in life force, known to the Chinese as chi and to Hindus as prana. The Inuit have a similar concept, known as sila, an all-pervasive, life-giving spirit that connects every living being with the rhythms of the universe. When a person is out of touch with sila, they are disconnected from their spirit.

"fortune", associating clouds with good luck. It is also said that wispy dawn clouds brought the five Chinese elements (fire, water, air, earth and metal) down from the five sacred mountaintops, and that clouds were formed from the union of yin and yang. In Taoism, they are symbols of the state that humans must pass through before reaching enlightenment – the mental fog that exists before clarity is attained. The colloquial expression "head in the clouds" suggests someone who is lost in fanciful ideas and out of touch with reality, while "living under a cloud" suggests a burden or disgrace. The Maori name for New Zealand – Aotearoa – means "Land of the Long White Cloud".

STORMS

Violent winds such as hurricanes, whirlwinds and tornadoes are symbols of elemental and divine power. Storm deities are figures of awesome power who embody the forces of disorder and turmoil; they include the Japanese Susano-O, the ancient Greek Poseidon

and the Maya storm god, Huracán, from whom we get the word "hurricane". As bringers of rain, they may also be associated with fertility, as with Baal, the ancient Canaanite storm god. The Maori say that blustery winds and storms are created by the wind god Tawiri-Matea to punish his disobedient brother Tane-Mahuta (god of mankind and the forests), who separated their parents, the earth and sky, to create light. In the West, storms have been seen as the work of the devil. In some Native American traditions, moths are associated with whirlwinds because of the swirly pattern of their cocoons and the whirring noise of their wings.

Storms are often associated with warrior gods and supreme male deities: Indra, the Hindu warrior god, was known as Vajiri ("wielder of thunderbolts") as thunder and lightning were his chief weapons, and a thunderbolt was the main weapon of the supreme Greek god, Zeus.

In the Bible, thunder is the voice of an angry God. The Celts interpreted it as a cosmic disturbance, a punishment from the gods who were invoking the wrath of the elements. In Africa, thunder and lightning are also associated with earthly rulers. The Yoruba of West Africa believe that Shango, the great god of thunder, was the greatest of their warrior-monarchs, while in Benin, thunderbolts are symbols of kingship, sometimes shown as brass pythons zigzagging down from the turrets of high buildings.

In Hinduism and Buddhism, a diamond-shaped thunderbolt

(*vajra*) symbolizes destructive and creative powers – destroying illusions and wrongdoing so that clarity and good can prevail. In Native American myth, the spirit of thunder and lightning is symbolized by the thunderbird, a fierce beast but also a protector of humanity; thunderstorms are believed to be the sound of its battles against underworld beings.

THUNDER HAMMERS

In many cultures the hammer or axe is a symbol of thunder and lightning. The symbol of Shango, the thunder god of the Yoruba, is a double-headed axe, representing the thunderbolts of stone that the god unleashes from the heavens. In Norse mythology, Mjölnir was the hammer of the thunder god Thor. Mjölnir created lightning when struck against stone and could turn into a thunderbolt when it was thrown. It was also a symbol of Thor's beneficence and was used in ceremonies to bless infants and brides.

BELOW This relief of the Canaanite god Baal shows his status as the god of storms by depicting him holding a thunderbolt, but Baal was also associated with fertility because of his rain-bringing qualities.

FIRE

RIGHT A bonfire can have many associations and meanings: a place of the imagination; the primordial hearth fire; or a place of transformation where effigies may be burnt, or where rites of passage are performed.

The symbolism of fire is wide-ranging, though it repeatedly arises as a central motif for the life force. It can be an intimate and personal force of love, passion and warmth, or aggressively pent up in the form of hatefulness and revenge. But fire is also a universal symbol of divine power, wrath or truth, and also of the uncontrolled forces of nature wreaking destruction and bringing about renewal. In many world cosmologies fire is associated with both creation and apocalypse, shining in paradise and burning in Hell.

Fire has been harnessed by humans for protection, light and warmth, and as a focus for stories, trance and dreaming. It is an essential element of transformation in cooking, initiation and funerary rites, and in driving the physical and spiritual processes of alchemy and science. The Chinese associate fire, rising upwards, with yang, or male, qualities. It is an active element associated with creativity and upward striving, and never rests until it has consumed that which fuels it.

Fire is often associated with strong emotions, conflict and war. Conflict can be the source of great emotional energy, and, like a fire, can lead to warmth, heat, motivation and light, but can also burn, damage and destroy. In the alchemical sense, the fire of conflict can truly lead to transformation, as long as it is neither given too much air, nor deprived of air or consciousness.

FIRE THEFT

The theft of fire is a symbolic theme pointing to its origins and its value to humanity. The act separates humans from animals in harnessing a force unavailable to them. Australian Aboriginal myths tell of the secret of fire being stolen from the birds or animals. In Greek mythology, the cunning Prometheus stole fire for humankind from the supreme god Zeus. In revenge, Zeus ordered the creation of the first woman, Pandora, and presented her to Prometheus' brother. She brought with her a box containing great afflictions, which spread over the earth.

VOLCANOES

Every volcano in the world has a particular character or personality, from dormant giants erupting violently after long periods of time, to volatile fuming mountains that never quite simmer down. Whatever their character, volcanoes command both respect and fear. Psychologically they symbolize power, volatility and simmering or pent-up anger, followed by outbursts of violent aggression.

Vulcano was the name of a small island off Sicily, and also the chimney for the forge of Vulcan, the Roman blacksmith god. In his forge Vulcan beat out

BELOW Molten lava: the erupting wrath and passions of the gods, source of light, home and fertility, or a psychological symbol of strength and power.

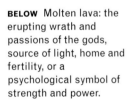

THE PHOENIX

A mythical bird of Arabia, the phoenix was the size of an eagle with magnificent scarlet and gold feathers. At the end of its life it made a fire from its own nest and was consumed in flames, then reborn from the ashes. The ancient Egyptians viewed the phoenix as a symbol of immortality, while Christians related the myth to the resurrection and for Romans it represented Rome's undying nature. The Chinese saw the phoenix as a gentle creature, feeding on dewdrops and, through the union of the energies of yin and yang, embodying the qualities of virtue, grace, wealth and power.

thunderbolts for Jupiter and weaponry for Mars, the god of war. Vesuvius in Italy is well known for entirely burying in ash the Roman towns of Pompeii and Stabiae in AD 79. The Roman poet Virgil (70 BC-AD 19) described its craters as seeping with the blood of giants, and wrote that a giant called Alyconeus lay beneath it. At the time of the eruptions, stories emerged of giants leaping through the smoke and ripping the mountainside to pieces.

In Hawaii, the islands have been formed by continuous volcanic activity, and legends tell of Pele, a most beautiful goddess of volcanoes, who is prone to periodic outbursts of anger. She caused earthquakes through the irate stamping of her feet and made volcanoes erupt by digging in the earth with her magic stick, the Pa'oa. Kilauea is the most active volcano on earth and is considered to be Pele's home.

Volcanoes are often associated with the wrath of the gods, but are also sources of light, power, and the tremendous fertility of volcanic ash. In British Columbia, the Tsimshian people believe that the trickster Raven brought light to humanity from a volcano.

The Aztec goddess of the hearth, home and fertility was also the goddess of the volcano. She was a symbol of both pleasure and pain, and was the ruler of wealth and precious stones. The Taal volcano in the Philippines, which enchantingly floats in the Taal Lake, is one of the smallest volcanoes and yet is considered to be deadly. It is said to symbolize the fearless strength of the people of the Batangas province, which is hidden beneath their apparent calmness.

FIRE IN RELIGION

In many religious traditions, fire is associated with the truths and illusions organizing spiritual experience. Zoroastrians consider fire to be the source of all creation, and each household has a sacred fire, the lighting of which is associated with a blessing. Zoroastrian fire temples are places of community worship, attended by priests who feed the sacred fires with incense. These fires symbolize interaction with Ahura Mazda, the lord of wisdom.

Judaism considers fire to be a fundamental element that should accompany all offerings made to God, and perpetual fires were kept burning at the altar of the Temple. The image of the angel of the Lord appearing to Moses through a burning bush illustrates the Hebrew belief that fire signifies true communication from God. In Christianity, candles are a reminder of the presence of God, and also represent hope and life. Fire is a powerful symbol of renewal and baptism, burning away sinfulness to leave only God's truth.

Buddhism often uses fire to symbolize forces that remove a person from enlightenment, such as desire, greed, hatred and ignorance, and therefore the extinguishing of these fires symbolizes nirvana. But Buddhism also uses an inner flame to represent enlightenment.

BELOW Jews believed that God's appearance in fire marked it as a true divine communication.

THE RAINBOW

ABOVE The rainbow has variously been associated with healing and good fortune, dreams and imaginary worlds, fertility and childbirth, and even with transsexual experience.

Elusive, ethereal and transient, the rainbow appears symbolically in myth and folklore, sacred tradition, art and science, as well as in contemporary Western culture, with a range of meanings as diverse as its colours. In different traditions the rainbow has been venerated as god and goddess, feared as demon and pestilence, seen as a symbol of optimism and hope, of divine covenant and peace and as an omen of war and retribution. Its arching shape links it symbolically with the circle, the bridge and the bow, while in some traditions it is also associated with the serpent.

THE RAINBOW BRIDGE

The bridge is an archetypal symbol of transition, and in this guise the rainbow is the pathway between Heaven and Earth, or a link between different worlds. In the Japanese creation myth, the twin deities Izanagi and Izanami stand on the Floating Bridge of Heaven to create the land, and a belief of southern Gabon states that human ancestors arrived on Earth by walking down a rainbow. In Norse myth, Bifrost was the rainbow bridge that connected Asgard, the land of the gods, to Midgard, the earthly realm. Bifrost was said to be very strong and built with more skill than any other structure in the world. Heimdall, the guardian of Asgard, lived beside it to alert the gods to enemy invaders.

The Navajo believe that the rainbow is a bridge between the human and spirit worlds, while shamanic traditions across North America believe that supernatural journeys to the land of the dead involve crossing a rainbow bridge. Shamans of the Buryat, in Siberia ascend to the spirit world via the rainbow, which they symbolize with a pair of red and blue ribbons tied to a ceremonial birch tree. Some rainbow bridges are manmade structures: the name was given to Chinese bridges of woven construction, spanning streams that were too wide or swift for conventional pier bridges – one built in the 13th century still bears traffic today. There are also rainbow bridges over the Niagara River and in Tokyo Bay.

DIVINE PRESENCE

The rainbow is often interpreted as a divine attribute and a sign of divine presence. Ishtar, the Babylonian goddess of love and war, wore an iridescent necklace, and the Inca believed that rainbows were the feather crown of Illapa, the god of thunder and rain. The bow – the archer's weapon – can betoken the god's wrath. Indra, the Hindu god of war, shot his thunderbolt from a

RIGHT The gods of the Vikings descend from Heaven to Earth using the rainbow bridge that the Norse legends named Bifrost.

rainbow, and in Cambodia and parts of India the rainbow is known as "Indra's Bow". Tiermes, the thunder god of the Lapps of Scandinavia, used the rainbow to fire arrows at evil spirits.

In contrast, in the Judaeo-Christian tradition the rainbow is a sign of peace and compassion, a symbol of God's promise after the Flood not to destroy humankind. Christ is sometimes shown enthroned on a rainbow at the Last Judgement, demonstrating

SEX AND GENDER

In some folklore traditions – such as Serbian, Albanian, Hungarian and French – the rainbow is associated with sex change. When two rainbows appear in the sky some cultures differentiate them by gender: the Chinese call the brighter, primary rainbow male, and the darker, secondary bow female. North African Berbers call the rainbow "the bride of the rain" or "the bride of the sky", whereas the Yámana in Tierra del Fuego refer to it as "the husband of the moon".

UNITY AND DIVERSITY

For some Native Americans, the rainbow symbolizes the coming together of the many tribes as "the rainbow nation", and this term is used in the same way in South Africa. The rainbow is also a pre-eminent symbol of the Western "New Age" movement, indicating a diversity of sacred paths, spiritual transformation and healing through its association with the chakra system.

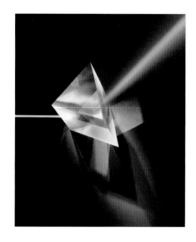

his heavenly power and his mercy. In Tibet, where rainbows occur at transitional times of the year and indicate changing weather, they are associated with blessings from the bodhisattvas of Tibetan Buddhism.

There is a widespread belief among Central African Pygmies that the rainbow is an instrument of divine communication, and in some cultures it marks the location of a divinity or person of high birth: in Hawaiian folklore the noblewoman Hoamakeikekula was tracked by following a rainbow. The rainbow was associated with Iris, the golden-winged messenger of the Greek gods, who is often depicted holding a caduceus, the messenger's snake-entwined staff. The Maya made offerings of gold and silver to the patron deity of women, Ixchel, goddess of medicine, fertility and the rainbow, who controlled the rain.

RAINBOW LEGENDS

There are many legends and customs surrounding rainbows. The Sioux say that the rainbow is where all the bright flowers are stored before and after their brief blooming period on earth. In Irish folklore, the leprechaun is a mischievous sprite who keeps a pot of gold at the end of the rainbow; in Celtic tradition, rainbow coins were to be found there, buried in the earth but revealed after heavy storms.

However, rainbows are not always associated with beauty and

good fortune. Ancient Peruvians claimed that if a rainbow were to enter a person's body, it would cause illness; a cure was to unravel a ball of rainbow-coloured threads to undo the rainbow's ill effects. Ideas of rainbow-borne disease also appear throughout Africa, Asia and Australia: for the Senoi of Malaysia, walking underneath a rainbow causes fatal fever, and Australian Aboriginals associate it with leprosy. Pointing at rainbows is considered foolhardy in many parts of the world: Hungarian folk belief insists the pointing finger will wither, while the Sumu of

Honduras and Nicaragua hide their children in huts to stop them pointing or even looking at a rainbow. Getting jaundice, losing an eye, being struck by lightning or even disappearing are some of the dangers associated with rainbows.

ABOVE When Christ is pictured with a rainbow in Christian art it is usually a symbol of the merciful aspects of his heavenly powers.

THE RAINBOW BODY

Related to the chakra system, the rainbow body may be thought of as fields of energy surrounding the human body, each associated with different qualities.

Level	Colour	Body	Qualities
1st outermost circle or layer	red	physical (temporal)	the foundation upon which all other levels are constructed
2nd	orange	etheric (temporal)	early emotional environment and formative influences; the body's energy pattern
3rd	yellow	astral (transitional)	influences of culture and society, such as religious and educational institutions, and how these shape thought and action
4th	green	mental (transitional)	achieves purpose in life through relationship with others; interface between the temporal and eternal
5th	blue	causal (transpersonal)	attuned to soul; repository of the soul's memories, empowers its journey
6th	indigo	diamond (bliss body) (transpersonal)	thinking superseded by intuitively received knowing
7th innermost layer or core	violet	celestial (eternal)	enlightenment; the individual soul merges into the cosmos, union with the divine

INDEX